Learning Disabilities

Learning Disabilities

An Overview of Theories, Approaches, and Politics

Roa Lynn

with Neil Gluckin and Bernard Kripke

THE FREE PRESS
A Division of Macmillan Publishing Co., Inc.
New York

Collier Macmillan Publishers
London

The Free Press
A Division of Macmillan Publishing Co., Inc.
866 Third Avenue, New York, N.Y. 10022

Collier Macmillan Canada, Ltd.

Library of Congress Catalog Card Number: 79-7477

Printed in the United States of America

printing number
1 2 3 4 5 6 7 8 9 10

Library of Congress Cataloging in Publication Data

Lynn, Roa.
    Learning disabilities.

    Includes bibliographical references and index.
    1. Learning disabilities. I. Gluckin, Neil, joint author. II. Kripke, Bernard, joint author.
III. Title.
RJ506.L4L93   371.9'26   79-7477
ISBN 0-02-919490-3

Contents

Acknowledgments

Excellent editorial suggestions and much encouragement were given to me by Susan Makiesky Barrow of the New York State Psychiatric Institute, Rowland L. Mitchell of the Social Science Research Council and Philip B. Flamm. Thank you.

Stevan Harnad, Editor of *The Behavioral and Brain Sciences*, and Jerome Kagan, Department of Psychology and Social Relations, Harvard University, read this manuscript critically before it attained its final form. I am most grateful for their very helpful comments and suggestions, most of which have been incorporated into the final draft.

Special thanks are due the many people who gave of their time to be interviewed for this report and who led me in turn to others. Especially helpful in expanding my circle of informants was Mario Pascale, Executive Director of the Marianne Frostig Center of Educational Therapy in Los Angeles, California, who contributed to the success of my entire West Coast trip.

I also want to thank David Jenness for helping me set up the administration of my grant at the Social Science Research Council and Eleanor Bernert Sheldon, President of the Council, who made its facilities available to me while this report was being compiled and written. And to all the SSRC staff who were such helpful, pleasant and stimulating company.

This report was supported by a grant from the Rockefeller Brothers Fund. I am most grateful to the Fund and especially to William C. Dietel and John C. Esty, Jr. for trusting my conviction that this study should be undertaken and for making it possible for me to do it.

I am pleased to acknowledge the help of all of these people, but the responsibility for the content of this report is mine alone, including the responsibility for any errors of fact or interpretation it may contain.

Preface

> *"That is to say, I was completely frustrated, completely at odds with my environment, a sort of fake who believed he was somebody, but could furnish no evidence to prove it."*
> Henry Miller

I was twenty five years old when I came across the above lines one Sunday in *The New York Times Book Review.* Miller was wearing the hat of a reviewer that day; I no longer remember the name of the book he reviewed, but the words hit me hard because I knew, somehow, that he was describing me. I copied down the words carefully and put them away.

For years I had hidden from parents, sisters, teachers, friends, even my husband, the fact that I can read only a few minutes at a time before becoming confused and exhausted. My problems extend beyond the inability to read well. Although I managed to earn a bachelor's degree and attend graduate school, I can neither recite the alphabet straight through nor do I know the multiplication and division tables. I add by surreptitiously counting on my fingers, and my spelling is bizarre. I have difficulty writing down the simplest note when someone gives me information—even a telephone number gets twisted in my hands. I am frequently bewildered by complex stimuli such as large parties, some kinds of music, and cluttered rooms. Although I have a good memory for events more than a few days old, I often cannot recall what I have most recently learned. When I move to a new city, it takes years before I can walk out the door confident that I will be able to find my way home. Despite such disabilities, I chose journalism as a career, and pursued it with intermittent successes.

Quite by chance some years later, Miller's words came back to me. At age 38 I was watching a news program on WNBC-TV in which Dr. Frank Field demonstrated a device to test for dyslexia. It struck me instantly that I had the symptoms discussed on the program. The very next day my self-diagnosis was confirmed by a psychiatrist specializing in dyslexia; and, somewhat later, it was reconfirmed after extensive testing by an educational specialist. She preferred to say that I was "learning disabled."

I cannot overemphasize the enormity of my relief when I finally had a name other than "stupidity" for the problems that were so painful and so central to my life. I had always feared that despite my high scores on intelligence tests, I was really stupid. Yet, at the same time, relief was mixed with despair and I sank into depression when I realized that the learning struggles, and therefore the life struggles, that had so tormented me would never go away.

Although I have managed to work for publications such as *Time* and *Newsweek,* my attempt to make a living as a reporter was, as one doctor put it, "like a paraplegic trying to become a professional football player." In fact, I was often unable to read through my own stories once they were published. Due to the exhaustion I experienced trying to keep pace with my peers, my career performance was extremely uneven; but it was consistent: I would start a new job after about six months of recuperation from the last one. In the first few months I would manage to do good, even outstanding, work. Taking note of my performance, my editors would naturally expect more of the same. For a short period I would succeed in meeting both my own high standards and those of my bosses. But then as the pressure to produce mounted while my ability to produce diminished, I would find myself unable to go on with my work. At this point (usually about four months into a job), I would panic and find some reason to quit so that I could leave before anyone realized that I was no longer productive. My most vivid memory of every work experience was the daily fear that the boss was going to call me into his office and fire me because he knew, just as I did, that I was too dumb to do the job.

Groping in the dark, terrified that I was really stupid, sometimes without money to buy the bare essentials of life because of my inability to hold a job, there were times when I considered suicide.

When I found out that I was not stupid, but dyslexic, I tried to rescue myself using the reporter's tools I had been able to master. I thought that an odyssey around the country, talking my way through a field I couldn't read my way through, might produce a more valuable statement pulling together a controversial field than would a conscientious literature review; and I hoped by understanding my condition to save my own life. I succeeded in obtaining a grant from the Rockefeller Brothers Fund to survey the field of learning disabilities from the point of view of one who was herself learning disabled. Already, my new knowledge helped me in some ways: From the start I arranged to be assisted by colleagues who transcribed my tape-recorded interviews and did the actual writing of the report. Knowing little about the field of learning disabilities at the outset, I set a journalist's pace and completed the entire project in approximately a year.

As my interviewing progressed, I realized that the things I was learning could be useful both to laymen and professionals. Therefore, this book is addressed to a dual audience. It is my hope that this information will be helpful to the millions of learning disabled people (and their families) who, like myself, lead troubled lives because of hidden handicaps. At the same time that I have tried to provide an overview for laymen, I have attempted to introduce the diverse professionals in the field to each other—the educators to the scientists, the scientists to the remediators, and the remediators to the administrators in Washington. My original report was circulated to more than 250 people concerned with learning disabilities. It now appears in revised form as the present book.

The reader must be warned that the terms "dyslexia" and "learning disabilities" are applied to diverse phenomena. I have encountered many people whose disabilities resemble my own or are even more severe, but these terms are equally applied to large numbers of people whose symptoms are much less distressing than mine or simply different. These individuals are also counted among the aforementioned millions of the learning disabled.

Since this report is based mostly on interviews, much of it is in quotation. The quoted individuals are clearly identified and their affiliations are given as of the time when the interviews were conducted. Each month some of the hundreds of people interviewed will move, so some of their reported affiliations will be out of date by the time this book is in press. There are also references to a variety of books, scholarly papers, public documents and written communications, which are referred to in traditional academic form. Unless a quotation is cited with a reference to the Bibliography, the reader may infer that the source was either an interview or some other personal communication with the author.

I approached the writing of this book as a reporter, trained to present the news, but not to evaluate it. What I offer here is the news, the bad with the good. I chose people to interview because they were representative of the state of the field. Even if I had wanted to do so, I would not have been able to confine my interviewing or reporting only to people doing the best work or having the best credentials. As the work progressed, I was drawn increasingly to view science as the key to the field, but my review of scientific research is intended only to be representative, not comprehensive. It was beyond the scope of my undertaking to review scientific work on normal cognitive function, important as that is to an understanding of learning disabilities.

While I conceived this project, found the network of people to talk to, conducted all the interviews which produced some 6,000 pages of transcription, organized the report, and drew the conclusions, my disabilities prevented me from doing more than a small part of the actual writing and editing. Most of the manuscript was written by my former colleague at *Time,* Neil D. Gluckin. Bernard Kripke, a neurophysiologist at the University of Utah College of Medicine, wrote the chapter on science and edited the manuscript. This book would not have been written without the contributions of these two dedicated professionals. Nonetheless, I found that when it came time to organizing the detailed outline, locating the sources of quotations, and recalling the details of laws, I hardly had to refer to the transcripts—all the information was stored in my head.

I believe my experience has important implications for potential employers of the learning disabled. While a learning disabled person (and recent estimates run as high as half a million of us coming out of the school system *every* year in the United States) can function effectively in some areas if given the chance, employers will have to make adjustments in their expectations to allow for individual differences in order to permit the learning disabled to use their intelligence to the best of their abilities without being castigated for their handicaps.

Roa Lynn
New York City
March, 1979

Chapter 1
The Problem

"To be different from everyone else . . . "

The exercise was brief but to the point: Sally Smith, Associate Professor of Education at American University and Director of the Kingsbury Lab School in Washington, D.C., was going to show a nonhandicapped audience what life was like for some learning-disabled people. Speaking in a normal tone of voice, Smith asked everyone in the auditorium to take out a piece of paper and a pen or pencil and to copy down a list of six words that she would read, spell, define, and display on cards. As Smith began to recite the words—and they were rare ones such as xyphoid or xyloid—graduate students started wandering aimlessly up and down the aisles and across the rows of seats in the auditorium, forcing people to shift their bodies or their chairs out of the way. Over by the windows, other graduate students played with the blinds, creating distracting, sudden shifts of light and shadow in the room. On the auditorium stage, a radio turned to full volume blasted out music, making Smith difficult to hear. Simple ornamentations bordering the display cards offered more visual distraction. When she reached the end of the list, Smith asked members of the audience to turn their papers over and reproduce from memory as many words as they could. No one in the room was able to recall all of the words; some found themselves unable to remember any. In the presence of so much sensory overload, their performance was much worse than it would have been without these distractions. When asked how they felt, the audience shouted back "stupid," "threatened," "frustrated," "angry."

A 14-year-old boy fills out the picture:

> To be dyslexic is to feel different from everyone else and to be constantly ridiculed because you're stupid and an idiot, and you really begin to wonder whether it's true because so many people say that. . . . When you're dyslexic the way I am it's so hard to play games that the other kids play, like baseball. I have the hardest time catching that stupid ball or hitting and even throwing it.
>
> I talk a lot, and they call that my way out—or hyperactivity, I think. In school I have trouble in English. I also don't get all the directions, like someone will send me out to get three things and I'll come back with only two, but one of them wasn't on the list. It is so frustrating to do everything wrong. . . . [Tec 1976, p. 89]

The reader will be struck by the fact that these are the words of a boy who is sensitive and intelligent, even though he has great difficulty learning to do things that most sensitive and intelligent people do easily and well. Educators, scientists, physicians, parents, and legislators have become concerned with the plight of such people; but they have not yet been able to reach consensus on the scope of their concern, or on the appropriate terminology to describe it. The terms most widely accepted in the United States to describe such disorders are "learning disabilities," "specific learning disabilities," "dyslexia," and "minimal brain dysfunction syndrome" (MBD). Some people in the field use all of these terms interchangeably, although they have different historical and etymological roots. All of them are applied to people of normal or superior overall intelligence whose performance on such learned tasks as reading, speaking, spelling, and calculating is surprisingly poor. Deficiencies due to physical impairments like deafness, blindness, and paralysis are excluded from the range of these terms, as are impairments in performance due to laziness, emotional problems, inadequate training, and variations in economic, social, or cultural background.

Since almost all standard measures of intelligence depend on the subject's ability to use the very same range of abilities that are affected by learning disabilities, the definitions of these terms virtually require that a learning-disabled person have superior abilities to perform some of these tasks to compensate for his impaired performance in others. Otherwise, his overall intelligence score would be below average and he would, by definition, not be counted as learning disabled. While such a definition has undoubted utility for educators and legislators, some scientists in the field complain that it begs the very questions they are attempting to answer.

Professionals in the field agree that there are millions of intelligent people (perhaps as many as ten million U.S. citizens) whose performance on some learned tasks is surprisingly poor. They do not agree on the boundaries between normal and pathological variations in performance. They do not agree how high a score on a standard intelligence test a child should have before one should be surprised at his poor performance in reading, spelling, or the like. They do not even agree whether standard intelligence tests are appropriate diagnostic tools. They do not agree that it is sound policy to characterize a disorder as being confined by definition to those of normal or superior intelligence. They do not agree whether it is useful to distinguish surprising deficits in scholastic performance from surprising deficits in such tasks as sitting still, interpreting facial expressions, and catching a baseball. They do not agree how many kinds of learning disabilities should be distinguished. They do not agree on the causes of learning disabilities (and the suggested causes range from birth injuries through food poisoning to asymmetries of the cerebral hemispheres). They do not agree how to distinguish deficiencies in performance due to organic brain disorders from deficiencies in performance due to laziness, emotional problems, inadequate education and training, or physical impairments. They do not agree on the means of remedying learning disabilities, or whether the accepted remediational techniques are effective. They do not agree how learning disabilities should be defined for the purposes of assuring fair access to social benefits and allocating financial resources to the learning disabled. They do not agree who is properly trained to work in the field.

The diagnostician's task is a difficult one. Learning disabilities are not characterized by neurological "hard signs" like paralysis, tissue pathology, or altered blood chemistry that have a well-understood connection with organic disease. Rather, they are characterized by difficulties in performing learned tasks and tend to be associated with other "soft signs" like clumsiness, abnormal distractibility, and unusual electroencephalographic rhythms. Although such soft signs are believed to reflect disorders of the central nervous system, their connection with specific organic disorders is poorly understood.

Faced with a lack of reliable diagnostic signs and a lack of well-established explanations for pathological symptoms, those who have had to define terms like "learning disabilities" and "dyslexia" have tended to attempt definitions by exclusion—for example, that the deficiencies in performance are not due to deafness or blindness. No one is fully satisfied with such a definition.

"Learning disabilities" is the most general of these terms. "Specific learning disabilities" is the term used in an important new piece of legislation, Public Law 94–142, which will be discussed at length below. It is intended to emphasize that the benefits of the law are reserved for those whose deficiencies are due to organic brain disorders rather than physical impairments, emotional disorders, inadequate education, or overall mental retardation; but it does not assist the diagnostician or administrator in deciding who is actually entitled to these benefits. "Dyslexia" was used originally to describe a reading disorder also called "word-blindness," but it is now more commonly applied to a broad spectrum of disorders of written and spoken language and, by some people, is used as broadly as "learning disabilities." "Minimal brain dysfunction syndrome" is a term preferred by some medical professionals. It emphasizes that the disorders to which it is applied *resemble* the disorders of some people who are known to have suffered brain damage due to injury or disease and underlines the belief that ab-normal behavior can be traced to abnormal functioning of the brain. It is applied especially to people who have trouble sitting still and maintaining attention. When we quote the people we have interviewed, we shall use their own termi-nology.

"If one were to evaluate 100 children with this condition (learning disabili-ties), he or she might find 30 or 40 different profiles of strengths and disabili-ties," writes Larry Silver, Chief of the Child and Adolescent Psychiatry Section at Rutgers Medical School (Silver 1979). Educational testing procedures often can determine with a fair degree of accuracy the type of specific learning disabil-ity that a person may have. Because learning disabilities can go, in a sense, wherever the brain goes, they can affect vision, hearing, muscle control, mem-ory, the capacity of the brain to organize information into proper sequences or abstractions, and the ability of the brain to coordinate operations that involve cooperation between different functions (as in using a hammer and nail, which involves cooperation between the visual and motor systems). Learning disabili-ties can interfere with any or all of the steps associated with the processing of information by the brain. They can affect the ability of the brain to receive in-formation, to produce information, or to carry out any of the many steps that lie between input and output.

Here are some of the characteristic signs of learning disabilities: in visual per-ception, an LD may confuse left and right, top and bottom, forward and back-ward, and other directions and positions; he or she may see the letter *d* as *b,* or the letter *p* as *q* (or vice versa); a dyslexic frequently sees whole words in reverse, i.e., *was* becomes *saw,* or sees letters transposed, i.e., *said* becomes *siad, spaghetti* becomes *psaghetti.* In open spaces, such as a gym, an LD may become dizzy; he or she may have trouble simply sitting in a chair or have difficulty discriminating an object from its background. Depth perception is often another problem area: unable accurately to gauge the proximity or distance of objects, LDs are fre-quently clumsy. Any action that involves hand-eye coordination may be difficult or impossible for them to perform.

By the same token, learning disabilities may affect auditory perception: dif-ferences in sounds, such as *tap/tab* or *wish/witch,* may be difficult to distinguish. There may be figure-ground problems, as in distinguishing one voice or sound against a noisy background. Auditory-motor problems, such as carrying out verbal instructions or repeating sounds, are also common. In some instances, LDs simply hear more slowly; it takes longer for a sound message to be proc-essed by the brain.

LDs frequently have trouble organizing information. Being unable to put data into proper sequences, for instance, may show up in spelling, in telling time, in remembering the order of days, months, seasons, or in repeating a story—an LD may start in the middle, then tell the beginning, then the end. Numbers are fre-quently reversed (23, for example, becomes 32). Similarly, LDs may have trouble organizing their belongings, scheduling or anticipating events, or interpreting their own behavior patterns as well as those of others. After reading or hearing a story about a dog, an LD may not be able to build on that story to a discussion of other dogs or all dogs. An LD may grasp material perfectly during a lesson, then forget it all within a short time.

Learning disabilities can affect a person's ability to retrieve information stored in his brain. This can be seen, for example, in a classroom situation when a teacher asks an LD to answer a question; the response, if there is one, often comes slowly. (This symptom often confuses teachers and sometimes leads them to conclude that an LD is simply a lazy student, for the child may readily raise a hand to answer a question when he or she knows the answer yet remain unable to perform in a demand situation.) So-called output deficits are also frequently seen in motor activity: clumsiness or poor coordination in walking, running, sports, and other gross motor activities are common characteristics of the learning disabled. Fine motor deficiencies frequently present themselves in an LD's inability to do puzzles or perform other acts in which the eyes must direct the hands, particularly handwriting. Speech production may also be affected. An LD child may not begin to speak as early as other children do, and articulation may remain a lifeling problem.

The above list is a very general one, intended only to suggest the range of problems with which LDs have to contend. Rarely does every sign show up in one person. As suggested above, the symptomatology of the disorder is highly varied, not only in terms of specific disabilities, but also in terms of the severity of any given deficiency. On the basis of clinical experience, however, professionals have found that symptoms tend to occur in clusters. For example, psychiatrist Silver observes that the disabilities associated with the syndrome tend to be grouped in one of two basic patterns. One relates to disabilities in visual perception, visual integration, visual memory, fine motor and/or visual motor areas. The other pattern is characterized by disorders of auditory perception, auditory integration, auditory memory, and language output (Silver 1979).

The fact is, of course, that at various stages of their development, most children display some traits of learning disability: clumsiness, difficulty pronouncing words, spelling and reading errors, and the like. From a diagnostic point of view, however, it is the persistence rather than the temporary appearance of symptoms that points to a child at risk. Moreover, as Silver suggests, in LD children difficulties tend to present themselves in clusters, rather than as isolated weaknesses.

Many, but not all, LD children are hyperactive and/or distractible. The hyperactivity refers to general motor restlessness, inability to sit still, to sleep at night, and often also an incapacity to restrain impulses. The hyperactivity associated with MBD is evident in school and at home, during the day and during the night, on week days as well as weekends. Anxiety-based hyperactivity, such as may be displayed only in specific anxiety-causing environments—in the classroom, for instance, or on the school bus—is not considered symptomatic of MBD. Distractibility is a condition in which a child's attention is easily drawn away—by light and shadow, sounds, random movements, even by his or her own body sensations. Thus, the child is unable to concentrate on any given task for more than a short period of time. Hyperactivity/distractibility can be treated with medication. For reasons not yet known, certain drugs (dexedrine, for example) calm down hyperactive/distractible children, adolescents, young adults, and, it has been reported, even mature adults in whom the condition has persisted. It is important to note, however, that these drugs do not improve learning per se; they simply make the child, in Silver's words, "more available for learning."

As a result of repeated failures and frustrations in the classroom (and elsewhere), many dyslexics develop secondary emotional disturbances that express themselves in myriad ways, such as hostility, regression, withdrawal, resistance to reward and punishment, a hot temper, depression, anxiety, stubbornness, and low frustration tolerance. Psychotherapy often helps to relieve these problems but will be of little value if the learning disabilities themselves are not carefully— and promptly—attended to. Without psychotherapy or educational remediation, the consequences of dyslexia can, and often do, grow more severe. Silver, referring again to his clinical experience, estimates that in 30 to 40 percent of all school dropouts, juvenile delinquents, and adolescent psychiatric hospital admissions, the psychiatric problems are secondary to unrecognized and untreated learning disabilities and/or hyperactivity. Among adults, serious psychiatric disorders—alcoholism, hysterical symptoms, and sociopathy, to name a few— may be typical outcomes of untreated learning disabilities. Both homicides and suicides by LDs have been reported in newspapers, with strong suggestions that these acts were outgrowths of frustration and poor self-images. Many in the learning disabilities field suspect that LDs may be more prone to delinquency than non-LD people. In a careful preliminary study commissioned by the Office of Juvenile Justice and Delinquency Prevention, Law Enforcement Assistance Administration (Murray et al. 1976A), it was found that there was sufficient evidence of an association to merit further investigation (which is now in progress), but that there is not yet any proof of the suspected relation.

In a thumbnail sketch, then, an LD may have some, or (in extreme cases) most, of the following symptoms. He or she may be unable to process visual or auditory information properly—in themselves serious handicaps in a literate and technological society; he or she may not be able to rely on memory, to speak or write fluently, to handle numbers, to abstract, to deal with concepts, or to express thoughts. An LD may be physically clumsy or awkward, unable to tolerate an open space, to thread a needle, hit a nail with a hammer, pour water neatly into a glass, or filter out irrelevant stimuli. He or she may have difficulty understanding or interpreting subtleties, nuances, gestures, or facial expressions—and often be unable to tell the difference between a loving touch and a threatening one. Consequently, he or she may endure a life devoid of satisfying human contact. Because their intelligence is at least normal and sometimes superior, LDs sense that something is wrong, but neither they nor anyone else can explain exactly what the problem is. The tragedy of the syndrome is that it so often goes unrecognized, and, when that happens, frustration grows steadily, poisoning a capable and healthy mind, extinguishing ambition and hope.

It cannot be stressed often enough that learning disabilities affect all of life, not just school. In every area of his or her life, an LD is vulnerable to deep emotional scars. LDs are, as the young man at the beginning of this section explains, "different from everyone else"—and constantly aware of that fact. In some cases, the simplest, and most vital, skills may remain forever beyond their grasp: not just classroom skills, but others, such as dribbling or throwing a ball, sewing, cutting up food, remembering a phone number, cleaning a room, dancing, driving a car. LDs are exposed to rejection and reminded of their disabilities by teachers, classmates, friends, relatives, parents, co-workers, employers, and—if they themselves become parents—even by their own children. Because they so often look normal, healthy, and capable, LDs do not receive the sympathy or concern that is so automatically extended to people with visible handicaps. Theirs is a suffering whose source is mysterious and whose shape is so unclear as to be virtually invisible—except, of course, to themselves.

Learning disabilities typically handicap people in performing some of the very same tasks that are measured by standard intelligence tests. Since, as suggested earlier, a learning-disabled person must by definition be able to achieve a normal or superior score on such a test, he must actually show superior performance on some parts of the test to balance his inferior performance on the parts where he is handicapped. Otherwise, he would be labeled "retarded," not "learning disabled." It is not surprising that professionals in the field of learning disabilities recognize that, along with their handicaps, LDs often possess unique coping mechanisms, survival strategies, and superior problem-solving potential. Many of them have rather strong egos and considerable persistence and motivation. Some of them are even strikingly superior to most people in some areas of performance: Leonardo da Vinci, Albert Einstein, Niels Bohr, Thomas Edison, and General George S. Patton, Jr. are all thought to have suffered from learning disabilities. Nelson Rockefeller was known to be dyslexic.

On one hand, such observations are in part merely consequences of the definition of learning-disabled people as people who, despite handicaps in some areas, are able to manifest at least a normal overall intelligence. On the other hand, it is a striking fact that some people with severe handicaps can do extraordinarily good work. Society has much to gain by ensuring that their potential contributions are not lost because of their handicaps.

Neuropsychiatrist Lauretta Bender, herself a dyslexic, has observed that the learning, and possibly the general behavior, of dyslexic children is characterized by a too great or too-long-continued "plasticity," meaning that they carry within themselves potentialities that are slow to become fixed. "This very plasticity," writes Margaret Rawson, past President of the Orton Society, "is one of the most valuable ingredients in human adaptability. Brought under control, it emerges as flexibility, a necessary condition of innovation and creativity, and is one of the several positive traits associated with the dyslexic constitution" (Rawson 1975, p. 238).

In the unraveling of learning disabilities, therefore, a great deal stands to be gained. For one thing, much suffering will be alleviated. For another thing, some of the unusual intellectual potential that many suggest may be associated with the condition might prove to be a valuable resource in a society whose continued existence depends more and more on imaginative and intuitive solutions to complex problems. Finally, there is an abstract and tantalizing reward that may lie wrapped somewhere in the convolutions of this disorder—nothing less than an understanding of the age-old puzzle of the brain and its role in human intelligence.

Definitions
"A great many things tried and discarded . . ."

The Commissioner of Education shall, no later than one year after the effective date of this subsection, prescribe—
(A) regulations which establish specific criteria for determining whether a particular disorder or condition may be considered a specific learning disability for purposes of designating children with specific learning disabilities;
(B) regulations which establish and describe diagnostic procedures which shall be used in determining whether a particular child has a disorder or condition which places such a child in the category of children with specific learning disabilities; and
(C) regulations which establish monitoring procedures which will be used to determine if State educational agencies, local educational agencies, and intermediate units are complying with the criteria established under clause (A) and clause (B).

Behind this deadpan and unequivocal language of subsection 620 of section 5, Part B of Public Law 94–142, the Education for All Handicapped Children Act of 1975, lay a task of staggering complexity. The assignment for carrying out Congress' mandate fell largely on the shoulders of Frank King, a psychologist by training, a seasoned bureaucrat, and a State Plan Officer, Division of Assistance to States, in the Bureau of Education for the Handicapped, Office of Education, U.S. Department of Health, Education, and Welfare. The ultimate goal was to establish a system that would allow states and local educational districts to determine which children were eligible for special help under the sections of P.L. 94–142 that deal with specific learning disabilities. But, in effect, Frank King had one year to accomplish the following: define, if necessary, and devise uniform procedures for identifying a condition that has no single agreed-upon cause, no single agreed-upon treatment or remediation, and no single professional home. As King observes, the Congressional mandate "specified that we would provide information that was beyond science at this stage."

The U.S. Congress had already taken a crack at a definition of terms. A specific learning disability, according to P.L. 94–142, "means a disorder in one or more of the basic psychological processes involved in understanding or in using language, spoken or written, which may manifest itself in an imperfect ability to listen, think, speak, read, write, spell, or to do mathematical calculations." Recognizing that disorders such as these can be traced to a number of causes—ranging from a simple head injury to cerebral palsy, with many possibilities in between—Congress added that the term "specific learning disability" did not "include children who have learning problems which are primarily the result of visual, hearing or motor handicaps, of mental retardation, or of environmental, cultural, or economic disadvantage."

In a field teeming with more than a score of different professional and special interest groups, a definition even as broad as this was bound to raise at least as many questions as it tried to answer. Indeed, of the hydra-headed conditions that are variously referred to not only as specific learning disabilities but also as perceptual handicaps, brain injuries, minimal brain damage, cerebral dysfunctions, developmental aphasia, dyscalculia, dysgraphia, and dyslexia of the (to name a few) genetic, environmental, developmental, dysmetric, dysphonetic, and dyseidetic varieties, only one thing seemed reasonably clear as Frank King began his year-long quest: nobody, including the U.S. Congress, believed that children with specific learning disabilities could be accurately identified or diagnosed on the basis of a definition that, for all practical purposes, spelled out primarily what the condition was *not*.

Looking back on his labors, King recalls: "The major problem that we encountered was the same as the one everyone else has encountered, and that is that there have been no consistent definitions of learning disabilities across the country, across the states and, in some cases, even across communities. What we found was that many people have theories and had developed instructional programs based on those theories. But, on close examination, we found that there was very little if any research that was done on the theories as to whether or not they were, in fact, accurate. Thus, many of the concepts of learning disability have been based, in part at least, on opinion rather than on established research. This gave rise to some real problems for us when we attempted to bring about any kind of consistency, particularly because the research that *has* been done has been done on varying populations—that is, the definition of learning disabilities was different in most of the studies we looked at, so that you couldn't compare one study with another."

King met with small groups, and King met with large groups. He addressed meetings of the Council for Exceptional Children (CEC), the Association for Children with Learning Disabilities (ACLD), and the Orton Society. He touched base with 34 out of 50 state consultants in learning disabilities, with professionals, with academics, with parents. He, or someone else from his office, conducted public hearings in San Francisco, Denver, Chicago, Atlanta, Washington, D.C., and Boston. In the space of a year, he prepared or read more than 50 separate memos, wrote two draft concept papers, distributed them, and reviewed all the comments. "There were an unbelievable number of policy issues that had to be checked, and financial issues that had to be addressed, and professional issues that had to be dealt with," says King. "We had numerous conferences," he relates, "and a great many presentations. And, of course, the one thing that came out over and over again was that there was very little agreement when you got to specifics. It just wasn't there. The medical people had one view, the psychologists had another. And within each of those subgroups there was disagreement. There was just not enough from any one group to be able to say with a degree of certainty that these are the factors that are specifically involved in learning disabilities, and if we examine these factors we can make a determination as to whether a child actually has a specific learning disability. And, of course, the literature is notably lacking in specific information like that." Adds King, "It's not the fact that people aren't interested in it. It's such a complex problem that we ran into the situation that the research that needs to be done hasn't been done. We haven't evolved to that extent."

Since the principal users of the procedures would be in the field of education, it was necessary that the regulations be based on, and usable in, an educational setting. But it still took King fully six months—with, as he notes, "a great many things tried and discarded" along the way—to come up with a practical, education-oriented characterization of a specific learning disability. The key finally proved to be the observation that all learning-disabled children appear to have one thing in common: they achieve at a rate considerably below that which might be expected when intelligence, age, and prior experiences are taken into account. According to this so-called discrepancy model, then, a specific learning disability could be identified as a gap between expectation and achievement. To this model, King added—again, after many hours of discussion with interested and knowledgeable parties—a quantitative element: the discrepancy between expectation and achievement had to amount to 50 percent or more.

On November 29, 1976, exactly 365 days after the Congressional mandate went into effect, the Office of Education published the regulations in the *Federal Register.* Due to the controversial nature of the area being regulated, the Office of Education allowed 120 days for public comment—twice as long as is normally allowed. And, as it turned out, the task of developing characterization of specific learning disabilities was not quite completed. For, while the public exhibited strong support for the discrepancy model itself, the 50 percent requirement drew very heavy fire. Opposition to the quantification of the discrepancy model centered on a formula included in the regulations to illustrate how the disparity could be measured. Five more hearings were held. Negative comments poured in from as far away as Belgium. In fact, the formula itself attracted more than 1,000 letters. Chief among the objections were: the standard of measurement would vary depending on the particular test or tests used; statistically, comparing intelligence and achievement is like comparing apples and oranges; quantifying the discrepancy meant reducing children to mere numbers. Comments made at a Washington, D.C. hearing by Walter H. MacGinitie, then President of the International Reading Association, convey some of the flavor and fervor of the objections heard: "Clearly," he concluded, "the use of the formula in the manner proposed is unworkable and a disservice to children. The defects in the proposed procedures are so great that they cannot be mended. Many of the defects are not just technical flaws but conceptual and methodological flaws. The introduction to the proposed rules," MacGinitie continued, "is quite correct in stating that there is little agreement on what constitutes a learning disability and that the data are not available from which criteria can be developed. In these circumstances, the appropriate action is to move to obtain the data, not conjure up an unsupportable procedure."

From his unique vantage point at the eye of this storm, King came to suspect that not a little of the opposition to the formula had to do, quite simply, with the way proposed regulations were printed. The way the columns on the page are laid out makes it easy for the reader to get lost before reaching the paragraph that explains that the formula does not have to be used in every instance and that specifies how the evaluating team can carry out its work without it.

In their final form, the regulations pertaining to specific learning disabilities under P.L. 94-142 appeared in the *Federal Register* on December 29, 1977. The act authorizes $375 million to be spent on educating handicapped children, including the learning disabled, in the 1978 fiscal year, and it escalates to $3.16 billion by 1982. Based on the regulations that it took more than a year to hammer out, learning-disabled children who are eligible to be counted for assistance will be identified on this basis: "it must be established [by an appropriate multi-disciplinary team including the child's regular teacher] (a) that a severe discrepancy exists between ability and achievement; (b) that there is a severe achievement problem in one or more of seven areas relating to communication skills and mathematical abilities; and (c) that the discrepancy is not the result of other known handicapping conditions or of environmental, cultural, or economic disadvantages." Towards the end of his assignment, King observed, "The problem is, as it has been all along, that we just can't define learning disabilities in terms that are discrete enough to separate out each child, in terms of the degree of disability, and in some instances, even in terms of the type of disability that's involved. We don't know as much about learning as we need to know, so we know less about the disabilities in learning."

Frank King had to struggle to define "learning disabilities" to meet the demands of legislation that allocates resources to the learning disabled, but he was not the first to wrestle with the choice of appropriate definitions and terminology in this field. The first observations of bright children who were nevertheless unable to read, write, or spell were recorded in England during the last decade of the nineteenth century. In the 1920s, Samuel T. Orton, an American psychiatrist and neurologist, made a number of important contributions to the study of reading-related disorders through his extensive observations of Iowa school children who, though intelligent and apparently neurologically intact, tended to be unusually clumsy, to have difficulties in spoken language, or to reverse or transpose the order of letters in reading so frequently that Orton coined a special term, "strephosymbolia," to describe the phenomenon. It was not, however, until the early 1960s that the phrase "learning disabilities" came into use to subsume conditions that had been previously recognized by about 100 different names. It was at about this time that the field began to take its present shape.

The reasons for the sudden spurt of activity and interest in learning disabilities are complex and beyond the particular concern of this book. What does concern us is the fact that, over the past 10 or 15 years, there has been a marked trend in the field that includes the following features: a number of different theories have been advanced—but none universally accepted—to explain the etiology of specific learning disabilities; a variety of remediation techniques, some old and some new, have become more or less solidly established and used to treat the condition, or particular aspects of it, in children and adults alike; government spending in the area of special education has steadily increased; professionals all over the country have been reporting that they see more cases of specific learning disability each year; and the transfer of information across professional boundaries has remained difficult, if it has not actually worsened with the passage of time, with the explosion of information in the field and with the growth of money available to support work or research on aspects of learning disabilities. A related but tangential trend is the increasing general dissatisfaction felt in many parts of American society with the job being done—or, it is argued, not done—by public education systems.

As the saga of Frank King suggests, one of the most salient characteristics of the learning disabilities field taken as a whole is the lack of consistency in terminology and procedure. This inconsistency may have consequences for such diverse areas as diagnosis and treatment, for the status of the various professional groups in the field, for the success of research efforts, and for the effectiveness of political lobbying on behalf of the learning disabled. From a diagnostic point of view, for instance, what does "learning disability" or "dyslexia" mean? "To my mind," says pediatrician Sylvia O. Richardson, Chairperson of the ACLD's Professional Advisory Board and Assistant Director of the Learning Disabilities Program at the Cincinnati Center for Developmental Disorders, "there is no child with 'learning disabilities.' It has to be spelled out. To say LD doesn't say very much other than the child is having difficulty in school, and we've got to find out what are his symptoms and what problems he is having." Similarly, psychiatrist Larry Silver of Rutgers Medical School explains that "if someone can't read, that doesn't help me. Some people are dyslexic because they have visual-perceptual-fine motor problems; others are dyslexic because they have auditory language problems; some are dyslexic because they have sequencing problems. Dyslexia is a general term."

Some researchers have coined new terms in an attempt to describe more precisely the symptoms associated with a particular condition. Pediatrician Elena Boder of the University of California School of Medicine, Los Angeles, for instance, refers to "dysphonetic" and "dyseidetic" dyslexia (as well as to a "mixed category"), with each subgroup manifesting a specific pattern of reading or spelling errors. Other professionals are concerned about the etiological implications of one or another set of diagnostic terms. "[Boder's] classification is interesting," says Drake D. Duane, neurologist and President of the Orton Society. "But whether or not it tells you what is going differently in the nervous system, or whether or not those are meaningful dichotomies within the reading retardation category, is difficult to state." The Orton Society, in fact, has its own favorite terms: "Developmental dyslexia," to imply, in Duane's words, "that this is something that the child is born with, and that is in evidence in early life"; and, instead of "specific learning disability," "specific *language* disability," to suggest that the problem involves more than just the reading and writing process. "Kids could have articulation problems, or problems in oral speech other than just articulation," Duane explains.

The many terms and linguistic preferences currently in circulation reflect some of the divisions—real and apparent—among the different disciplines at work in the field. "As far as I'm concerned, there's some sham going on here that's being sold by the hospitals," says Larry Lieberman, Assistant Professor of Special Education, Division of Special Education and Rehabilitation at Boston College. "It comes in the form of something like the 'Cortical Function Test Laboratory' at Massachussetts General Hospital. If you look at the reports that come out of the 'Cortical Function Test Laboratory,' you see that the tests they do—the ITPA [Illinois Test of Psycholinguistic Ability], the Peabody Picture Vocabulary Test, the Detroit Test of Learning Aptitude, the Gray Oral Reading Test, the Wide Range Achievement Test—are all tests that can be given by educational specialists out in schools who are as well qualified and as well trained as any of the people they get into those hospitals to do it. When they say 'Cortical Function Test Laboratory,' it implies to me, and to an unknowing or naive parent, that they have the ability to open up kids' heads with can openers, take a look in there, and tell them exactly where the wires are crossed or not connected." Lieberman adds, with a trace of irony, "I found myself going to conferences and listening to physicians talk about learning disabilities, and any time they ever made any sense whatsoever—in the sense of being pragmatic or practical about the situation in terms of what do we do with it, instead of 'Let's just admire the problem together'—they were talking like educators. And, as I was sitting there, I was saying to myself, 'Why do we have to listen to a neurologist talk like an educator? Why don't I go listen to an educator talk like an educator?'"

A similar concern for professional integrity prompts William Healey, Director of the School Services Program of the American Speech and Hearing Association (ASHA) to reject "learning disabilities" as a diagnostic category of any value and to characterize it instead as little more than an "umbrella term." His reason is quite straightforward: changing the label on a child from "aphasic," for instance, to "learning disabled" very often means that, by law, "a whole series of new regulations become imposed on the delivery of services to children. That's one of the reasons we've had to become concerned, because in many instances a person in the field of speech and language pathology and/or audiology—if you take those rules and regulations literally—will now be excluded from being the primary provider of service to the children." Healey acknowledges that this position can be criticized by saying, "You're trying to protect your turf, your territorial rights, et cetera. That is partly true. However, said another way, and maybe more positively, what we're trying to do is maintain the appropriate role of these professionals as we see them in terms of their training and their competencies and their experience. And very often, by an act of law or a state rule or regulation, people arbitrarily are being catapulted out of the roles for which they have been prepared."

On occasion, terminology hampers communication between and within disciplines just because it is so vague. Psychiatrist Paul Wender of the University of Utah College of Medicine, complains, for instance, that many published research studies on learning-disabled children fail to make clear whether the children are hyperactive, minimally brain damaged, purely learning disabled, or some mixture thereof. By the same token, Janet Switzer, Executive Director of the Switzer Center in Torrance, California, argues that, as a result of the "democratic" trend away from the use of labels, it is becoming increasingly difficult to maintain the integrity of diagnostic terms. (Switzer, incidentally, considers dyslexia to be a form of aphasia.) The rebuttal to the argument that labels are important, however, is that if the behavior itself is described, then everyone will know what the problem is. "I often wonder," University of Arizona professor of special education Samuel A. Kirk once said, "why we tend to use technical and complex labels when it is more accurate and meaningful to describe behavior. If we find a child who has not learned to talk, the most scientific description is that he has not yet learned to talk. . ." (Hallahan and Cruickshank 1973, p. 6).

Indeed, as Frank King discovered, one of the most troubling aspects of the research being conducted in the area of learning disabilities is the absence of adequate characterizations of the populations—normal or disabled—being treated and studied by different people. For example, UCLA education professor Barbara Keogh notes that "one of the problems with the research literature and the clinical literature in this field is that some people are talking about the kids with neurologically based problems—probably a relatively small number—who have a set of symptoms, one of which is the problem of reading. Other people are talking about very poor readers. I think there is a critical need for some kind of comparison studies that allow decisions as to whether we're dealing with the same kinds of children."

To better differentiate the various subgroups that come under the LD label, a number of studies have been or are being conducted that involve very carefully chosen populations of children. At the John F. Kennedy Institute for Handicapped Children in Baltimore, Maryland, for instance, experimental psychologist

Paula Tallal and speech and language pathologist Betty Stark are studying four groups of children: normal, language delayed, dyslexic, and verbal dyspraxic (who exhibit a severe form of misarticulation in speech), with 60 children in each group. "What we've done," explains Christy Ludlow, Research Speech Pathologist of the Communicative Disorders Program, National Institute of Neurological and Communicative Disorders and Stroke (NINCDS), who is monitoring the Baltimore project, "is selected one very well-controlled, uniform group of dyslexic children. And now we're looking at every hair on their heads to find out what corresponds to their major problem. In other words, these children all have the same degree of dyslexia and the same pattern. Now, what else do they have in common?"

Whether any patterns will be found remains, of course, a major question. It is equally pertinent to wonder how the results would be received, even if patterns eventually do show up. A case in point: in California, Elena Boder has been attempting to subdivide dyslexics into categories based on reading-spelling patterns. Boder (1973, p. 673) first identified 300 children who fulfilled an operational definition of "specific developmental dyslexia" that she had established at the outset of her study (she uses the terms dyslexia, specific dyslexia, specific developmental dyslexia, and developmental dyslexia interchangeably). Then she whittled the group down to a final sample of 107 children (92 boys, 15 girls), ranging in age from 8 to 16, reflecting a variety of socioeconomic backgrounds and including 39 siblings from 16 families. Leaving aside for now Boder's actual findings, how well designed was her study? Too narrow? Too broad? UCLA psychology professor Morton Friedman's assessment: "She was careful, I think, with those 107 kids, to sort out the primary emotional problems and the neurological cases and the more psychiatrically oriented and the low IQ and whatever. That's why it isn't clear when you take an unselected group of kids in school, how many of them will fall into her categorization." But while Friedman worries that the Boder subcategories are perhaps still too refined to serve as a diagnostic net, psychologist Howard Adelman, Director of the Fernald Laboratory at UCLA, comes to a radically different conclusion: "I think she's just too convinced too soon and she hasn't done the scientific process. It's clear that she's making no differentiations within this [learning-disabled] population." In the realm of research, then, it is not only the territorial disputes between professionals that hamper the development of a shared terminology: the confusion over labels is closely tied to the procedural question of how adequately to distinguish or differentiate one labeled group from another.

What It Means to Have a Label
"The consumerization of learning disabilities"

There is yet another area of the LD field where terminology looms as a problem, and that is in the sphere of politics. The background to this state of affairs, Frank King points out, is that, when the category "Learning Disabled" was created, many parents saw it as the answer to their questions why their children weren't doing well in school. Parents, King says, had heard about remarkable educational techniques that were being used with handicapped children, and many of those parents concluded that those same techniques would help their own nonhandicapped children. "And so they pushed and they pushed and they pushed," King notes, "and schools began to include a higher percentage of non-handicapped children under the rubric of 'learning disabilities.'" Nothing has happened to dampen this trend, which might be termed "the consumerization of learning disabilities." Howard Adelman recounts that, in the state of Texas, the law required that for children to be placed in LD programs, some sort of clear brain dysfunction had to be demonstrated. "The pediatricians of course cooperated en masse," says Adelman, "and they had the largest number of brain-damaged children in the country. It starts to become a little ludicrous in terms of understanding what's going on. It's fine for dealing with the problem of kids' placement, but it doesn't tell you what's really going on, what's wrong."

No one is likely to take issue with Adelman's suggestion that the use of the handiest or most politically expedient label makes it difficult, if not impossible, to differentiate diagnostically one kind of learning disability from another, but some would say that there are other factors to be considered. "There's a con-sumer demand to have your problem 'medicalized,' to come in here and be told it's not your fault—which I think is all right," says pediatrician Melvine Levine, Director of the Medical Outpatient Department at the Children's Hospital Medi-cal Center in Boston. "We've too often taken adversary positions with parents, we've too often been too accusatory. And one of the things I like about working in this field is that I love being redemptive rather than accusatory—I like taking people off the hook, especially children but also parents." In the opinion of Larry Lieberman of Boston College, however, many learning problems can be traced to poor parenting, and, therefore, medical LD labels—as opposed, for in-stance, to "mental retardation" or "emotional disturbance"—simply give parents "a license not to have to face their own involvement with the child."

In some parts of the country, a kind of labeling backlash can be discerned. Not long ago, for instance, a chapter of the ACLD in Westchester County, New York, came to the conclusion that to use the term "learning disabled" was to place an ineradicable stigma on a child. The group opted instead for the milder "learning differences." Says Roy Lasky, Executive Director of the New York Association for the Learning Disabled: "That movement is indicative of a major problem that we have, and that is that people are constantly trying to lessen the impact of the learning disability on a child—'it is not a handicapping condition; it will go away,' etc., etc. And that translates into a political problem for us." To the general public, Lasky points out, a label like "brain injured" sounds severe and dramatic. But, he says, "'learning disabilities' means absolutely nothing, and 'learning differences'—I can't even try to sell that!" In effect, Lasky found him-self dealing on the one hand with legislators and members of the public whose interest in and positive response to LD depends largely upon the extent to which they perceive "learning disability" as a serious handicapping condition, on the other hand with parents and teachers who want to minimize the stigma of a handicap.

The conflicting views within the LD field concerning labels thus reflect some very real dilemmas which go beyond professional self-interest and jealousies. One promising approach to the labeling problem—or at least to a part of it—has been pioneered in Massachusetts. Chapter 766 of the Acts of 1972 (of Massachusetts), widely hailed as a model piece of legislation, mandates educational services for handicapped children and, at the same time, "decategorizes" all the various groups who are eligible for services. Instead of referring to children as mentally retarded, learning disabled, or emotionally disturbed, Chapter 766 speaks of children with mild, moderate, or severe problems, or of children "with special needs." Decategorizing handicaps in this way might also serve to weaken the oft-noted and, to many, distressing links between the use of specific labels and the socioeconomic status of the people or groups being labeled. H. Wayne Johnson, Director of the Southwest Regional Resource Center in Salt Lake City, cites a study conducted in St. Louis a few years ago in which it was found that, while white children were most frequently labeled "learning disabled," black children tended to be labeled "mentally retarded."

As Leon Oettinger, Jr., a San Marino, California, pediatrician, suggests, the labeling problem is connected at many points to philosophical questions. "The concept that you are born with a reading disorder and that you may never be able to do anything about it, or the best you can do is likely to be minimal regardless of what you do, goes against everything in the American system," Oettinger notes. Nor is an abstract notion such as this merely a theoretical concern. It gives rise to a conflict that can be clearly seen—and felt—in the areas of education and remediation. William Halloran, State Plan Officer, Division of Assistance to States, Bureau of Education for the Handicapped (BEH), explains: "If you look at someone with a disability, and you make the assumption that that disability is a life-long problem, then you have to start structuring academic and occupational training to identify occupational areas in which that person can succeed in spite of the disability. In other words, you would want to find the areas where the abilities can be optimized and the disabilities won't interfere. But the paradox is that other people would say, 'Forget that, because what you're doing is giving up. You're operating off the notion that this thing we're talking about is incurable.'" Halloran complains, in fact, that one of the big problems he sees in both junior and senior high school remediation programs is that they ignore the skills—occupational, behavioral, social, and others—that people will need when they leave school and concentrate instead on bringing academic achievement up to a predefined, normative level. "The assumption is, in many cases, that if you raise the achievement, you're doing away with the disability," says Halloran. From a philosophical point of view, this assumption—

or one very similar—lies at the heart of the regulations prepared by Frank King
for inclusion in P.L. 94-142.

An alternative line of thought is based on the argument that inflexible expectations regarding academic achievement that are built into the educational system are responsible for much of what is now being identified as learning disability. Bill Adams, Headmaster of the Carroll School in Lincoln, Massachusetts, a
private school specializing in reading problems, puts it succinctly: "I maintain
that the only reason we have something called dyslexia is because of educational
expectations—that we have this arbitrary expectation that everybody learn to
read at the same time. If we didn't have that, if we had flexibility, we wouldn't
have this problem." (Subsequent to this interview, Adams left the Carroll
School. The current headmaster, Allan Forsythe, argues that Adams' statement
is much too broad.)

Whether or not the truth of Adams' sweeping statement can be demonstrated,
it is true that the inadequacy and inflexibility of the educational system in the
United States is a topic of major concern in the LD field from coast to coast.
Some of the arguments, which will be examined in greater detail in a subsequent
portion of this book, are: many children are being required to learn to read
before they are developmentally ready; educational reforms in the past few years
have put pressure on children to adapt to teaching styles, rather than forcing
educators to adapt to learning styles (particularly in kindergarten through third
grade); the entire educational system—not just special education—needs to be
upgraded, because when education is bad, it's bad for normal and LD kids alike,
and when it's good, it will be good for both.

But even if education is widely regarded as a primary influence on the development (and definition) of learning disabilities, specifically educational remediations are not universally accepted as the best way to deal with the problem.
Floyd Estess, currently Professor of Clinical Psychiatry at the Stanford University School of Medicine and former Medical Director of the Marianne Frostig
Center of Educational Therapy in Los Angeles, explains that the Frostig Center's method of treatment grows out of the concept of a "global" dysfunction,
i.e., one that affects the entire range of mental functioning, all sensory systems,
motor control, and so on. Thus, says Estess, "we tried to help the child at all
levels of his existence, and I don't think we could ever parcel out what part of
our therapeutic program was effective in contrast to some other part. It was a
shotgun thing: do everything you can to help this child. And I think we got
excellent results. Especially if we got them young."

A narrower, but not necessarily less valid, viewpoint is expressed by Eli Tash,
a past president of the ACLD, who is the founder and current Administrator of
the St. Francis Children's Activity and Achievement Center in Milwaukee,
Wisconsin. "We prefer not to look at either the neurological or the emotional
aspects of [LD]." Tash explains, "We say that's none of our business, and we
hold that at arms length." The staff at St. Francis works with all children with

any kind of handicapping condition from birth on, according to Tash, "provided our staff believes they have an internalized learning problem that we could work with them on."

The Rationale of Treatment
"If we could wipe out dyslexia with a pill . . ."

Such differences in philosophy and concept do have implications for remediation strategies. But whether it is meaningful to approach and remediate learning disabilities from a global perspective; or as a complex of components—educational, neurological, emotional, etc.—that can be divided and conquered; or as a problem that responds best to eye muscle training, stimulation of various parts of the nervous system, dietary manipulation, drug therapy, or other methods; or even from the point of view that a learning disability is not actually a problem at all remains to be seen. "You're caught," laments Christy Ludlow of NINCDS, "because you've got a population that you've got to serve—you can't just ignore them and let them go away. But then at the same time, by trying to treat them on the basis of hunches, you may be doing them more disservice and creating more frustration in the long run."

Yet hunches and unsupported theories continue to be the best the learning disabilities field has to offer in response to the still-open question of what, in fact, a learning disability is. A few prevalent theories are the following: learning disabilities are birth defects of a biochemical or anatomical nature; learning disabilities are caused by poisoning by environmental toxins; learning disabilities are within the range of normal biological variation; learning disabilities are a result of bad teaching (for which the term "dyspedagogia" has been coined). Many people in the field assume that learning disabilities are incurable, but not all do. Susan Trout, Chairperson of and Associate Professor in the Department of Learning Disabilities at the School of Medical Sciences, University of the Pacific, San Francisco, says that some LDs recover from their learning disabilities —or at least learn to cope with them successfully—although many others remain severely disabled in adult life. "Rather than viewing this whole thing as a learning *disability,*" she says, "the day's going to come when it will be viewed as different ways of learning." Others in the field advance similar views; indeed, more than a few contend that people with learning disabilities develop compensatory skills and abilities of significant value and creativity. "If we could wipe out dyslexia with a pill," says Charles Drake (a dyslexic himself), Headmaster of the Landmark School in Prides Crossing, Massachusetts, a private school which specializes in LD children, "I'm not sure whether I would give the pill or not." Noting that the dyslexics he has seen are superior problem solvers, Drake argues —only half jokingly—that "dyslexics are the wave of the future" because, as life becomes increasingly complex, "the world's going to demand people who see relationships and who have problem-solving potential." Perhaps the most extreme form of the "wave of the future" argument is the conclusion reached by Grace Petticlerc, a West Coast remediator, after 40 years of working with educationally handicapped children. "We forget that we evolve," says Petticlerc, "and these kids are coming in with the right side of their brain more open and stronger than the left side, which takes care of the static learning that you get in school." The right-brain development, according to Petticlerc, "is the new evolutionary pattern of the human structure. It's a perfectly natural thing." Petticlerc's speculations receive little support from experts on hemispheric localization.

One possible explanation why learning disabilities remain so difficult to define is that a major piece of the puzzle has yet to be described. There is at this point an almost total lack of reliable longitudinal data—i.e., how does a learning disability manifest itself and affect a person over a long period of time—and there is a concomitant lack of precise information as to what the condition looks like in an adult. Even when adult LDs can be located, most of them, as one educator notes, seem to just "fade into the population." It is still extraordinarily difficult, Elena Boder notes, to tease apart the core symptoms from the emotional and psychological overlays and complications that develop after years of failure and frustration.

Nevertheless, the fact that such complications are almost always seen in LD adults (and, of course, in children as well) has given impetus to a perspective on learning disabilities whose significance is only now beginning to gain wide acceptance. In the words of psychiatrist Larry Silver, "the child with the Minimal Brain Dysfunction Syndrome does not have just a school disability—he or she has a *Life Disability* [Silver's italics]. The same group of learning disabilities that interfere with normal learning processes also impinge on self-image, peer relationships, family relationships, and social interactions. The same hyperactivity or distractibility that affect the child's abilities in the classroom interfere with his adaptation to home and neighborhood" (Silver 1979).

That failure in the classroom can have wide-ranging consequences was explained in the following way by clinical psychologist Roger E. Saunders, a past president of the Orton Society:

> . . . academic failure at any age can corrode a person's personality and self-esteem, leaving the dyslexic increasingly vulnerable to stress. For example, a normal reaction to a problem of everyday life may, in the dyslexic, become exaggerated as he attempts to adjust emotionally to almost constant frustration and anxiety over failure. And so the dyslexic in the classroom may respond to his dilemma by choosing "fright, flight, or fight"—noncompetitive withdrawal or denial, a don't-care attitude, or rebelliousness—(the acting-out of nonconforming behavior) [Saunders 1977, pp. 64–65].

The complications of academic failure, Saunders adds, can be of lifetime duration.

Incidence

"It's big money."

Such observations become especially significant when they are considered in the light of estimates (however inflated they may be) that the incidence of learning disabilities among prison populations is as high as 80 or 90 percent. Indeed, both the General Accounting Office and the Law Enforcement Assistance Administration have recently undertaken studies of the possible links between learning disabilities and juvenile delinquency (see pp. 122–126). While early results indicate that the estimates of 80 to 90 percent are—as many have felt them to be—gross exaggerations, the more moderate recent estimate that 32 percent of incarcerated juveniles are learning disabled remains a dramatic indicator of the possible cost of learning disabilities both to society at large and to individuals who, due to their inability to read, balance a checkbook, deal with stress, hold a job, or develop or maintain a healthy self-image, are forced to go on welfare or turn to crime. (But see the cautionary remarks below on the use of statistics to establish cause.)

Estimates of the incidence of learning disabilities among the general population (by which is usually meant the school-age population) range from 1 percent or less to 35 percent or more, although most assessments fall in the 3 to 16 percent range. The variations primarily reflect differences in the definition used and in the experience of the estimator. It goes, perhaps, without saying that there is currently no way to estimate the extent of LD with any degree of precision, not only because of the confusion as to how many subgroups and syndromes are really involved, but also because LD has become something of a fad. "There was a time," recalls Sylvia Richardson, "when it was very difficult to convince the field of medicine and also some in the field of education that there were such children with specific learning disabilities and children with dyslexia. And now I find that the pendulum's gone full swing the other way, and now it's very hard to convince people that all children don't have LD." Educator Don Hammill, past President of the Division for Children with Learning Disabilities (DCLD) of the Council for Exceptional Children (CEC), who is currently conducting independent research in Austin, Texas, is not alone in his view of why estimates of LD tend to go so high. "See, you can't divorce specific learning disabilities from the institutional aspects. It's big money. There's big money in materials. There's money in the schools. There's big money in this delinquency side. If LD becomes 3 percent instead of 30 percent, there are people who will be out of business." To put this numbers game in perspective, Orton Society President Drake Duane has pointed out that, even if one accepts an estimate "of five percent of the school-age population demonstrating specific language disability, this would mean that reading retardation constitutes a greater health problem than the combined occurrence of mental retardation, cerebral palsy, and epilepsy" (Duane 1974, p. 33).

Our approach to the numbers, statistics, and other pieces of data that appear in this volume has been one of "cinema verité." The inconsistencies among the estimates—of anything—speak for themselves. The authors are inclined to believe that the incidence of specific learning disabilities is relatively low, but, at this point, no figures—high or low—can be taken as reliable.

Statistics are frequently mentioned in this field in a way that invites the reader to infer a causal connection from a statistical association. The reader should take pains to avoid this logical error. Consider, for example, the figure quoted above that 32 percent of incarcerated juveniles are learning disabled. Even if we suppose that this figure is reliable, we cannot logically conclude that these juveniles are incarcerated because they are learning disabled, nor can we logically conclude that teaching them to read would have kept them out of jail. These guesses may be correct, but, on the other hand, it might be true, for example, that both the learning disabilities and the deviant behavior are consequences of some third factor such as low socioeconomic status. Curing the learning disabilities without improving the low socioeconomic status might have no effect on deviant behavior. The figure of 32 percent LDs among incarcerated juveniles is also difficult to interpret without knowing how many juveniles would be classified as LD by the same criteria out of a nonincarcerated population.

For reasons such as these, the reader should exercise extreme caution in interpreting statistical associations. They may suggest causal relations, and they can be expected to be present when causal relations are there, but they can never be proof of cause.

Explanations of why more LD is being seen now than in the past are just as varied as estimates of the extent of the condition. It's not that the incidence of LD is actually increasing, argues psychiatrist Floyd Estess of the Stanford University School of Medicine, but simply that more of it is being detected now. "High civilization begins to worry more about its creatures," says Estess. "There used to be dumb kids who didn't learn, and nobody cared. Now we're affluent enough in this country to begin to care." But Learning Disabilities Professor Susan Trout offers a contrary finding. She reports that, in the past three years, she and other educators with whom she has spoken have noticed that the problems they're seeing in children are becoming steadily more severe. Trout puts the blame primarily on increasing stress in the environment—as do many others. Although it is widely accepted in the field at this point that boys turn up with learning disabilities far more frequently than girls do (estimates range from four boys for every girl to ratios as high as 9 to 1), Trout says that she is now seeing equal numbers of both, possibly as a result of a shift towards greater expectations for girls than has been the case in the past. Some people suggest that learning disabilities can be caused by environmental toxins which have been increasing in prevalence.

Another frequently heard hypothesis for the rising incidence of LD is the fact that premature infants are surviving today who, 20 years ago, would not have survived. Increasing sophistication on the part of educators, physicians, and others in diagnostic roles is another frequently adduced explanation. The trend toward the consumerization of learning disabilities, as discussed above, is pointed to as still another factor. Many suspect that the incidence of learning disabilities in urban areas is greater than in suburban or rural parts of the country because of socioeconomic or cultural conditions, or, as San Francisco child psychiatrist John Sikorski suspects, because in suburbs and small towns, "the value systems of the parents are more coincident with the value systems of the teachers and school administration."

Finally, a number of people in the field explain the growing incidence of learning disabilities in terms of narrowing educational options. Hofstra University Reading Professor Harvey Alpert points out, for instance, that, 50 years ago, a person could enter a profession such as medicine or law through an apprenticeship. Today, however, says Alpert, "we have closed off everything to the point where if you cannot read—and read reasonably well—you're not going to succeed easily." Ironically, Alpert notes, the emphasis on reading exists alongside numerous information-presenting media that are at society's disposal. Similarly, Larry Silver notes that a shift in the basic educational model away from "structure" and memory-oriented learning to abstract thinking and language-oriented techniques has made many students vulnerable who would not have been formerly. As examples of the shift, Silver mentions modern math, whose emphasis on language disadvantages the student who used to get by by memorizing the "times tables," and the increasing tendency to teach such foreign languages as French in elementary school.

Sharing Knowledge
"The right hand doesn't know what the left hand is doing."

Given the almost limitless span of theories, hypotheses, hunches, and opinions on almost every conceivable topic in the learning disabilities field, it is not at all surprising to hear people make comments like, "the right hand doesn't know what the left hand is doing," or "everyone has been in their own discipline, not reading the journals from the others," or "here are these tremendous learning problems—they're really serious things. And yet here are at least half the professional people putting down anyone who's trying to do anything. We fight against solving the problem."

To begin to remedy this state of affairs, Edward M. Glaser, President of the Human Interaction Research Institute in Los Angeles, submitted a research proposal to the National Science Foundation (1976). The proposal suggested that a group of eminent researchers and practitioners in learning disabilities be brought together for the express purpose of creating a collaborative state-of-the-art monograph on dyslexia, following steps previously devised and applied by Glaser in an earlier project concerning chronic obstructive airway diseases. Among the benefits of the state-of-the-art paper that the proposal described were (1) better identification of issues in the field, (2) a "much-needed integration" of what is and is not known about dyslexia, and (3) "enhanced communication between researchers and practitioners" in the field, "and between the numerous federal funding agencies that sponsor dyslexia research or treatment programs."

The NSF turned the proposal down. While the arguments in favor of Glaser's approach are strong (and Glaser notes in his very thorough proposal that results from the NSF-funded chronic obstructive airway diseases project "have been extremely positive"), there are at the same time a number of reasons for wondering whether such a strategy would work in the field of dyslexia. Over the past decade or so, a number of organizations, among them the Ford Foundation, have sponsored conferences and programs aimed at bringing about some agreement among professionals over the characteristics, treatment, or other aspects of learning disabilities. The results have been consistently disappointing. For instance, Steven Larsen, coordinator of the Learning Disabilities Program at the University of Texas, Austin, and President of the DCLD, relates that, a few years ago, at the instigation of the DCLD, a group was assembled consisting of high-ranking representatives of such organizations as the Orton Society, the American Speech and Hearing Association (ASHA), the DCLD (as well as another CEC division, the Division for Children with Communication Disorders), the International Reading Association, and others. The primary objective of the group, which was initially chaired by Larsen and called the Joint Committee on Learning Disorders, was to work together in preparing a list of competencies that teachers had to have in order to work with children with language, reading, math, spelling, written expression, or other types of learning disorders. Getting the committee to begin working, Larsen recalls, "was a very difficult and arduous undertaking because there was so much animosity, both overt and covert, among the groups. Everybody thought that their constituency was the best prepared to work with these kids." The committee never achieved its goal.

As a number of people in the field note, conflict among professions, which Larsen describes as "ethnocentrism," is not necessarily negative, nor is it unusual in the field of human services. Furthermore, some argue convincingly that there actually is a degree of consensus to be found in the field, although, as Howard Adelman observes, the points on which the most agreement is to be found "are so broad that it's like God and mother and the flag." This being the case, UCLA psychology professor Morton Friedman suggests that, rather than spend money in pursuit of consensus, it makes far more sense to spend money on actual research. Upon hearing about the Glaser proposal, Friedman responded, "I think it would be a waste of time and money, because what you're getting is the least common denominator. By the time you're done, if you're going for consensus, you're going to end up with what people already know."

An alternative approach to bringing about better coordination in the LD field might be to establish a national linking network or organization that would function as a kind of clearing house. An enterprise of this nature would keep tabs, in effect, on everything going on in the field, would disseminate information on a regular basis, and would be available as an information or data resource to all interested parties. There is, in fact, an organization of this sort already in operation on a small scale, the National Learning Disabilities Assistance Project (NALDAP), with headquarters in Andover, Massachusetts. NALDAP is a branch of the Network of Innovative Schools, Inc., which was founded in Massachusetts in 1969.

During its first few years of operation, Network acted as a designated "state facilitator" in Massachusetts, linking various educational projects and services with schools that needed them and also doing consulting work, teacher and management training, developing or reviewing curricula, and also disseminating information—all for schools in Massachusetts. In 1975, when the Bureau of Education for the Handicapped released an RFP (Request for Proposal) for a technical assistance agency to serve federally designated learning disabilities "model demonstration projects" (or CSDCs—Child Service Demonstration Centers) all over the country, Network filed a proposal—even though the organization had not, up until that date, had any experience with learning disabilities per se. And the proposal was accepted. Thus NALDAP came into being in July, 1975, funded under P.L. 91-230, the general Education for the Handicapped Act, and since then has been functioning on a national scale to link together the demonstration centers (there are currently 53 in operation in 33 states), providing them with resources and various kinds of assistance, including on-site consultation, workshops, and a monthly newsletter. There are a number of other information clearing houses and regional technical assistance agencies currently providing services similar to those of NALDAP.

According to NALDAP Project Director David "Max" McConkey, a national linkage and dissemination network for learning disabilities could apprise people in one part of the field of work going on elsewhere. "It would no longer be an excuse that the right hand didn't know what the left hand was doing," he says, "because it would be the responsibility of this coordinating technical assistance agency to find out who's doing what, to make sure that information gets fed in, and then is fed back to the field—not only to those people themselves who are doing the work, but also to parents, teachers, and to administrators, and to those folks who are going to have to comply with the regulations of 94-142-in an easy to understand, palatable form that's not just education-ese." McConkey adds the qualification that it is necessary for this agency to originate outside of the field, "because all experience that we have indicates—and not just in special education, and not just in learning disabilities, but in every other area of education—that when an organization like ACLD or DCLD or even CEC attempts to coordinate work in the field, they in fact tend over time to exclude, if not explicitly, then implicitly, a certain portion."

Just as with the proposed state-of-the-art monograph, the NALDAP concept raises questions. Exactly how useful and desirable would such a network be? Steven Larsen complains that a great deal of the work going on in the field, especially work that BEH has funded, is "so very definitely without value that it's almost sickening," and therefore concludes that there is a great deal of information that is simply not worth disseminating. Jean Ayres, occupational therapist and psychologist whose clinical work is generally highly regarded but whose theories concerning the role of the vestibular system in learning disabilities (see pp. 106-108) remain controversial, wonders whether progress in the field has not been more hampered by a lack of people willing to share information and results than by the absence of a national linking organization. Indeed, UCLA education professor Barbara Keogh notes that "the field is plagued by too many people with advocacy stances" and admits that she prefers her own communication system. "I have a set of people that I interact with, and so we sort of have an informal network," she says. "I don't know that I would want to sacrifice it for a formal network—selfishly."

Even if a NALDAP-type facilitator is not the right answer for now, there is, nevertheless, a general longing in the field for better communication. Some professionals see better communication in such scientific terms as more accurate and universally applicable testing and labeling procedures, better identification of groups being diagnosed and served in different parts of the country, or more rigid adherence to the language and procedures of the scientific method. Others think of communication in more humanistic terms. When asked what she would do if she could wave a "magic wand" in the field to bring about a result she desired, regardless of the money that might be involved, Jean Ayres answered, "The first thing I'd like to see done in the field—although money won't do this— is to see people free enough of their emotional hang-ups and feelings of threat and all those psychodynamics that interfere, and then let some people work together. We could make such headway." In response to the same question, West Coast developmental optometrist Larry A. Jebrock—a member of a profession whose role in the remediation of learning disabilities is currently a matter of considerable debate—wished that educators, medical people, optometrists, and others could be brought together in a "one-roofed clinic" where they "could all open their eyes and see what the other person is doing."

This book hopes to be a kind of one-roofed clinic. It is clear that, up to now, some professions have contributed more to an understanding of learning disabilities than others, but it is also clear that the field as a whole is nearing, if not at, a crucial juncture. Membership in professional societies involved in the field is continuing to grow; billions of new dollars are about to start flowing into the field, not only from P.L. 94-142, but from state and local budgets as well. Increasingly, skilled scientists are focusing their interests and talents on the puzzle of learning disabilities and, not at all incidentally, on the larger question of human intelligence. Special education has also grown enormously over the past decade, to the point where it is now being referred to as "the erogenous zone" of education.

Indeed, there may never be another time such as this, when so much is ready to happen and when so much can still be encompassed within the scope of a single overview. It is tempting to think of the LD field as a kind of metaphor for the condition itself: information is not, at this time, being processed effectively, although the potential is clearly evident. To extend the metaphor one step further, it is also tempting to suspect—as many do of LDs—that impressive abilities are available to be applied to the problems posed by learning disabilities and that their activation awaits only the appropriate stimulus. The federal government is attempting to provide such a stimulus, as are several private organizations—a matter which we will discuss in the next chapter.

Chapter 2
The LD Establishment

"Too far too fast . . . ."

For the learning disabilities field, September 1, 1978 represented a true high-water mark. On that day, Public Law 94-142, the Education for All Handicapped Children Act (henceforth the EHC Act) took full effect: states wishing to qualify for assistance from the federal government must have established programs for providing a free appropriate education to all handicapped children between the ages of 3 and 18 (handicapped children between the ages of 18 and 21 must be served by September 1, 1980). For learning-disabled children, the law is especially significant. Up to now, those children (who, according to the Bureau of Education for the Handicapped [BEH], account for 1 to 3 percent of the United States population aged 3 to 21) have made up the largest single category of handicapped children not being served in education programs. In the academic year 1974-75, according to Office of Education statistics, 88 percent of the learning disabled children between the ages of 0 and 19 were not receiving services. At the other end of the scale, for comparison, the Office of Education estimates that only 19 percent of the speech-impaired children in the same age group were unserved.

First introduced in Congress in May 1972, then reintroduced in January, 1974, and finally signed into law by President Gerald Ford in November, 1975, P.L. 94-142 can be said to make learning disabilities "legitimate." Although

28

there has been legislation dealing with the education of handicapped children on the books at least since 1966 (see below), in the EHC Act, specific learning disability is for the first time given full status as a handicap and is listed along with the other categories of disabilities to be served. In earlier legislation, LD had always been treated under separate sections or titles.

Where learning disabilities are concerned, P.L. 94-142 is both a beginning and an end. It represents, in the first place, the culmination of a long and unremitting effort on the part of parents, professionals, and civil servants to win recognition for and acceptance of LD as a full-fledged handicap. The struggle stretched over three decades, and its roots tap not only science, medicine, and education, but also civil rights. Partly a cause of the so-called LD Movement and partly a legacy are a number of organizations, associations, and government agencies that constitute a sort of LD "Establishment," in the sense that these groups have been—and continue to be—highly influential in determining both the government's policy towards and the public's perception of learning disabilities. Today, as we will see below, the LD Establishment faces a challenge that grows in large part out of its present triumph. For, while LD is now officially recognized as a handicap, it is, as we have seen, far from fully understood—even as the enormous legislative and administrative gears of P.L. 94-142 begin to turn. In a sense, the field has more momentum than direction. And it is to this paradoxical situation that many of the current debates in the field can be traced.

Indeed, though the etiology, symptomatology, and treatment of learning disabilities are baffling and controversial, learning disabilities are now to be one of the focal points of a far-reaching, multibillion-dollar effort on the part of local school districts, states, and the federal government to assure that all handicapped children receive equal educational opportunities. It is in this sense that P.L. 94-142 is a beginning. The machinery is in place; the task now is to see that it works.

The EHC Act is not the federal government's first commitment to the education of learning-disabled children. Since the creation by Congress in 1966 of the Bureau of Education for the Handicapped within the Department of Health, Education, and Welfare (HEW), the federal legal and fiscal roles in the LD field—as in the wider area of educating handicapped children—have grown steadily. The bulk of the money spent in the LD field today—on research, demonstration, and the delivery of services—is spent by the federal government and, more specifically, by HEW.

Since learning disabilities projects are in many instances subsumed under programs that deal with the education of handicapped children, it is virtually impossible to prepare a comprehensive balance sheet that shows exactly how much, program by program, the government spends on learning disabilities. Gross expenditures look like this: the Bureau of Education for the Handicapped estimated that its total fiscal 1978 spending in the area of learning disabilities would amount to some $118 million (total projected BEH spending for education of the handicapped in fiscal 1978 was $622,825,000); the National Institute of Neurological and Communicative Disorders and Stroke gave $1,450,000 as its current total outlay for LD-related research (out of a total fiscal 1978 budget of $178,414,000); the National Institute of Child Health and Human Development allocated $16,471,000 for work in the LD area in fiscal 1978 (out of a total of $166,380,000); and, finally, the National Institute of Mental Health spent, in fiscal 1977, $2,337,525 on major and minor programs relating to learning disabilities (out of a total of $451,754,000). (The figures were provided by these agencies.)

Rather than try to pursue each of these dollars to its destination, what we plan to do in this chapter is to take a broad view. First, we will outline briefly the legislative background to P.L. 94-142—to highlight the nature and context of the public sector's role in the LD field; then, we will describe the EHC Act itself; and, finally, we will mention some of the more important government funded programs that have (or could have) a bearing on learning disabilities.* In the second half of this chapter, we will look at the private side of the LD Establishment and detail some of the chief policy positions found there.

The Federal Government

The federal government's firm commitment to the education of the handicapped dates back at least to 1966, when Congress added a new Title VI to the Elementary and Secondary Education Act passed the previous year. The major impact of that title was to create the Bureau of Education for the Handicapped to provide leadership in what had been a leaderless field. In 1971, Congress repealed Title VI and put in its place the Education for the Handicapped Act (P.L. 91-230), which authorized grants to the states and outlying areas to assist them in initiating, expanding, and improving programs for the education of handicapped children. Although that act did not recognize learning disabilities as handicapping conditions per se, part G of Title VI of that act authorized funding for learning disabilities projects and for a technical assistance agency.

According to the June 2, 1975, report prepared by the Senate Labor and Public Welfare Committee to accompany the Senate version of what was to become P.L. 94-142, prior to 1971, statutes mandating the education of handicapped children were in effect in only 11 states. Following the enactment of P.L. 91-230, however, most states adopted programs of one sort or another—either through court orders or legislative action—to provide educational opportunities for handicapped children. (By 1972, Mississippi and Ohio were the only states without mandates.)

Nevertheless, the delivery of services to handicapped children continued to be

*Projects in basic science are for the most part excluded from this list; many of them are described in the chapter on science.

uneven between and within states. One reason was that some states specifically excluded certain categories of handicapped children from their mandates. The mandate in Pennsylvania, for example, covered only the mentally retarded, while the mandate in Georgia covered all but the profoundly retarded. Another reason, explains Frank King of BEH, was that many states simply failed, as a matter of routine, to appropriate sufficient funds to carry out their own mandates.

The need for further legislation was clear, and the chief impetus arose from a number of landmark court cases that firmly established the rights of handicapped children to receive a free appropriate public education. The two most frequently mentioned cases are *The Pennsylvania Association for Retarded Children* v. *Pennsylvania,* in which the court upheld the right of mentally retarded children to receive a free appropriate education, and *Mills* v. *Board of Education.* In that case, the federal district court in the District of Columbia ruled that the lack of financial resources available for education cannot be used as a reason for depriving handicapped children of their educational rights. The courts, in effect, defined the education of the handicapped as a civil rights issue: discrimination against children on the basis of their handicaps. Among the other key doctrines to emerge from the courts were: (1) that, regardless of the nature of severity of the handicap, a child may not be denied a free appropriate education; (2) that schools must provide equal educational opportunities for handicapped children, meaning an education specifically designed to help them reach their fullest potential; (3) that handicapped children must be educated with nonhandicapped children to the maximum extent appropriate to their needs; and (4) that the child, parents, guardian, or "surrogate" for the parents or guardian are entitled to be notified of any special educational placement before that placement is made and given a chance to influence that placement.

The Elementary and Secondary Education Amendments (P.L. 93-380), passed by Congress in 1974, incorporated most of these doctrines. In addition, P.L. 93-380 substantially increased the appropriation for grants to the states in order that the states would be able to meet the Congressional mandate "to identify, locate, and evaluate all handicapped children, to establish a policy of providing full educational opportunities for all handicapped children, and to establish a time-table for accomplishing this goal" (U.S. Senate Committee Report 1975, p. 6). As the Senate Labor and Public Welfare Committee report explained, P.L. 93-380 was intended to lay the groundwork for "comprehensive planning, the delivery of additional financial assistance to the states, and the protection of handicapped children's rights by due process procedures and assurance of confidentiality" (p. 6).

But the states continued to move slowly. In spite of substantial progress at the state and local levels during the preceding few years, the Senate Committee report noted, "the parents of a handicapped child or a handicapped child himself must still too often be told that adequate funds do not exist to assure that child the availability of a free appropriate public education. The courts have stated that the lack of funding may not be used as an excuse for failing to provide educational services. Yet, the most recent statistics provided by the Bureau of Education for the Handicapped estimate that of the more than 8 million children (between birth and 21 years of age) with handicapping conditions requiring special education and related services, only 3.9 million such children are receiving an appropriate education. 1.75 million are receiving no educational services at all, and 2.5 million are receiving inappropriate education" (p. 8).

Thus, the 94th Congress enacted the EHC Act "to establish in law a comprehensive mechanism which will insure that those provisions enacted during the 93rd Congress (P.L. 93–380) are expanded and will result in maximum benefits to handicapped children and their families" (U.S. Senate Committee Report 1975, p. 6). In the words of P.L. 94–142, "It is the purpose of this Act to assure that all handicapped children have available to them . . . a free appropriate public education which emphasizes special education and related services designed to meet their unique needs, to assure that the rights of handicapped children and their parents or guardians are protected, to assist states and localities to provide for the education of all handicapped children, and to assess and assure the effectiveness of efforts to educate handicapped children."

When it was signed into law, the EHC Act specified that, in applying for grants, states could not count more than 12 percent of all children in the state aged 5 to 17 as handicapped and that children with specific learning disabilities could not make up more than one-sixth of the percentage, or 2 percent. But the act also said that, once Congress had accepted the BEH regulations establishing specific criteria for determining whether a particular condition may be considered a specific learning disability, the 2 percent "cap" would be lifted. Since Congress accepted the LD regulations prepared by BEH, there is now no limit (other than the overall 12 percent) on the number of children that any state may count as learning disabled for the purposes of receiving assistance. Some other key features of P.L. 94–142:

The act defines "special education" as "specially designed instruction, at no cost to parents or guardians, to meet the unique needs of a handicapped child, including classroom instruction, instruction in physical education, home instruction, and instruction in hospitals and institutions." "Related services" means transportation, speech pathology and audiology, psychological services, physical and occupational therapy, recreation, and medical and counseling services (medical services may be for diagnostic purposes only, not for treatment). Also included under "related services" are "the early identification and assessment of handicapping conditions in children."

Beginning in fiscal 1979 (i.e., October 1, 1978), states will receive grants equal to the number of handicapped children between the ages of 3 and 21 who received a special education (in the fiscal year preceding the application for the grant) multiplied by 5 percent of the national average per pupil expenditure in fiscal 1978; by 10 percent of that expenditure in fiscal 1979; by 20 percent in fiscal 1980; by 30 percent in fiscal 1981; and by 40 percent in fiscal 1982.

Based on the current national average per pupil expenditure, the authorizations generated would be as follows:

Fiscal 1978 $387 million
   1979 775 million
   1980 1.5 billion
   1981 2.32 billion
   1982 3.10 billion

Beginning October 1, 1978, each state must pass 75 percent of the federal grant along to its local school districts. Those monies can be used to pay only for the *excess* costs of educating handicapped children (in other words, the state and local school districts must first spend as much money on each handicapped child as they did on each normal child). If a state or local school district is already providing a free appropriate education for all handicapped children, it can use federal grants under P.L. 94-142 to pay for certain other activities, such as locating or screening children, or training special education personnel.

The act encourages states to provide services for handicapped children between the ages of 3 and 5 by offering incentive grants of an additional $300 for each such child receiving services.

In evaluating handicapped children, public agencies are required to provide and administer tests that are not racially or culturally discriminatory and that are in the child's native tongue. No single procedure or test can be used to determine an appropriate educational program for a child. And the evaluation must be made by a multidisciplinary team that includes at least one teacher or other specialist with knowledge in the area of the suspected disability.

One of the innovations of the act is the requirement that local school districts must, in consultation with teacher, parents, and child, prepare a written, individualized education program for each handicapped child. That plan must describe the child's present level of educational performance; state annual goals (including short-term instructional objectives); state the specific educational services to be provided and the extent to which the child will be able to participate in regular education programs; and, finally, indicate when the services will begin, how long they are likely to last, and on what basis and with what procedures the child's progress will be evaluated (the plan must be reviewed at least once a year).

The act also requires that handicapped children must be educated in the "least restrictive environment," meaning that states must develop procedures to assure "that, to the maximum extent appropriate, handicapped children, including children in public or private institutions or other care facilities, are educated with children who are not handicapped, and that special classes, separate schooling, or other removal of handicapped children from the regular educational environment occurs only when the nature or severity of the handicap is such that education in regular classes and with use of supplementary aid and services cannot be achieved satisfactorily."

The EHC Act refines and strengthens the due process procedures established in P.L. 93-380, the Education Amendments of 1974. These safeguards protect the rights of parents and children in all matters pertaining to the identification, evaluation, and placement of the handicapped and also provide for the opportunity to protest educational decisions made by school officials.

Indeed, the act places heavy emphasis on parent involvement, not only by requiring that at least one parent play a role in the development of the individualized education plan, but also by specifically giving parents the right to obtain independent evaluations and to be fully informed, in their native language, whenever an educational agency proposes or refuses to make a change in "the identification, evaluation, or placement of the child" or in "the provision of a free appropriate education. . . ."

The act also authorizes appropriations for grants to states and school districts to remove architectural barriers that might impede the handicapped.

Members of Congress and staffers at BEH alike are highly supportive of P.L. 94-142, reports Edwin W. Martin, Deputy Commissioner of Education, BEH. In the House of Representatives, those who were most conspicuous in their backing of educational programs for handicapped children include: Indiana Democrat John Brademas, Minnesota Republican Albert Quie, Kentucky Democrat Carl Perkins (all members of the House Education and Labor Committee), Wisconsin Democrat David R. Obey, and Massachusetts Republican Silvio Conte. Senate supporters included New Jersey Democrat Harrison Williams, California Democrat Alan Cranston (the majority whip), West Virginia Democrat Jennings Randolph, New York Republican Jacob Javits, Massachusetts Republican Edward R. Brooke, Maryland Republican Charles R. Mathias, Jr., and Washington Democrat Warren Magnuson.

As for the bureaucracy, says Martin, "most of us who work here at BEH have been advocating the program for years, so there's tremendously strong support for it. My policy with the staff is to urge them to be vigorous in implementing the law and to set high standards—hopefully just a little bit higher than the states will be comfortable with—so they'll have to stretch a bit to satisfy the Bureau."

States need not comply with P.L. 94-142. If they do not, they simply do not receive federal assistance. To date, only one state, New Mexico, has chosen not to comply. But even if states or local school districts decide to forego the aid offered by the EHC Act, any educational program receiving federal financial assistance must comply with a separate set of HEW regulations that are similar in spirit to, and, in fact, designed to be compatible with P.L. 94-142: the regulations for implementing Section 504 of P.L. 93-112, the Rehabilitation Act of 1973. Section 504 provides that "no otherwise handicapped individual . . . shall, solely by reason of his handicap, be excluded from the participation in, be denied the benefits of, or be subjected to discrimination under any program or activity receiving federal financial assistance." The 504 regulations are detailed and broad. They cover employment practices; preschool, elementary, secondary, and postsecondary education; health, welfare, and other social services. The central requirement of the 504 regulations is that programs or activities operated by recipients of federal financial assistance must be readily accessible to handicapped persons.

In order not to discriminate against the handicapped in education, recipients are required to comply with provisions that closely resemble those set forth in P.L. 94-142. Recipients operating public education programs must provide a free appropriate education to each child in the least restrictive environment; they must "undertake to identify and locate every qualified handicapped person residing in the recipient's jurisdiction who is not receiving a public education" (Section 504 Regulations 84.32); evaluation procedures must be non-discriminatory, and evaluation data must be interpreted by more than one person before a placement is made; and procedural safeguards must be established for the benefit of parents or guardians. In the areas of education, the 504 regulations actually go somewhat beyond the EHC Act insofar as they cover preschool education or day care programs, postsecondary vocational education, and adult education.

Equally relevant to the learning disabled are the provisions of the Section 504 regulations that deal with employment. These bar discrimination by recipients of HEW assistance "in recruiting, hiring, compensation, job assignment and classification, and fringe benefits."

Several other sets of regulations established to implement sections of the Rehabilitation Act of 1973 also apply to situations where learning-disabled individuals could conceivably confront discrimination on the basis of their handicap. Section 501 of the act requires affirmative action plans for disabled employees. It creates an Interagency Committee on Handicapped Employees that consists of the heads of government agencies. They are ordered to meet periodically to discuss recommendations for improving affirmative action programs within the government.

The Civil Service Commission has published regulations (1978) prohibiting discrimination in federal employment against handicapped persons, specifically including the learning disabled. Agencies are required to "make reasonable accommodation to the known physical or mental limitations of a handicapped applicant or employee unless the agency can demonstrate that the accommodation would impose an undue hardship on the operation of its program. Reasonable accommodation may include, but shall not be limited to . . . job restructuring, part-time or modified work schedules . . . appropriate adjustment or modification of examinations, the provision of readers or interpreters, and other similar actions" (Section 713.704).

The regulations for Section 502 of the act (1976) create the Architecture and Transportation Barriers Compliance Board. These regulations may have a bearing on the learning disabled, because, as Paul Ackerman, Chief of Central Region Branch, Division of Personnel Preparation of BEH, points out, the question of what constitutes a "barrier" is more complicated than it might at first appear to be. "In a school system," he wonders, "if there are no provisions for curriculum materials or special library facilities where the learning disabled can listen to books rather than reading them, is that accessible?"

Finally, the Section 503 regulations (1976), administered by the Department of Labor, require contractors with contracts of over $2,500 from the federal government to establish affirmative action plans for the handicapped.

These regulations make provision for grievance procedures by means of which handicapped persons can seek recourse: under the 501 regulations, for instance, disabled government employees can use the grievance procedures in their own agencies. But, according to Debby Kaplan, Director of the Disability Rights Center in Washington, D.C., "The agencies usually rule against the person and there's no appeal to any higher authority past the agency." Under the 503 and 504 regulations, individuals may file complaints with the Department of Labor or the Office of Civil Rights, respectively, in their federal region.

Hearings are now being held in Congress on amending and extending the act for another five years (the current Rehabilitation Act of 1973, as amended, expired September 30, 1978). An amendment to Title V of the act (which concerns handicapped persons), introduced by former Congressman Edward Koch of New York, would strengthen considerably the legal rights of the handicapped. It would explicitly extend to them the right to go to court to seek recourse against discrimination—a right that has been disputed in the past—and it would also require that, if a handicapped person wins a discrimination suit in court, his or her lawyer's fees be paid by the guilty party.

To what extent this (or other amendments), or the 501 through 504 regulations as they now stand, work to the benefit of learning-disabled individuals is difficult to determine. At the moment, it seems that few if any LD persons have used the law to seek reasonable accommodation. "I would imagine," says Debby Kaplan, "that a lot of learning disabled people have just been taught that that's tough and that's the way it is and you can't expect people to bend over backwards to take care of your needs—especially since until recently learning disabilities hadn't really even been recognized. And I would also imagine that traditionally, learning disabled people haven't thought of themselves as handicapped or coming under the coverage of handicapped affirmative action law."

Kaplan is not alone in surmising that learning-disabled people do not consider themselves handicapped in the same way that individuals in other categories do, and we will return to this important issue below. More to the point in this discussion is the fact that the government itself is currently using—or not using, as the case may be—a number of different definitions of learning disability in the various laws, regulations, and programs that offer assistance to LD individuals. According to a background paper written by Donald Freedman, "the nature of the definitions of disability varies with the type of program involved. Definitions for programs which provide individual income supports tend to be the most narrow and rigid. Definitions tend progressively to be broader among programs of the following types: individual remedial programs; . . . individual insurance programs; . . . grant-in-aid programs; planning and advocacy programs; and federal standards requirements for facilities and programs" (Freedman 1977, p. 37).

Indeed, in seeking assistance from a state or federal agency, a learning-disabled person faces a wide, if not bewildering, variety of definitions, standards, and priorities. For instance, the Section 504 regulations for the 1973 Rehabilitation Act (Section 84.3) defines a "handicapped person" as "any person who (i) has a physical or mental impairment which substantially limits one or more major life activities, (ii) has a record of such an impairment, or (iii) is regarded as having such an impairment," and it defines a "mental impairment" as "any mental or psychological disorder, such as mental retardation, organic brain syndrome, emotional or mental illness, and specific learning disabilities." The definition of "handicapped individual" used in the act itself is "any individual who (A) has a physical or mental disability which for such individual constitutes or results in a substantial handicap to employment, and (B) can reasonably be expected to benefit in terms of employability from vocational rehabilitation services." The act, however, requires that priority be given to severely handicapped persons in any of 20 categories (e.g., spinal cord injury, epilepsy) from which specific learning disabilities are excluded. Thus, a learning-disabled person can use Section 504 regulations of the Rehabilitation Act to challenge discrimination in an employment situation, but only with great difficulty could that same person use the act itself to seek assistance in becoming employable.

Tom Skelley, Director of the Division of Special Populations in the Rehabilitation Services Administration (an agency in the Office of Human Development Services of HEW), explains that, in order to gain assistance from the state/federal program of vocational rehabilitation, a learning-disabled person would have to demonstrate that the handicap had a clear neurological basis. Once a person had been certified as having a neurologically based learning disability, says Skelley, he or she would be, in theory, eligible to receive "virtually any services that are required to enable a person to become gainfully employed, from a comprehensive evaluation, vocational training, counseling, pre-vocational adjustment training, or physical or mental restoration services" (which can be anything from surgery to psychotherapy). Even so, Skelley continues, a person with a certified neurological learning disability might still not receive services, since, even though the Rehabilitation Act itself does not stipulate that an applicant be financially needy, many state rehabilitation agencies impose economic needs requirements.

For school-age children, the stringent requirements of vocational rehabilitation agencies do not close off all avenues of aid (although a clear-cut symptom can sometimes be enough to qualify a person for a college education financed by the state rehabilitation agency). Skelley reports that many people, including some in BEH, interpret the mandate in P.L. 94–142 to include "comprehensive life adjustment services, including job placement," and that a task force composed of representatives from BEH, the Rehabilitation Services Administration, special educators, and state administrators is currently working together to coordinate the programs established under P.L. 94–142 and the Rehabilitation Act of 1973. Skelley adds that, with school-age individuals, one of the problems involved in helping them get onto the right career track is that special education—rather than vocational rehabilitation—is usually the best answer. "The main difficulty so far as our program is concerned," he notes, "lies with the LD adult. It seems to me that that's the area where we should be helping out, rather than trying to do much for the in-school LD whose needs should be met by special and vocational education." Of the 291,000 individuals served by the state/federal program of vocational rehabilitation in fiscal 1977, Skelley estimates that learning-disabled individuals amounted to no more than a few hundred.

Definitional complexities similar to those in the Rehabilitation Act of 1973 are found in the Developmental Disability, or DD, program which, like the Rehabilitation Services Administration, operates out of HEW's Office of Human Development. The DD program is not, at the moment, a service program per se but rather a mechanism through which a target population—those defined as developmentally disabled—achieves better access to existing programs and through which new programs are developed where existing ones are inadequate. How that target population has been defined, however, has been a matter of considerable controversy. The only learning disability mentioned in the Developmentally Disabled Assistance and Bill of Rights Act of 1975 (P.L. 94–103) is dyslexia, and, under the act, dyslexics do not qualify for a full range of services. Whereas the Rehabilitation Act of 1973 makes organic dysfunction a criterion for eligibility, the DD Act requires that dyslexia (and other developmental disabilities) "be closely related to mental retardation because such a condition results in similar impairment of general intellectual functioning or adaptive behavior to that of mentally retarded persons or requires treatment and services similar to those required for such persons. . . ."

At the time it passed P.L. 94–103, Congress was aware of the turmoil surrounding the question of who should and who should not be included in the DD target population. And so it included in the legislation a provision that a report be submitted to Congress on an "appropriate basis" for a definition. A contract was awarded to a private firm, Abt Associates, Inc., of Cambridge, Massachusetts, and subsequently a National Task Force was organized to work on the problem. The report submitted concluded that the appropriate basis was as follows:

A developmental disability is a severe chronic disability of a person which:
1. is attributable to a mental or physical impairment or combination of mental and physical impairments;
2. is manifest before age 22;
3. is likely to continue indefinitely;
4. results in substantial functional limitations in three or more of the following areas of major life activity:
   (a) self-care
   (b) receptive and expressive language
   (c) learning
   (d) mobility
   (e) self-direction
   (f) capacity for independent living, or

(g) economic self-sufficiency; and

5. reflects the need for a combination and sequence of special, inter-disciplinary, or generic care, treatment, or other services which are:

(a) of life long or extended duration, and

(b) individually planned and coordinated [Abt Associates 1977, p. 9].

The Task Force estimated that, under the new definition, approximately 200,000 "chronic, socially impaired" LD individuals would be eligible to be served (Abt Associates 1977, p. 21).

At this writing, Congress is holding hearings on the DD program, whose authorization expires October 1978. The DD program is operating on a $60 million budget for fiscal 1978, which is scheduled to increase to $62 million in fiscal 1979. The House of Representatives, however, is considering increasing the appropriation for fiscal 1979 to $103 million and keeping the program—and the current definition—intact. In the Senate, on the other hand, a bill has been introduced that would turn DD into a straight service program, would incorporate a new definition similar to the one proposed by the Task Force, and would appropriate $241 million for fiscal 1979. In the meantime, the White House is said to be preparing its own recommendations. Thus, the fate of the program and the kind of assistance it is likely to make available—on whatever basis—to the LD population will be uncertain for a time.

In any event, whether the old definition is maintained or a new one developed, some groups are going to be dissatisfied. The trend in legislation seems to favor ever-broader and more inclusive definitions. However, the state and local administrators who must determine which applicants are eligible for these services complain that noncategorical definitions are difficult to use in practice. For instance, of the 12 signers of the minority report that accompanied the DD Task Force recommendation, the majority are or have been responsible for interpreting and implementing the DD program at the state and local levels. They did not believe "that the program can be successfully administered without identifiable categories of disability. A generic definition necessitates endless interpretation of who is not developmentally disabled and serves to increase the potential for not serving those most in need of services" (Abt Associates 1977, p. 25).

Another HEW effort with LD implications is Early and Periodic Screening, Diagnosis and Treatment (EPSDT), which is administered by the Health Care Financing Administration. EPSDT is also trying to coordinate its activities, which are national in scope, with DD, the Rehabilitation Services Administration, P.L. 94–142, Head Start, Title I in the Office of Education, Maternal and Child Health, and other programs.

Initiated in 1967, EPSDT, a component of Medicaid under Title XIX of the Social Security Act, is a comprehensive health care program for needy children and youths from 0 to 21 years of age. The program provides for early and periodic screening, diagnosis, and treatment of physical and developmental problems. The program is operated by the states and localities. Emphasis is placed on prevention through early identification of physical and developmental problems. Innovative techniques of outreach and case management are being employed to reach eligible children and youths and to provide the supportive services needed to follow though on diagnosis and treatment of identified problems. Although federal guidelines provide for minimum requirements for physical screening, states have been following their own plans for developmental assessment pending the issuance of federal guidelines. The American Association of Psychiatric Services for Children has been awarded a contract to study and make recommendations in this area and has issued an interim report, "Developmental Review in the EPSDT Program" (1977).

Federally Funded Educational Research

Aside from these services, civil rights, advocacy, and global screening programs, the federal government also funds a number of smaller programs that tend to focus on educational research and program innovation and development. The bulk of these programs are administered by the Bureau of Education for the Handicapped. Again, precise dollar figures for the amounts spent on LD per se are hard to break out, because most of the programs are involved simultaneously with more than one handicapping condition.

For instance, BEH spent $45 million or so in 1978 to support the training of personnel to work with handicapped children; a portion of that sum will be used to develop specialists in the area of learning disabilities. By the same token, a percentage of the $22 million fiscal 1978 budget for the Handicapped Children's Early Education Program was earmarked for LD-related projects. This program, also known as First Chance, supports demonstration—not service—projects. The purpose of First Chance is to develop programs for 0- to 8-year-old handicapped children that can serve as models for public and other agencies that need information on how to provide a variety of special services for children and their families. First Chance activities include not only model service programs but also dissemination of information, replication, and evaluation (of activities, not children). In 1977, First Chance encompassed more than 200 projects that served approximately 12,000 children. Of those, 1,500 were learning disabled.

Now being phased out is a BEH "Model Programs" project aimed exclusively at learning-disabled children between the ages of 5 and 21.* This project dates back to 1971; at that time Congress enacted P.L. 91-230, and, because that act did not formally recognize learning disabilities as a handicapping condition, it included a separate section (Part G of Title VI) that authorized funding for LD model programs and for a technical assistance agency (since 1975, that agency

*There are no "model programs"—and, indeed, few of any other kinds of service or development programs—for adults.

has been NALDAP). In fiscal 1977, the BEH budget for funding the 53 Child Service Demonstration Centers operating under Title VI–G and administered by the Program Development Branch of BEH was approximately $9 million. BEH describes the LD Model Programs project as one that seeks to stimulate state and local comprehensive identification, diagnostic and prescriptive educational services for all children with specific learning disabilities through the funding of model programs, as well as supportive technical assistance, research, and training activities. It also provides for early screening programs to identify these children and for dissemination of information about the learning disabilities programs.

The project is being phased out—but not discontinued—because, since P.L. 94-142 recognized LD as a handicapping condition, Congress saw no need to maintain a separate authorization for LD programs. Thus, Congress eliminated part G of Title VI and moved the LD Child Service Demonstration Centers to part E (the research component of Title VI). In effect, a new model programs project is being built by BEH. Educational Program Specialist Gary Lambour explains that the new model programs "will be for the establishment of demonstration programs of a three-year length, for service to any type of handicap that is recognized by P.L. 94-142." At present, there are 53 demonstration centers in 33 states operating under old model programs authorizations. These will all live out their funding and may then reapply for support under the new project. Lambour points out, however, that "we do not intend to just re-fund the same old things, so old projects would have to come in with a variation of what they're doing—a new population, or maybe a new approach; something that makes it a different project." Lambour reports that Model Programs is now considering putting out a new RFP for a technical assistance agency, which would mean that, if NALDAP reapplied, it would have to compete against other applicants.

The first-year budget for Model Programs is $3 million which is being split up into grants of $115-120,000 for each of the two-year projects being funded. Lambour feels certain that the budget will increase significantly once the project picks up steam because it has received a strong response in terms of applications for funding. In the coming year, Lambour estimates that Model Programs will receive 800 to 1,000 applications (last year, he reports, the project received 225 applications for LD programs) and that it will spend $4-4.5 million on learning disabilities.

Through its experience with projects like LD Child Service Demonstration Centers, BEH became aware of two broad problems in the field. One of them was administrative: individual study projects, operating on relatively short-term funding, were unable to plan ahead for either personnel or facilities in order to establish ongoing research programs. The other problem had to do with the substantive nature of research and particularly with the need for combining research and development activities with "real-world service delivery settings." One of the obstacles to this kind of integrative programmatic research, the BEH observed, was the fact that researchers tend to be divided into narrow disciplines. To try to overcome these problems, the BEH awarded contracts to nine organizations to conduct research programs along the lines of an institute format. In essence, this means that the programs would be comparatively long-term, would be given sufficient funding to support a core staff that would carry out planning activities and also to support personnel in addition to the core staff once the program became operational, and would involve both a basic research and applied component. The projects got under way in 1977, with research activities falling into two categories of concern to professionals in the special education field: early childhood education of the handicapped, and the education of children with learning disabilities.

Four institutes are receiving grants of about $150,000 a year for the planning years and $400–500,000 for each operational year to conduct research leading to improved educational intervention for newborn to five-year-old handicapped children. The grantees, whose programs will stretch over five years with a renewal option for another five years, are the University of Kansas; the Educational Testing Service; the University of North Carolina; and the University of California, Los Angeles.

The other five institutes are conducting research on the nature and education of children with specific learning disabilities. These programs, funded at approximately the same levels as the early childhood projects, are three years in length with a three-year renewal option. The institutes and their projects are: Teachers College at Columbia University, carrying out "basic academic research and development work," according to Max Mueller, Chief of the Research Projects Branch at BEH; the University of Illinois at Chicago Circle, focusing on the identification and diagnosis of LD in kindergarten, first, and second grade students; the University of Kansas, looking at the problems of adolescents with learning disabilities; the University of Minnesota, concentrating on the diagnosis of LD; and the University of Virginia, placing its emphasis on attention as a major problem in LD children.

In each of these programs, as we mentioned above, there must be a provision for applying the results of research in a delivery setting. Moreover, the contracts require that research results be published in professional journals. For its part, the BEH intends to hold annual meetings at which the researchers from the various institutes can share ideas. The funding for these projects derives from the research and demonstration provisions of P.L. 94–142.

To assist in the development of educational specialists in the area of the education of handicapped children, BEH has been maintaining, since 1975, a "Dean's Grants" program. According to Thomas Behrens, Program Officer, Division of Personnel Preparation at BEH, the purpose of these grants is to stimulate a reconceptualization of teacher training curricula and also to support faculty in-service training, "so that in the future, regular classroom teachers will come out of school with a good amount of knowledge as to how to accommodate handicapped children in their classrooms. The goal is to redesign curricula so that the handicapped child isn't an add-on kind of thing in the teacher's training, but rather that the handicapped child's needs would be a more integral part of the whole training process." The grants, which average about $50,000 apiece, are given to university deans or their equivalents, since they are in a position to make the decisions that lead to actual changes in training programs. The Dean's Grants program is currently funding about 120 projects.

Obtaining Information from the Federal Government

A persistent complaint among both professionals and consumers in the LD field concerns the difficulty of obtaining information on relevant laws and regulations, available programs and resources, and research. There is no single source for all the data that pertains to specific learning disabilities, but there are a number of organizations, most of them operating with government funding, that fill in some of the gaps. Only one of these organizations is explicitly designed to answer questions from parents of handicapped children (though it also serves professionals): the BEH-funded National Information Center for the Handicapped, also known as Closer Look. In operation for the past seven years and serving all 50 states, Closer Look supplies parents and other interested persons with free information on how to obtain services for handicapped children. Part of the Closer Look budget covers public relations costs; a contract is awarded to a PR firm that places public service ads in magazines, periodicals, and on television.

Typically, Closer Look hears from parents or professionals by mail. Many of the print ads are accompanied by a coupon, which can be sent in and on which the type of handicap can be specified. Sometimes, reports Closer Look staffer Mary Lowry, a parent will simply write "problem," in which case Closer Look will send back a letter asking for more information. When the problems specified are difficult or complex, Closer Look will send back a personal "special attention" letter; as a rule, however, Closer Look can answer inquiries with specially assembled packets that have been gradually refined to be relevant to a wide variety of handicaps. To keep the packets current, the Closer Look library receives —and staff members screen—some 300 periodicals a month.

The LD packet, for instance, contains a number of booklets dealing with learning disabilities,* as well as a general "steps-to-take" pamphlet called "Practical Advice to Parents"; a reading list of books on LD; a reprint of a Closer Look newsletter (which is published three times a year) that explains P.L. 94-142; the addresses of local chapters of the Association for Children with Learning Disabilities; and a brochure that explains a child's legal rights to services, how these rights can be used, and also how to use due process of law. Only about 15 states have prepared rights brochures for parents that explain how the rights

---

*If "dyslexia" is specified, Closer Look will include in the packet material prepared by the Orton Society.

work in the state in question, Lowry notes. In answering inquiries from states which have no such brochures, Closer Look sends a general explanation. In addition, Closer Look encloses in each packet the name of the state Director of Special Education and other relevant officials in the state from which the inquiry has come, and it is now preparing lists that give the names of county or regional special education officials and administrators.

In order to avoid the appearance of giving an endorsement and, also, to avoid discouraging parents or professionals from seeking out programs that were not on the list, Closer Look does not send out lists of programs. What it does suggest is that parents begin by seeking services in the local school system.

Another BEH-funded clearinghouse system is the Regional Resource Centers, located in 16 offices around the country. In the current funding period (budget for fiscal 1978: $9.75 million), the mission of the Regional Resource Centers is to assist states and local education agencies with educational appraisal and programming for the handicapped child. In particular, the Regional Resource Centers are charged with giving assistance in connection with the individualized education plans required by P.L. 94–142.

Computer Information Retrieval Systems

Funding from the National Institutes of Health (NIH) of the Department of Health, Education, and Welfare supports two computerized information retrieval systems: CRISP and MEDLARS. CRISP, Computer Retrieval and Information, Scientific Projects, is designed to provide by research category (e.g., dyslexia), the names and addresses of the principal investigators working on projects related to that category, as well as a brief description of, and the amount of money allocated for, each project. CRISP indexes projects funded by the National Institute of Child Health and Human Development (NICHD) and the National Institute of Neurological and Communicative Disorders and Stroke (NINCDS), as well as other NIH institutes. MEDLARS stands for Medical Literature Analysis and Retrieval System. The system performs literature searches by subject, and it maintains "Medline" regional centers all over the country that are linked to the main computer in Washington.

The Scientific Project Analysis and Retrieval System (SPARS) is operated by HEW's Alcohol, Drug Abuse, and Mental Health Administration to index the work of its division in the National Institute of Mental Health (NIMH). Overlapping somewhat with CRISP, SPARS provides by subject the abstracts of NIMH research grants and Research Career Program Awards, as well as the name and address of the principal investigator.

The National Institute of Education (of HEW) funds 16 ERIC (Educational Resources Information Center) clearinghouses, one of which—the Clearinghouse on Handicapped and Gifted Children—is operated by the Council for Exceptional

Children (CEC). Other clearinghouses provide information on such topics as teacher education and educational management. The ERIC clearinghouse at CEC is a literature search system for all exceptionalities, including dyslexia and specific learning disabilities. Four times a year, it publishes Exceptional Child Education Abstracts, which covers and indexes publications in the field of special education. ERIC also makes those documents available through microfiche.

A privately funded clearinghouse—more accurately, a linking organization—is NEXUS, which is a part of the American Association for Higher Education. NEXUS keeps track, primarily, of programs in postsecondary education. As Rona Hartman of the NEXUS staff explains, if a learning-disabled person were looking for a college that has a program for, say, dyslexics, then NEXUS would put that person in touch with one of the organizations, such as the ACLD, that keeps lists of such programs. Or, if a professional wanted to set up a program for the learning disabled, NEXUS would provide information on similar programs already in existence.

Other Federal Programs

One other ongoing program that has a bearing on LD is the Right to Read Effort, which is located in HEW's Office of Education. The program, now 6 years old, is designed to serve an estimated 1.9 million adults in the United States who are functionally illiterate and 7 million elementary and secondary students with severe reading problems. Among the components of the Right to Read Effort, whose funding in fiscal 1977 was $26 million, are programs aimed at the development and implementation of innovative reading programs for pre- and elementary school children; at determining the effectiveness of reading instruction provided by reading specialists in the classroom setting; and at providing, through "Reading Academies," appropriate reading instruction for in-school and out-of-school youth and adults who otherwise do not have access to such instruction. Although the Right to Read Effort has, some say, gotten tangled up in a welter of small programs that have blunted its initially strong thrust, there is some reason to believe that it may regain some of its former effectiveness under the leadership of its new director, Gilbert Schiffman. An optometrist from Johns Hopkins University, Schiffman is a past board member of the Orton Society and has also been very active in the International Reading Association.

The White House

Rounding out the Washington scene are two broad initiatives aimed at developing policies and recommendations for dealing with learning disabilities and other handicapping conditions: the President's Commission on Mental Health, chartered by President Carter; and the White House Conference on Handicapped Individuals, organized during the Ford administration.

The President's Commission on Mental Health included, among others, a panel of experts and authorities known formally as the Task Panel on Learning Failure and Unused Learning Potential of the President's Commission on Mental Health. At the end of April, 1978, the panel submitted a report based on the following set of orders:

> School failure is known to be associated with ongoing emotional distress for the affected students and their families. When failure persists, the individual becomes a discouraged, damaged adult who lacks the necessary skills for effective adult functioning. Knowledge is currently available to help a great many of these children. It will be the task of this panel to: (1) review the state of knowledge in the various disciplines that relate to learning disorders and learning failures; (2) [carefully define] meaningful categories of unused learning potential, extrinsic and intrinsic factors that may apply; (3) describe with as much specificity as possible what is known to be effective for each of the specified categories of learning failure; (4) describe models of effective interdisciplinary teamwork in meeting the complex needs of long-term learning problems; (5) review what is known of effective programs to achieve early detection and appropriate intervention or prevention of some of the categories of learning disorder [Task Panel on Learning Report, 1978, p. 60].

The major theme to emerge from the 17-member panel's report is that the best way to reduce the incidence and impact of learning and emotional disorders is by changing the "goals and practices" of the American public school system. In particular, the panel concluded:

> ... at present, most teachers have had little or no preparation in their undergraduate training to recognize and to respond appropriately to the learning problems of the individual child. ... It is the consensus of the Task Panel that this is the most important area for policy change in the goals and practices of the school system in the United States [Task Panel on Learning, Report 1978, pp. 45–46].

The panel specified a number of "options for action" to implement in effecting this change. One major option is an increased emphasis on the screening and the delivery of follow-up services to infants and children. The panel recommends that the office of the secretary of HEW design "an integrated, comprehensive plan to unify at the federal level" screening and service delivery programs currently administered by health and education agencies.

The comprehensive educational assessment of children in school, the panel suggests, should be conducted for every child—not only the handicapped—prior to each school year. Following this assessment, parents and school personnel should meet to work out "an educational plan and expectations for the individual child." One of the strongest benefits of such a policy, the report argues, is that it will identify learning-disabled children early in their educational careers, when the prospects for remediation are more favorable.

Meeting the needs of individual children in the classroom will require competencies that are not as a rule imparted to educators in current undergraduate teacher education or in-service training programs. These programs, the panel recommends, should be "restructured and redesigned," and teacher certification requirements revised to reflect this new emphasis (Task Panel on Learning, Report 1978, p. 47). At the same time, the panel concluded, minimal standards to govern the development of appropriate individualized education programs should be established by the U.S. Commissioner of Education or by state departments of education.

The panel goes a significant step beyond P.L. 94–142 in its view of the advocacy rights of parents. For one thing, the panel recommends that information, referral, and advocacy services (i.e., advice in "due process proceedings") be provided "from a base independent of the schools or the school system." One option listed in the report would make the secretary of HEW "responsible for developing a plan and for formulating a funding model to implement parent resource and child advocacy offices in states and localities" (Task Panel on Learning, Report 1978, p. 49). Moreover, the panel recommends that, in addition to having the right to demand a comprehensive assessment of their children's ability and performance (as is stipulated in P.L. 94–142), parents also be ensured the right "to initiate formal evaluations of educational personnel and/or of the program at the child's school."

Failure to learn, says the report, can be the result of a number of factors. Among them, for instance, are inadequate or inappropriate educational practices; lack of screening and assessment programs for preschool and school-age children; widespread ignorance of the role of diet, exercise, substance abuse, and other factors in the birth and subsequent health of children; inadequate prenatal and postnatal care of mothers and infants; and even insufficient preparation of adolescents and young adults for parenting.

Concerning the learning problems known as specific learning disabilities or developmental dyslexia, the report quotes a number of definitions but puts them all in perspective by emphasizing the fact that a great deal remains to be learned about the basic process involved in the use or understanding of language. Still, the report contains a suggestion by Jeanne McCarthy, Assistant Executive Vice President of the University of Arizona, to the effect that children with specific learning disabilities (estimated by McCarthy to account for 1 to 3 percent of the school-age population) may also have sensory, motor, intellectual, or emotional problems or may be environmentally disadvantaged. These children, McCarthy argues, may require federally subsidized multiple services (Task Panel on Learning, Report 1978, p. 17).

Whereas the Task Panel of the President's Commission on Mental Health was limited by its charter to a concern with learning disabilities and disorders, the

White House Conference on Handicapped Individuals was concerned with, and designed to be a forum for, all handicapped groups. Originally created by Congress and the White House in 1974, the Conference was not actually activated until 1976. Its purpose was to give all handicapped groups a chance to air their grievances and express their needs and thus to give both Congress and the White House an idea of what further legislative and policy action was needed.

In advance of the national meeting that took place in May, 1977, each state held at least one preparatory mini-conference (Paul Ackerman of BEH was Director of Planning and Evaluation of the Conference staff and reports that most states held four or five such mini-conferences). Then the delegates from the states convened in Washington.

Among the recommendations to emerge that pertain to LD, reports Ackerman, were the following: for preschool handicapped children, high-risk registries should be established that might lead to early intervention (a problem with this idea, Ackerman notes, is that the record keeping involved in screening and registry programs might pose a threat of invasion of privacy); and, for preschool-age children, stronger interdisciplinary intervention programs should be developed.

For school-age children, there was a very strong sentiment for more research in all areas of handicapping conditions. The Conference delegates also called for the creation of a national computerized clearinghouse that would collect all research data, laws, and information on services pertaining to the handicapped in order that that information could be disseminated to those who have direct contact with the handicapped, including parents. A related notion was that schools should provide information to parents through in-service workshops in local education agencies and universities to disseminate research findings and to demonstrate their applicability for parents, parent groups, advisory committees, and handicapped adults.

For both school-age and postschool-age handicapped individuals, Conference delegates expressed a strong concern for better vocational education. "They feel," Ackerman says, "that vocational and pre-vocational training and counseling for all types of handicapped children were minimal in most schools." Also, they felt that better training of teachers was necessary in both regular and special education to work with handicapped children.

For postschool handicapped persons, the Conference recommended more research, more programs for adults, and incentive grants to community colleges to make their programs more accessible to the handicapped. "At this level," Ackerman says, "they wanted more handicapped individuals in education planning and policy making," and particularly in adult and postschool vocational education. This theme of input from the handicapped, Ackerman notes, "is particularly relevant to the learning disabled because there are very few advocates for the learning disabled on any advisory groups."

The applicability of these suggestions notwithstanding, Ackerman reports that, of the literally thousands of recommendations and resolutions to emerge from the Conference,* only one dealt explicitly with learning disabilities:

> ... whereas a continuum of educational services is required for a learning disabled person with mild, moderate, or severe handicapping conditions from ages 3–21, and whereas individualized educational prescriptions require effective teaching and the use of carefully selected materials and techniques, be it resolved that educational resources in both general and special education for the learning disabled be provided and coordinated in order to effectively ensure such a continuum [The White House Conference on Handicapped Individuals 1977, p. 245].

Ackerman then ascribes the fact that there was only one resolution on LD— and that it was so weak—to a "provincialism" that pervades the entire movement for stronger rights and better services for the handicapped. On the bureaucratic level, for instance, Ackerman points out that there was no coordination or communication between the White House Conference and the LD panel of the President's Commission on Mental Health, even though there were many areas where their concerns might have overlapped. But the provincialism that Ackerman describes is even more pronounced among the various groups that make up the handicapped population. Ackerman had hoped that the White House Conference might lead to a sort of "coalition of people with handicaps" that could unify for major improvements. "It's been estimated," says Ackerman, "that if an issue were to come before Congress that affected 'the handicapped' and the handicapped were unified behind it, they could probably rally 50 million votes, what with their families and friends." This possibility was not lost on members of the administration. According to Ackerman, "all the relevant cabinet members came to our conference because they saw us as a potentially huge voting bloc." But no such coalition emerged; instead, each handicapped group pursued its own interests, and there was little attempt made at coordinating efforts.

Even so, Ackerman points out that, at the Conference, a movement of sorts developed for better recognition of "hidden handicaps." At the heart of this movement were the groups representing cystic fibrosis and epilepsy. "Very intelligently, systematically, and powerfully," Ackerman observes, "these groups got together and proposed some very strong resolutions about the need for special concern for hidden handicaps—for people whose handicaps did not show but who were discriminated against in all sorts of civil rights ways and in education also." But the participation of LD groups in this movement—if there was any participation at all—was low, Ackerman says. And in the view of Ackerman (and many others), one handicapped group that is badly in need of advocacy at this point is the dyslexic or learning-disabled adult.

---

*These have been put into an Implementation Plan that will be monitored by a White House Conference Action Unit within HEW (The White House Conference on Handicapped Individuals 1978).

Indeed, at the Conference there was only one LD advocate (and seven advocates for language disorders). Not only did LD groups make a weak showing at the Conference but also at the preparatory state mini-conferences. And the reason for this, Ackerman suggests, has to do with a phenomenon that we noted briefly above and that is becoming a major issue in some parts of the field today: there is a stigma attached to being handicapped. There were so many physically disabled people at the Conference, says Ackerman, that "the wheel chair was almost the Conference symbol." Many people, he notes, were put off by "what appeared to be the sort of physical nature of the disabilities represented. And, editorializing, I think that learning disabilities has always been a sort of nice, clean, hidden, middle class disability. As adults, a lot of people 'pass' and build up all sorts of defenses, and all of a sudden to be thrown in a room with two thousand other people, many of whom are very severely multiple handicapped, brings one up short about 'Am I really handicapped? Do I fit into that generic classification?'"

From the start of the LD Movement at the end of the 1950s, the question of classification has been a critical issue, and it still is today. Each of the major special interest groups in the field—the Orton Society, the Association for Children with Learning Disabilities (ACLD), the Division for Children with Learning Disabilities (DCLD) of the Council for Exceptional Children, the American Speech and Hearing Association, and the International Reading Association—answers the question of classification in a somewhat different way. But members of the medical profession—whose role in LD is growing—express doubts whether this question can be answered at all now (Palfrey 1978, pp. 819–824).

Private Organizations

The three most "establishment" groups in the LD Movement are the Orton Society, the ACLD, and the DCLD. Of these, the Orton Society is the oldest, having been founded in 1949. It is also the narrowest in terms of its stated interest. With 21 branches in the United States and members in every state as well as in a number of foreign countries, the Orton Society is, according to one of its pamphlets, "the only international organization devoted exclusively to helping children with Specific Language Disability (Dyslexia)." Named for Samuel T. Orton, a neurologist and pioneer in dyslexia research, the Orton Society is particularly interested in the neurological aspects of dyslexia and, more broadly, in the "use of scientific discipline in educative treatment." The membership of the society (5,000 at last count) is predominantly professional, explains current President, Drake Duane, a Professor of Neurology at the Mayo Medical School and Consultant in Neurology at the Mayo Clinic; "that is," he continues, "most of its members come from psychology, medicine, and education." Members with educational backgrounds predominate, says Duane, but there is a higher proportion of members from the fields of psychology and medicine in the Orton Society than in either the ACLD or the DCLD. The society's membership, however, also includes parents and others.

"Our purpose," explains Duane, "is an educational one. We're interested in seeing to it that there is greater recognition of the problem of dyslexia throughout the United States and the world." To this end, the Orton Society holds a meeting each year at which professionals and parents speak on a wide variety of technical and nontechnical subjects. Although the society does not endorse specific schools, institutions, or teaching programs, it does hold the position that the most appropriate form of remediation is an academic one closely associated with the Orton-Gillingham approach (see p. 103).

In a manner of speaking, it is the ACLD that put the term "learning disabilities" on the map. Until the early 1960s, children with perceptual problems (the general term then in use) were classified under a host of labels, some of them reflecting presumed etiology (brain injury, cerebral dysfunction, etc.), some of them reflecting behavior manifestations (hyperkinesis, perceptual or conceptual disorders, etc.); and the interests of those children were championed by a variety of small organizations. In April, 1963, concerned parents held a conference in Chicago to explore the issue of perceptual handicaps and particularly to find a better label than those in use—a term broad enough to draw the various small organizations then in existence into a large and politically powerful group.

The main speaker at that conference was Samuel A. Kirk (then at the University of Illinois, now Professor of Special Education at the University of Arizona). "Recently," Kirk told the parents, "I have used the term 'learning disabilities' to describe a group of children who have disorders in development in language, speech, reading, and associated communication skills needed for social interaction. In this group, I do not include children who have sensory handicaps such as blindness or deafness, because we have methods of managing and training the deaf and the blind. I also exclude from this group children who have generalized mental retardation. . . ." (Hallahan and Cruickshank 1973, p. 6).

The following day, the parents voted to organize themselves as the Association for Children with Learning Disabilities. In February, 1964, a Professional Advisory Board was appointed (which did not meet for the first time until the spring of 1965). Hallahan and Cruickshank* write: "The nine members of the Professional Advisory Board, together with the parents themselves, failed to appreciate what had been created through the term *learning disabilities*. Few observers recognized that in the creation of a new term the undergirding of research, competent professionals, and appropriate conceptualization of intervention processes were almost completely lacking. . . . The term learning disabilities quickly took on meanings never anticipated by the newly formed

---

*William Cruickshank was one of the original Advisory Board members. The others were Raymond Barsch, Ross Beall, Marianne Frostig, William Gellman, Newell Kephart, Laura Lehtinen, and Helmer Myklebust, with Kirk as chairman.

Professional Advisory Board to the Association" (Hallahan and Cruickshank 1973, pp. 7-8).

In part, the proliferation of meanings attached to the term learning disabilities can be traced to parental pressure. That the term—and the organization—struck a responsive chord among parents is suggested by the fact that, as Hallahan and Cruickshank note, "from a state of practically no visibility in 1960, the annual conventions of the [ACLD] drew registrations of several thousands before 1970." Increasingly powerful parental pressure at the state and local levels on superintendents of schools and school board members led to developments that Hallahan and Cruickshank describe as "unequaled in professional education in the United States." Classes were organized; teachers with an interest in learning disabilities became specialists, "often with no more than three weeks of informal, summer-workshop training." School psychologists "found a whole new arena for the application of their tests, in spite of their lack of a fundamental understanding of the problem" (Hallahan and Cruickshank 1973, p. 3). Moreover,

> despite the lack of a large reservoir of trained professionals in this field [including both teachers and teacher-trainers] and the dearth of research and writing to provide a common definition, children with all sorts of problems, related or unrelated, were placed into classes for the "learning disabled" under the guidance of inadequately trained teachers. Personnel conducting diagnosis and placement often had no adequate concept of the problem [Hallahan and Cruickshank 1973, p. 8].

In effect, conclude the authors, throughout the 1960s, the parents were ahead of the professionals.

Today the ACLD is a large and politically powerful organization with over 200 state and local affiliates. Membership of the ACLD is 50,000. It played an influential role in the passage of P.L. 91-230, the first piece of federal legislation to give recognition to specific learning disabilities. The mission of the ACLD, according to past President Eli Tash, is "to create community awareness of what learning disabilities are and of the need to remediate learning disabilities in children from birth on through adulthood. Our job," says Tash, "is not to mount programs or train personnel, but to stimulate interest in doing this by holding broad, general conferences once a year to which we invite all the top professionals in the world to present their latest insights and knowledge. We also invite administrators to tell us what they are doing and to share their successes, experiences and failures with other administrators and teachers." The ACLD, says Tash, is neither professionally nor service-oriented. "Our group is strictly consumer-oriented. We are parents who have children who we thought could learn if someone could learn how to teach them. We take an eclectic point of view. We never advocate or sponsor any particular product or technique or technology or theory. We create a forum for all points of view."

The most educationally oriented of the three "establishment" groups in the LD field is the DCLD or Division for Children with Learning Disabilities of the

Council for Exceptional Children. Founded in St. Louis in 1967, the DCLD has a membership of approximately 10,000 members, most of them from the fields of education, speech and hearing, medicine, psychology, and nursing. "Dedicated to promoting the education and general welfare of children with specific learning disabilities," the DCLD is primarily concerned with supporting efforts to resolve research issues in the field, particularly issues that have a bearing on the delivery of educational services. Prior to the annual convention of the CEC, the DCLD sponsors open forums and discussion groups on LD-related topics.

The actual differences between these three groups have as much to do with style as with substance. In fact, leaders of both the ACLD and the DCLD claim that their positions are fairly close to that of the Orton Society. For instance, Eli Tash of the ACLD sees a similarity between his group and the Orton Society insofar as both have members who are either consumers or consumer advocates, whereas the DCLD is primarily concerned with providing, rather than consuming, services. Steven Larsen, President of the DCLD, observes that, though there is a great diversity of views to be found among the DCLD's membership, the elected leadership of the organization sees eye-to-eye with the Orton Society insofar as the neurological basis of most learning disabilities is concerned, and also insofar as learning disabilities tend to manifest themselves primarily in language disorders. Don Hammill, a past President of the DCLD, adds that both the DCLD and the Orton Society assume the incidence of specific learning disabilities is low (2 percent or less), and that the two groups are also similar in that they concentrate on remedial approaches that involve "on task" reading instruction. The ACLD, on the other hand, is said by many to be more open to a variety of remedial techniques—proven and unproven (perceptual training, motor integration, diet, biofeedback, etc.)—which gives the ACLD a reputation for being "faddist."

Indeed, criticism from various parts of the field are leveled at all three groups. The Orton Society, for instance, is felt by some to be ineffective in the field of education because its orientation is towards more of a medical than an educational model. The DCLD is said to be overly "academic," a posture that serves to exclude interested regular classroom teachers and parents. And, in addition to being "faddist," the ACLD is judged by some to be overly concerned with preserving LD as a nonstigmatizing label, which leads it to avoid contact or cooperation with groups representing more severe handicaps.

In contrast to the heterogeneous membership of the three major private organizations, associations like the American Speech and Hearing Association (ASHA) and the International Reading Association (IRA) represent more specialized professional constituencies. To say that the ASHA and the IRA are particularly concerned with maintaining their territorial rights in the LD field is not a criticism but a statement of fact. Both groups have been arguing that unduly narrow interpretations of the definition of specific learning disabilities by states and local school districts have resulted in the exclusion of competent personnel from the areas of evaluation and remediation of LD students.

The ASHA, whose 30,000 members are for the most part speech and language pathologists and audiologists, adopted an official policy statement on learning disabilities in November, 1975, that argued, in effect, that many learning disabilities involve impairments in auditory and language processes that speech pathologists and audiologists are trained and certified to remediate. More than 20 state departments of education, the statement points out, have used the definition of learning disabilities developed in 1967 by the National Advisory Committee on Handicapped Children (NACHC)—the same definition that is used in P.L. 94–142—"to describe one category of handicapping condition. In most of these states, children with communicative disorders in speech, language, or hearing are defined separately." The result, according to the statement, is an oversimplification of "complex language and learning problems in children," the fragmentation of services, and conflicts among professional personnel. The statement goes on to note that

> some state and local education agencies that have employed a rigid application of the NACHC definition in their program rules and regulations tend, also, to permit only those personnel certified as learning-disability specialists to provide the primary instructional services for these handicapped children. Because of the limited certification criteria in many of these states and the varying state and local interpretations of the definition, such educational agencies are in jeopardy of unnecessarily restricting or preventing appropriate services for some children whose learning disabilities may very well result from conditions that require competencies of personnel certified in other disciplines.

The 70,000-member IRA (composed primarily of reading teachers, school administrators and superintendents, psychologists, and psychiatrists) officially entered the LD field in May, 1976, when it formally activated a Disabled Reader Special Interest Group. The membership of that group had exceeded 500 within a year. Just as the ASHA argues that many learning disabilities involve speech and hearing disorders, so does the IRA contend that many learning disabilities involve severe reading problems—problems that IRA-certified remedial reading teachers are competent to treat. The IRA statement on learning disabilities argues that the present trend to define and fund learning disabilities according to a "pathological model" leads to the inappropriate labeling and classification of children simply in order to obtain resources; that it limits funds for the greater number of children with severe reading problems that are not pathological but rather expressions of the

> extreme end of natural variation . . . [and that] federal, provincial and state governments, because of special interest groups, are allocating the limited available resources to programs for children classified within the pathological model, compelling local education agencies to employ professional persons whose preparation is for the pathological model, which displaces reading/language specialists whose preparation would serve the total range of natural variations.

The ASHA and the IRA were not alone in feeling that excessively narrow interpretations of the definition of learning disabilities and the law were likely to deprive children of services they might need (not to mention depriving professionals other than LD specialists of jobs). The Joint Committee on Learning Disabilities (JCLD), composed of three representatives each from the ACLD, the ASHA, the IRA, the Orton Society, the DCLD and the Division for Children with Communication Disorders (DCCD)—which, like the DCLD, is a division of the CEC—adopted a similar position on a list of recommendations submitted to the Bureau of Education for the Handicapped in the spring of 1976. To begin with, the JCLD recommended that the definition of specific learning disabilities be omitted from the EHC Act. Among the reasons they cited in support of this move was the fact that "the definition has led some to assume that learning disabilities represents a homogeneous group of children, when in fact the learning disabled constitute a heterogeneous population"; while the ASHA representatives held that "some state and local educational agencies, by a rigid interpretation of the definition, developed criteria for service delivery that ignored professional preparation and expertise and required delivery consistent with the definition as implied in the law" (Joint Committee on Learning Disabilities 1976).

Furthermore, the JCLD formally agreed on a number of concepts that they felt should inform any regulations pertaining to learning disabilities. The JCLD argued that "interdisciplinary knowledge" should be brought to bear in the evaluation and placement of children with learning disabilities and that the assignment of primary and secondary providers of service and instruction should be based on a careful—and prior—matching of the preparation, experience, and competence of personnel with "the needs and disability(ies) of each individual." The JCLD also agreed that "federal and state regulatory provisions should make it clear that individuals, depending on the type and severity of their disability, may best be served by such personnel as learning disabilities teachers, speech and language pathologists, audiologists, reading specialists, psychologists, etc." (Joint Committee on Learning Disabilities, no date).

A little less than a year later, the JCLD sent another list of recommendations to Washington—this time to the Committee on Education and Labor of the House of Representatives. Once again, the JCLD urged that the definition of specific learning disabilities be dropped from the EHC Act and also that the act be technically amended to permit federal reimbursement to the states based upon "the number of different services provided for each child rather than on the basis of unduplicated pupil count." The reason for this suggestion, said the JCLD, was that "assessment of an individual with specific learning disabilities may indicate the requirement of a multiplicity of services, e.g., learning disabilities specialist, reading specialist, speech and language pathologist, etc." (Joint Committee on Learning Disabilities, no date).

Frank King at BEH had reservations about the dividing up of learning-disabled children's needs into categories defined in terms of these various professional approaches. "A great many people believe," he said, "that learning disabilities programming is an approach to teaching, rather than an approach to teaching children with learning disabilities. They see this or that approach as being applied to any child who is not learning in the manner he should be learning. In effect, they make no distinction between those children that are handicapped and those that are not. It's that they're all children on a continuum, and they all need this technique at this time and to this extent, and as you move up the continuum, they need the same technique to a lesser extent. The problem is," King has observed, "that the kids change. They may need this today and something else tomorrow and something else the next day, and that's where you need the skill of a trained teacher in the area of learning disabilities, somebody who has as a part of their repertoire of instructional techniques the ability to shift from one technique to another according to the particular demands of the particular child for that particular day."

Ultimately, the final regulations prepared by BEH for evaluating children with specific learning disabilities acknowledged the role that professionals other than LD specialists might play. In evaluating a child suspected of having a specific learning disability, the final rule ordered, each public agency must include on its multidisciplinary evaluation team "at least one person qualified to conduct individual diagnostic examinations of children, such as a school psychologist, speech-language pathologist, or remedial reading teacher" (P.L. 94–142, regulations 1977, Section 121a.540).

Health Professionals

One group of professionals who will be affected by P.L. 94–142 in a variety of ways, but whose responsibilities under the law are only vaguely defined, is made up of physicians and other health professionals. Dr. Judith S. Palfrey points up some of the implications of the EHC Act for the medical profession. She writes that physicians can expect to be asked by local education agencies to assist in both the identification and evaluation of handicapped children, but the precise extent to which health information will be used is left up to the school districts to decide. P.L. 94–142 assigns no central role to physicians in either of these processes. Indeed, Palfrey reports, "many health professionals involved in the care of children are disturbed by the lack of emphasis placed on developmentally oriented medical input. The American Academy of Pediatrics Committee on Children with Handicaps has issued a statement recommending that the basic team for the evaluation of developmental disabilities be composed of representatives from 'medicine (preferably pediatrics), psychology, education and audiology/speech.' It is not accidental," Palfrey adds, "that medicine is listed first" (Palfrey 1978, p. 821).

While some health professionals are upset by the possibility of their being underutilized in the P.L. 94-142 program, there are others who fear that the emphasis that the act places on evaluation and individualized education plans may mean "that already busy developmental-evaluation clinics will be overwhelmed by requests from parents and education agencies for definitive diagnoses." In addition, there is the danger, Palfrey warns, that specialized school staff such as doctors and nurses will be forced to give so much time to the review process that they will have less time to actually serve children.

As child advocates, physicians will also be affected by P.L. 94-142. One problem they encounter is that school systems, caught between pressure to fulfill the law and the likelihood that special education budgets will not be greatly increased, will respond by attending to "the more visible and accountable aspects of compliance (identification of target children, committee evaluation and preparation of individualized education plans). Thus," says Palfrey, "it will not be an uncommon experience for a physician to hear from a family that a formal evaluation has taken place, that handicaps have been identified, but that little change has taken place in their child's school program." A somewhat more delicate problem may be created for physicians by the fact that children they have been carefully following for years return from evaluations bearing diagnostic labels like "disabled" or "minimally handicapped"—and parents will want an explanation. The heavy emphasis that the EHC Act places on parent involvement will also have a bearing on the medical profession. Physicians will have to be prepared not only to help parents make decisions during the appeals process but also to perform the independent evaluations that parents have the right to request.

A final—and major—impact of the law on the medical profession, explains Palfrey, will be one arising from the fact that the act "assumes a high level of diagnostic sophistication—in effect, mandating physicians to expand their training, to develop more accurate diagnostic instruments and to foster better communication between medicine and education. . . . Although physicians treat children with various developmental disabilities within their practices and clinics, many are not sufficiently trained for the kind of assessment called for (even if obliquely) by P.L. 94-142 legislation and directly by some state laws. The American Academy of Pediatrics Committee on Children with Handicaps suggests that training should be acquired through participation in formally designated fellowship or training programs or through several years of clinical experience working with a multidisciplinary team." And beyond the need for further training is the question of whether the medical profession and other specialists in the area of child development "have yet devised diagnostic tools of sufficient predictive value to enable them to prescribe programs for handicapped and developmentally disabled children." Indeed, she concludes, "the state of the diagnostic art may not be advanced enough for the optimum functioning of a program like P.L. 94-142."

Weaknesses in Terminology

This question, of course, is especially significant in the LD field. The meaning of the term "learning disabilities," and therefore its diagnostic import, remains vague. "Classes for mentally retarded children have often been criticized as being 'dumping grounds' for the benefit of school personnel who could not solve certain problems in children. This criticism could apply a hundred fold to the typical public school program for learning disabilities" (Hallahan and Cruickshank 1973, p. 8). Even special programs for the learning disabled appear to be using broad and imprecise diagnostic criteria. In an editorial in the *Journal of Learning Disabilities,* Louise Bates Ames of the Gesell Institute at Yale University writes: ". . . the term 'learning disabilities' caught on and swept the country —long before we had reached a really satisfactory definition of what it meant, and certainly before we knew what to do about it. . . . Of the supposedly learning disabled children brought to our clinic because they are having trouble in school, the largest number are simply academically overplaced. [I] t seems possible that perhaps half of the children classed as LD and taught and treated accordingly, actually suffer from . . . correctible [physical] difficulties. . . . I personally do not feel that society or the local communities have failed the learning disabled child. Rather, I suspect that the leaders in the field have gone too far too fast, and the parents have been led to expect too much" (Ames 1977, pp. 328-330).

The leaders in the field have been predominantly educators, and it has been through the educational system that local communities and society at large have predominantly been made aware of learning disabilities as a category and have tried to deal with them. This system will be the subject of our next chapter.

Chapter 3

The Educational System

"Through the needle's eye. . . ."

Tailoring the Teaching to the Child

"In the early days at Columbia," recalls Sylvia Richardson, a Cincinnati pediatrician who also trained as a speech pathologist, "if a child couldn't learn, it was because he had a Freudian or psychiatric problem. Later, if a child couldn't learn, it was because he was brain injured. Bull! If a child can't learn, why don't we examine what we're providing for the child to learn and see if we can help him instead of giving him a label and sloughing him off into a special category?"

Increasingly, professionals in the field of learning disabilities are echoing Richardson's challenge and beginning to insist that many children who are labeled "learning disabled" are actually handicapped, not by brain disorders, but by school environments whose standardized expectations are too narrow or rigid to accommodate a wide variety of learning styles. According to the so-called "environmental" model of dyslexia, the hard-core neurological or constitutional instances of dysfunction represent a relatively small percentage of the total number of learning disability cases. It is argued that the bulk of the problems are created by, or at any rate stem from, inappropriate educational practices, expectations, and strategies.

Not everyone, it should be said, finds this perspective a productive one. Pediatrician Melvin Levine of the Boston Children's Hospital describes the approach that focuses on changing society rather than on remediating children as "nihilistic." "In the meantime," says Levine, "what does a kid do?" Concern with the role of learning environment, however, does not necessarily mean that children with learning problems are to be left to their own devices until education in the United States has been sufficiently reformed. What the growing concern with the role of the learning environment does suggest, as we document below, is that (1) changes in educational practices may make it possible to *prevent* certain types of learning disabilities from developing into serious handicaps; (2) as a corollary, those changes may also make it possible to diagnose or locate more accurately the truly severe cases of specific learning disability (specific in the sense that it originates in a neurological deficit of one type or another); (3) inflexible, unresponsive, or overly demanding learning environments may not only contribute to the misdiagnosis of LD on a massive scale but also result in misdiagnosed (and, perforce, unjustly labeled) children receiving services at the expense of those who are most in need of specialized attention and remediation; and (4) within the learning disabilities field, a number of concepts are beginning to emerge that have important implications for traditional notions of teaching, learning, and education in general. Among these evolving perspectives, for instance, is the idea that the range of normal learning styles in children is significantly wider than is currently held to be the case in regular education and the belief that educational techniques geared to helping learning-disabled students will also be of value to nonhandicapped students.

Many specialists in learning disabilities would like to reallocate the resources of society at large and change the practices of schools in general—but their aims and interests are sometimes in conflict with those of other constituencies. Specialists in learning disabilities are concerned, by definition, with children who are not "stupid" but who nonetheless have great difficulty learning some things. They are much concerned not to stigmatize their clients as "stupid," but they tend not even to address the problems raised by students who really are stupid. In their concern to protect the interests of their special constituency, they may sometimes work against the interests of genuinely stupid students or of students who find everything in the school curriculum easy to learn. If public school programs often are not constructed the way specialists in learning disabilities would like them to be, this happens not only because school administrators sometimes are ignorant of trends in special education but also because those who manage the schools must balance a variety of conflicting interests and must compete for resources with claimants outside the field of education. It is no trivial matter to construct a learning environment that is stimulating but not distracting, fosters cooperation but is tailored to individual needs, doesn't put too much pressure on students who lag in development but challenges advanced students, and does all this while putting everybody together in the "least restrictive environment."

Assuming, then, that the environment is a factor in the development of a learning disability, how should that environment be changed and at what stage of the educational process? The Early Recognition Intervention Network (ERIN), an innovative program currently operating in the state of Massachusetts and being funded by the BEH, is focusing on the three-year block of time stretching from the beginning of kindergarten through the end of second grade. Working with over 50 Massachusetts school systems and preschool agencies, ERIN is attempting to refine a model and a practical method for the prevention of learning disabilities. While ERIN's methods are sophisticated and extensive— they include materials for parents, consultations with school administrators and specialists, curriculum ideas, and teacher training techniques and exercises—its ambition is simple. Project Co-Director Marian Hainsworth explains: "Our goal is to provide kids with such a good educational experience in the first two or three years of school that they will learn to handle their problems so well that they will never have to be labeled as learning disabled."

The ERIN prescription for a successful school experience breaks down into two concepts of equal weight. First, by providing children at risk for LD with abundant opportunities to build up their skills and understand their own learning styles, ERIN strives, in Hainsworth's words, to help children "cope as effectively as they can with the demands of regular education so that they can learn how to function in a regular classroom." At the same time, ERIN helps teachers "see how they can broaden their expectations and the ways that they teach things so that children can learn them."

In operational terms, Hainsworth says, "we're really trying to do what we call a diagnostic teaching job. That means understanding a child and his learning style, and understanding the learning environment. Our framework binds these two together, so that you can look at the skills the child has, and you can look at the demands of the environment at one particular point in time, and try to make a match." Although ERIN uses specially developed tests of information-processing abilities to screen young children for those at risk, no labels are used in the program. (P.L. 94-142 may, however, force a change in that policy.) "I don't want to call any of these kids 'learning disabled,'" Hainsworth insists. "I want to say that this educational experience they're about to encounter will need modification for a certain portion."

It is in this light that the implications of the ERIN program, and, more generally, of the environmental model of learning disabilities, begin to take on some startling dimensions. For while Hainsworth estimates that no more than about 5 percent of the portion she refers to are truly learning disabled—and therefore unable to remain in the regular education mainstream—she points out that "if you ask the question of how many kids will need a modification of the learning environment in order to function successfully, that's a fairly good-sized proportion: between 20 and 30 percent is what we think."

The modifications envisaged in the ERIN approach to forging a match between a child's skills and a learning environment are not particularly drastic. For example, Hainsworth explains, an LD child cannot usually produce the amount of written material required by a first grade math or writing lesson. A typical adjustment under such a circumstance might entail helping the teacher understand that the child is not, as Hainsworth says, "stupid, lazy, and trying to get out of the work." Alternatives might be offered, such as reducing the writing demands or allowing the child to use a tape recorder or to select words from a prewritten list and to use those words in a sentence. Some of the modifications that ERIN suggests are simply common sense but nevertheless require a teacher to abandon old concepts. Certain children, for instance, need a calm, quiet place to study. In the past, teachers have isolated students from one another as a punitive measure—because the child is bad or a bother to other students in the class. But setting up table dividers to create individual study carrels, explains ERIN Training Coordinator Donna Carroll, need not be a punishment at all. "Now," says Carroll, "we're seeing it more as, well, the child needs it, and given a choice, he will use that space so that he can study."

Ideally, after a teacher has worked long enough with the ERIN model, materials, and exercises, the framework becomes internalized as part of the teaching setting. "You then are able to look at what's happening from moment to moment and to make the kinds of adjustments that are necessary," Hainsworth says. But in spite of the time and study involved—for parents as well as for teachers—the ERIN model is not a mere set of formulas. "What it comes down to eventually," Hainsworth concludes, "is that you need a lot of ideas to draw on when you're working with these kids. What we find is that every child that we deal with is different. You can recognize certain patterns and that gives you an idea where to start, but each child is unique."

Education based on the insight that all children are unique—nonhandicapped as well as learning disabled—sounds like nothing more than first-rate teaching. Even so, argues Howard Adelman, Associate Professor of Psychology and Director of the Fernald Laboratory at UCLA, teachers have a hard time accommodating to differences in children, particularly in the large classes that are so common in public education today. Rather than tap whatever it is that leads each child to want to learn, Adelman contends, education is structured along behaviorist lines in the sense that the emphasis is on the modification of behavior through external rewards and pressures—with "token learning" and even aversion to particular subjects the frequent result—rather than on the modification of the learning environment to accommodate and stimulate "intrinsically motivated behaviors."*

A fundamental tenet in Adelman's thinking, then, is the notion advanced by such writers as R. D. Laing, Thomas Szasz, and Ivan Illich that society's institutions may themselves produce disorders in individuals and in the whole fabric of our sociocultural life.

*These are defined as "behaviors in which a person engages to feel competent and self-determining. They are of two general kinds: (a) the seeking of stimulation, and (b) the conquering of challenges or reducing of incongruity/dissonance" (Adelman and Taylor 1978).

To put this philosophizing in practical language, it is the lack of sensitivity in education to the uniqueness of each child that, in Adelman's view, accounts in large part for the fact that people in the LD field "spend a lot of time dealing with what wouldn't be here in the first place if we could change the educational system." Adelman zeroes in on what he calls "set-ups," situations that occur when, for instance, a teacher tries to get a large class of first or second graders to line up for recess. Many of those teachers, according to Adelman, are unprepared to cope with children, especially boys, who have a hard time standing perfectly still. "And that," explains Adelman, "sets up an environment. Who's getting in trouble in those situations? Certain boys are sort of fidgety, they start getting a reputation, and pretty soon, by second grade, we're seeing some of those kids [at the Fernald Laboratory]."

To explore the phenomenon of set-ups in some detail, Adelman has been experimenting at Fernald with "model classrooms," by which he means "just a regular good classroom—not much different from what goes on in most public schools—that would accommodate not just developmental differences, which most of the field tends to look at, but also motivational differences." In classrooms such as these, Adelman finds that, with the children he sees, "for about 75 percent, as soon as you've changed around the environment, there's nothing wrong." Findings such as this have prompted Adelman to propose that there is a continuum of learning problems in schools today that can be divided into three broad types: Type I, at one extreme of the continuum, "really has no disorder at all," Adelman says, "and never did." When these children came to school, they were perhaps a bit different "in terms of developmental factors, or maybe they were different in terms of the motivational match with what they were being asked to do, and it started a process of failure going. By the time those children are seven or eight," Adelman observes, "they are virtually indistinguishable from anybody else who's having a learning problem, given the assessment tools that we have to work with today."

Adelman's Type II marks the point in the continuum where minor deficiencies begin: "minor weaknesses in some areas," Adelman explains, "that predisposes them, given one environment, to learning problems." Given another environment, Adelman says, those minor deficits would be no handicap. Type III, at the other end of the range, includes the relatively small proportion of children with serious disorders. These disorders stem either from neurological problems, or from emotional disturbances severe enough to precipitate a learning dysfunction.

Adelman thus indicts education on two counts. In the first place, the bulk of children who are labeled "learning disabled" are not actually disabled at all but represent instead a failure of the education system to accommodate "a very wide range of normal differences." As a result of education's excessively narrow conceptualization of normal differences, Adelman complains, "We're asking certain kids to do certain types of tasks before they are capable of doing them, which is to say before they are developmentally ready or motivationally ready. And we need to stop doing that because for every kid we do that to, we produce a failure that doesn't have anything to do with any major disorder."

As strongly as they may point to weaknesses in the educational system, neither Adelman's finding that 75 percent of the learning disabilities he sees disappear when the environment is changed, nor Hainsworth's estimate that the standard school experience needs to be modified for 20 to 30 percent of the children she works with, fall into the category of hard data. But, then again, what does? "What validity do we have for regular education?" asks Larry Lieberman, Assistant Professor of Special Education at Boston College. "Give me the data. Half the data that they give you is achievement testing. The achievement testing is geared right to the curriculum, and the curriculum is geared to the achievement tests; you're in a circular kind of thing, with one feeding the other."

Partly in an attempt to get away from both rigidly statistical and purely anecdotal characterizations of learning disabilities, Michael Cole, Professor and Director of the Laboratory of Comparative Human Cognition at the Rockefeller University in New York, is collecting retrievable yet nonnumerical information on the organization of learning environments by recording large samples of student behavior on videotape. The only statistical data that Cole has compiled comes from the battery of tests that he gave, at the beginning of the project, to the student participants.

In contrast to Adelman, who seeks to construct environments that inhibit learning disorders, Cole is looking hard at the problem of "what is it about the different environments that we put the kids in that makes manifest a particular difficulty, a particular deficit?" Rather than restrict himself to studying the classroom environment alone, Cole has established a number of after-school "clubs" at the University—cooking, nature, Cub Scouts, etc.—where he can carefully watch students (who attend a nearby private school) in an assortment of social and cultural contexts. One of these students turned out to be dyslexic. In this way, it is possible to observe and precisely record not only the specific types of handicaps that dyslexia imposes on this child but also the coping mechanisms that a dyslexic develops to deal with a wide variety of obstacles. At this stage, Cole's work is intensive, small-scale, and qualitative. It focuses on systematically describing the interactions of one severely learning-disabled child with peers and teachers in nonschool, as well as school, environments.

There are immediate benefits to be derived from this methodology—to digress for a moment—even if the findings cannot yet be quantified. Chief among them is the force with which a visual presentation can make clear the fact that educational environments are not the only settings in which learning disabilities have an impact. Cole recalls, for instance, playing a segment of videotape that documented some of the difficulties faced by the dyslexic student in an after-school cooking club activity. "Even this kid's tutors, when we finished showing what this kid's life was like in environments they'd never seen him in, were stunned," says Cole, "just stunned. Because, when you watch it, it's like watching a horror movie. We have a scene where he's been sort of hard on another kid who's a social misfit. [The dyslexic] has a buddy, but the buddy's absent and he has to work with this other kid. And the other kid is very smart, but socially messed up. Now what the other kid does is to systematically hold out on the dyslexic kid until he reduces the dyslexic kid to tears in the most subtle fashion. Then he says, 'What's the matter?' And then he helps him and he works with him and they get the thing done. And we had the whole thing on tape," Cole notes, "so we can show the intimate dynamics of his day-to-day, minute-to-minute problems." There is no scientific way to describe the behavior recorded on tape. Cole admits at this point, "You use all your knowledge as a member of the culture to figure out what's going on." However, Cole is operating for now on the notion that it will eventually be possible to develop data analysis techniques for this relatively novel kind of data.

In setting forth the specific problem that he is now trying to unravel, Cole uses a metaphor that echoes through virtually every corner of the LD field and beyond: "How can you arrange the environments of severely learning disabled children to help them get the kind of information they would need," Cole asks, "information that's accessible to them as long as it's not presented through the needle's eye, where it just so happens that they're missing the needle?" For example, Cole observes, "It makes no sense at all to make American history, or civics, or a lot of literature have to go through kids' eyes. If they're having real difficulty with reading, we have all the capability in the world to integrate reading with other media and get all of this information in other ways. Right now," Cole concludes, "kids are doubly penalized, because reading is made the conduit through which all information has to come or you're no good."

Learning to read, as Cole suggests, amounts to more than simply acquiring an academic skill. In most schools today, reading ability is virtually the sole ticket to social and even moral legitimacy; the only alternate is success on the athletic field. Indeed, as Roy Lasky, Executive Director of the New York Association for the Learning Disabled, points out, "a normal child with athletic ability has much more money spent on him than a handicapped child does, and there's no law mandating it." But the fact remains that, within the broad cultural context of education, not to mention society in general, the consequences of not being able to read are in many ways analogous to the consequences of not being able to get or hold a job. Nonreaders are stigmatized and segregated from their apparently more capable peers; they are frequently ostracized by classmates, by teachers, and even by their own parents. Moreover, as with the unemployed, nonreaders are usually held accountable for their own failure. Speech pathologist Christie Ludlow of the National Institute of Neurological and Communicative Disorders and Stroke, puts it bluntly when she says, "I can remember that when I was in school, there were dumb kids and smart kids. And the dumb kids were dumb because they were dumb, and it was their fault that they were dumb. And so we used to make fun of them and everything else because they couldn't fit in." Hofstra University Reading Professor Harvey Alpert drives the same point home by pointing out that he has seen parents in Long Island who will not let their children play with kids who have been put in remedial tracks—"dummy classes" as they are commonly known.

It is in precisely this sense that the failure syndrome begins to take its heaviest toll on LD (as well as environmentally handicapped) children. For superimposed upon the distress and frustration of repeated lack of success in mastering the skills of reading is the emotionally and psychologically devastating impact of feeling different, set apart from one's classmates, and of being—as Ludlow put it —"dumb." In abstract terms, pediatrician Elena Boder puts the problem in perspective by noting that "a reading disability is a lack of talent, it's an extreme lack of talent that is penalized simply because it's required by society for all education, whereas if you have a lack of musical talent, you don't suffer as a result of it."

What is one person's failure can be another person's trial and error. Elizabeth Freidus, Educational Director of the Gateway School of New York (an independent school for LD children aged 5 to 10) and a pioneer in the field of special education, emphasizes the importance of teaching children the use of "feedback." Through this technique the children learn to become aware of the consequences of their actions. She tries to help them see unsuccessful attempts as opportunities to learn rather than as failures.

Freidus notes, "We spell it [feedback] out at every level; first the very concrete and then we move on to the abstract and the social. This self-monitoring is a particularly useful technique because our children are very afraid of failing *again*," she says. "We strive for positive feelings which come from a child's figuring out which way something works best, and we try to dispel feelings of doom if something goes wrong."

Some argue that children enter the failure syndrome not because of any intrinsic difficulties with reading but merely because they are called upon to read before they are ready. "We see many youngsters at my clinic*—and all over the country," says Sylvia Richardson, "who started school at the age of six, because that's the law, who simply neurologically did not have the maturation to start at that time, who were not ready for the academic material that was thrown at them. And now we have kindergartens teaching children how to read, which is ridiculous." Why all the pressure? San Marino, California, pediatrician Leon Oettinger, Jr. suspects that an illogical syllogism is at work: "Good readers read early" is where the argument starts, says Oettinger, adding that "this is true; they teach themselves. Therefore," goes the syllogism, "if we teach children to read early, they will all be good readers." But, says Oettinger, "this isn't necessarily at all true. In fact, it's probably the opposite because if you try to get a child to read before he's ready, he gets frustrated and upset and he'll start building up enough emotional disturbances to compound the problem." Suggesting a syllogism of his own, Oettinger notes that the best readers in Europe are the

---

*The Cincinnati Center for Developmental Disorders, which is affiliated with the University of Cincinnati Medical School.

Norwegians, who live in a country where formal education does not start until children reach the age of seven. The poorest readers in Europe, according to Oettinger, are in England, where education starts in infant schools.

The "needle's eye" of early reading is made even narrower, according to some, by the emphasis on fast reading. Edwin M. Cole, Senior Consulting Neurologist at Massachusetts General Hospital and long a prominent researcher in the area of dyslexia, argues that many learning problems could be headed off "if we get over this silly, superficial idea that everybody must read fast. Speed doesn't matter.* The point is that children read with understanding, and I think a lot of kids are turned off from reading because they're told they have to read quickly." Cole also argues for a simplification of the English language into a system of absolutely phonetic spellings.

Not all would agree with Cole's diagnosis. There are those who insist that, to be useful, reading must be automatic and that working on reading speed is one of the best ways to improve facility. At the same time, the irregularities of English orthography and pronunciation are not universally regarded as obstacles. What does seem to be widely agreed upon, however, is the general point made in a report prepared for the Task Panel on Learning Failure and Unused Learning Potential of the President's Commission on Mental Health: "A small but important body of knowledge [about reading acquisition] is becoming available for translation into instructional procedures for the classroom teacher. The problem as we see it now is that this body of knowledge is not reflected in the reading curricula commonly used in our schools" (Liberman 1977A). Another paper prepared for the same Task Panel makes a similar point about the curriculum and instructional inadequacies to be found in mathematics (Cawley and Fitzmaurice 1977).

Teacher Training
"Education is slow to change. . . ."

Of course the concern over reading (or math) failure is not a monopoly of LD specialists. The possibility that illiteracy is increasing in the United States, the steady decline in the Scholastic Aptitude Test scores of high school students, and the marked deficiency in writing expression now widely found among first-year college students—to name just a few current topics—are becoming standard fare in the news media, and matters of vigorous public debate. It cannot be said that educators are ignoring these problems; reforms in educational practices have followed one after the other for the past few years. The lack of convincing results from most of these reforms, however, raises the possibility that the

*It should be kept in mind that these comments are made in reference to a specific population of school children. Some children need to be pushed in order to become facile readers.

"needle's eye" is no wider on the teacher's side than it is on the student's side. Why have so many classroom reforms failed to bring about the hoped-for results? One explanation: "Education is slow to change," wrote Harriet Sheridan, Acting President of Carlton College, Northfield, Minnesota, and a member of the Committee on Public Literacy of the Association of Departments of English. "It has its shibboleths. When it does change, it changes in a radical swoop, from the narrowest kind of workbook grammar instruction all the way to electives in collage making. The middle ground—the ground on which students develop their skills and powers, the ground on which teachers use all techniques at their command to help individual students learn—is a barren one" (Sheridan 1977, p. 67).

One patch of barren ground has been glimpsed repeatedly during the recent past by Carolyn Compton, Educational Director of the Children's Health Council of the Mid-Peninsula in Palo Alto, California. She says that when she takes reports on dyslexic children to local schools and tells a teacher about a child who has difficulty in written language, the teacher will often say, with evidence to prove it, that the writing of the other students in the class is no better. In practice, says Compton, this circumstance makes it quite difficult to discriminate between LD children who have written language problems and normal children with the same problems (the Children's Health Council is now conducting research aimed at constructing better assessment measures of written language development). Compton's hunch of why it is so hard to differentiate between normal and LD kids on this basis is, quite simply, that "in the past several years, written language as such has not been well-taught in the public schools. So, when you take a random group of fourth graders, since no one has really been taught the skills, it's very hard to sift out who would have learned them had they been taught, and who wouldn't have learned them." If changes in education have put regular students at a disadvantage, their impact has been even more damaging for the learning disabled. Since some children with learning disorders often cannot block out nonmeaningful stimuli, for example, Leon Oettinger argues that in a so-called "enriched classroom, with junk all over the walls, and movies going, and six classes doing six different things, these children just go straight up the wall—and teachers wonder why these kids don't learn. These children," Oettinger explains, "can't focus, and when you present six stimuli, they're not going to understand any of them." Donna Carroll of ERIN draws the same conclusion.

As the ERIN program makes clear, a considerable amount of training and knowledge is required by the classroom teacher who is going to teach children with differing learning styles. And it now appears that an overwhelming majority of people in the LD field agree that the reorganization of teacher training is a top priority. Says pediatric neurologist Jerome Mednick, Medical director of the Child Development Center at Children's Hospital in San Francisco: "We believe that in the final analysis, to help kids with dyslexia, teachers are simply going to have to become more sophisticated, and so is the whole educational process, in order to be able to understand the disorder and to understand the process of intervention. And we can't do that with people who have not had the training or who are unwilling to be trained."

Nor is the training called for simply a matter of learning new pedagogical tricks. New attitudes are needed, for there is still skepticism in educational circles as to whether there is really any such thing as a learning disorder. Psychiatrist Leon Eisenberg of the Harvard Medical School observes that people interested in special education and dyslexia have had a difficult time convincing other educators that the problem exists. Revelations, however, do occur. Eisenberg remembers an incident that took place some 15 years ago when he was providing psychotherapy for an LD child who was "quite bright but not reading, and therefore regarded as stupid in the school system in Frederick, Maryland, which didn't recognize the existence of dyslexia. But while we had the child in treatment," Eisenberg recounts, "the child of a member of the Frederick school board was diagnosed as having dyslexia, and the system changed remarkably." Edwin Cole notes that revelations also tend to take place just after the passage of laws that offer money. "Before there was any public law to give support to dyslexic students," says Cole, "most schools, and schools of education around [Massachusetts] said 'Dyslexia? There's no such thing. What are you talking about?' But as soon as the law was passed and there was money in the bank for these programs, everybody flip-flopped: 'Oh sure, there is dyslexia, and we have a program.'"

Where skepticism exists in the system as a whole—but even where it doesn't—it can still be found among teachers who, as we have already indicated, often conclude that a child is not learning disabled but lazy, stupid, and trying to dodge the work instead. In all fairness, teaching some dyslexic children is a stiff challenge, in large part because they lack what ERIN's Marian Hainsworth calls "self-organization skills. I think that it is frustrating for people who deal with these kids—teachers and parents—because the problems don't seem to be consistent," Hainsworth says. "One time they'll have trouble with this particular thing and the next time they won't. One day they'll have a heck of a time, and another day they'll be functioning a lot better."

The heavy demands of teaching LD children are reflected in what some administrators report to be a high "burn-out rate" among special-education teachers. The demands for LD children for sensitivity and reassurance can often exceed the teacher's long-term capacity to give. Unless the teacher receives careful management and emotional support, he or she may be exhausted after a few years work with LD children.

Beyond flexibility and sensitivity, however, teachers also need sophisticated techniques at their disposal—and a broad background that helps them know when to use those techniques. "To me," says Sylvia Richardson, "the most important teachers in the school system, who should be the highest trained and the highest paid, are the primary teachers—K[indergarten] through 3[rd grade]—because they have to teach children. All the rest have to teach subject matter. And it's up to K through 3 teachers to teach the children the primary skills of reading, writing, and arithmetic." To do this effectively, argues Richardson (and others), a teacher needs a firm background in early childhood education (how do they know what to do with a 6-year-old, asks Richardson, unless they also know how he or she got to be 6?); in speech and hearing; in reading; and in special education and remedial techniques.

The strength and logic of this argument should not obscure the fact that children in secondary school also need highly skilled teachers. By the time a learning-disabled child has become a teenager, as Ernest Siegel makes painfully clear in his book, *The Exceptional Child Grows Up,* the accumulated burden of years of difficulty in school will have produced at least some emotional problems, and these are compounded in adolescence by the emergence of the turbulent maturational forces of puberty. Yet it is at this time, quite often, that parents, who have been hoping for years that their child would improve, begin to give up and withdraw their love and support, feeling that the time has come for the child to succeed on his or her own. At the same time, both junior and senior high school represent threatening new environments for the LD student, yet special education services that might help ease the transition diminish dramatically as the child gets older. It is also the case, Siegel argues, that high school teachers tend to receive less training in psychology and child development—and more training in specific subject areas—than elementary school teachers do and may therefore be less receptive to the problems of the LD student. "At worst," Siegel writes, "the junior-high and high-school experiences, instead of lessening the impact of the many environmental stresses already impinging upon the child, aggravate the problem and introduce new sources of tension, frustration, and self-doubt. Instead of being part of the solution, the school has become part of the problem" (Siegel 1974). The result of the accumulated pressures and the lack of specialized services at these levels of the educational process often produce school dropouts, or, as psychiatrist Larry Silver perhaps most accurately calls them, "school push-outs."

But dropping out of school is not the worst that can happen. At a recent meeting of the Scarsdale Organization for Learning Disabilities, Charles Drake, Headmaster of the Landmark School, told the story of a 14-year-old dyslexic in Toronto who, suffering terrible anxiety over his failures in school, tried to find help, failed, and finally committed suicide. Pediatrician Melvin Levine sums it up: "In elementary school, there's a lot of love for LD youngsters; when they get to junior high school and beyond, there is no love."

At the heart of the teacher training problem seems to be the organization of teacher training institutes. Territorial lines tend to be sharply drawn between elementary education, early childhood education, regular and special education, reading, speech, and hearing, and so on. The Bureau of Education for the Handicapped has been trying, through the use of grants, to persuade deans of colleges of education to rethink and reconceptualize teacher training curricula—"and in that reconceptualization," explains BEH Program Officer Tom Behrens, "to have the handicapped kid as an integral part." But progress has been slow. Even if progress were fast, though, the problem would be far from solved. "Based upon existing live births and the existing average age of teachers in America, the chances are we will hire very few new teachers between now and the end of this century," says John W. Porter, Superintendent of Public Instruction in the Michigan Department of Education and a member of the President's Commission on Mental Health. "Furthermore, the data indicates that better than three-quarters of the teachers in America are at the top of the salary schedules in their respective states and local districts and better than three-quarters of the teachers in America have earned all of the required credits they need in order to have life certificates. This means that we now have a labor-intensified industry where 85 percent of the cost of running schools is tied up in salary and wages. If there's going to be any modification, it's got to be where the 85 percent of the money is, and those are people who are now at an average age of 31. They will teach for at least 29 more years."

At least as important, therefore, as reorganizing teacher training curricula is setting up effective programs of in-service retraining. Many of the existing programs of this nature, according to Carolyn Compton of the Palo Alto Children's Health Council, are not working well. These consist for the most part of after-school lectures or demonstrations. "Teachers find this a burden," Compton says, "and they find the information hard to apply in their classrooms." Beyond this problem, some observers indicate that many teachers resent being forced to allow handicapped kids into their classrooms and also fear the effects of the evaluation procedures written into P.L. 94-142.* "One of the things I've been arguing about with OE [the Office of Education] is that there's nothing wrong with 94-142 as a policy," says John Porter, "the problem is that the people to implement the policy were never prepared to do it. What I said to OE was, once you adopted the policy, which is 94-142, you should have put out in front a requirement to retrain the two million teachers so that they can implement the policy."

Some feel that if training can catch up with the law, the results would be dramatic. "We have enough knowledge to help the current generation, if we just begin to use it," says Rutgers psychiatrist Larry Silver, who worries that it will take four or five years to train all the educators needed to carry out P.L. 94-142. "Such basic things as learning how to build on strengths, teaching parents to work with their kids, teaching school systems to be more flexible towards styles of learning: we already have that knowledge. It's just a matter of implementing it, and that requires a massive public relations program, in-service training for those who are already out, and changing curricula for those who aren't out of school—and I'm not just talking about educators, but also about pediatricians and other kinds of physicians who are involved with the problem."

On the education, as opposed to the medical front, ERIN is one example of the efforts presently being made to help schools put current knowledge to use.

---

*These procedures call for at least annual evaluation of the effectiveness of programs in meeting the educational needs (including individualized programs) of LD children.

Another example is Reach for Learning, a learning disabilities clinic operating in the San Francisco area. Reach for Learning offers consultation and in-service training on a contract basis to both public and private schools (and the clinic also evaluates and remediates children with specific learning disabilities). In working with schools, explains child psychiatrist John Sikorski, a partner in the clinic, Reach for Learning uses a "mental health consultation model" and stresses "the fact that half the job of the teacher is the relatedness to the child: how to engage the child at whatever level is appropriate and how then to use the child's strengths in working around the difficulties. We think that effective teaching/learning is always done within a relationship context."

The specifics involved in the information that Reach for Learning brings to schools include such factors as how teachers can increase their awareness and appreciation of learning disabilities in the classroom, how they can structure the classroom for maximum efficiency, and how they can "utilize educational materials—hardware—that's abundantly available but usually stacked up in closets because the teachers, after a year or two, rotate or quit or whatever and new teachers come in who don't know about that particular equipment that was purchased at great price," notes Sikorski, with open cynicism, "for the benefit of the booming educational product companies."

In working with schools, Reach for Learning uses task forces made up of members of the clinic's multidisciplinary staff (which consists of a child psychiatrist, two clinical psychologists, eight teachers at the master's level in either special education or learning disabilities, and a consulting neurologist). In addition, Reach for Learning often uses films on learning disabilities that have been made at the clinic. In discussing the program's role in the schools, Sikorski makes the interesting observation that at least a part of the staff's success derives from the fact that Reach for Learning is invited by schools, rather than forced upon them. In effect, Sikorski suggests, the battle is fought before the troops are called: "Somebody in the school has really had to bump heads with the administrator or the board of directors or somebody in order to get in some outside help. And so when you get invited in at that level and role, you can really be effective."

Making the System Work

In many, perhaps most, communities, however, programs like ERIN and Reach for Learning simply do not exist, or have not, at any rate, until quite recently. And under these circumstances, the responsibility for ensuring that learning-disabled children receive an appropriate education falls on the parents and the local school systems. Paul Ackerman, former staff member of the White House Conference on Handicapped Individuals and now Chief of the Central Region Branch, Division of Personnel Preparation of BEH, has devoted considerable thought and energy to raising the awareness of parents about the role they can play. He characterizes the plight of parents as "an Alice in Wonderland kind of thing: if you're a parent and you all of a sudden have found that your child has a learning disability, you don't know where to go. You have quacks to go to as well as reputable people; you can go to an optometrist, a psychologist, a shrink, a pediatrician, an educator. And they'll all have these strange theories, some with logic behind them, some without." Along with pediatrician Murray Kappelman, Ackerman wrote a book, *Between Parent & School,* that spells out how parents can deal with the often bewildering—and intimidating—complexity of school systems in trying to get help for their children. But, as the authors succinctly state, becoming a child advocate "is very hard work"—as Ackerman knows from first-hand experience. Trained in clinical psychology, he occasionally moonlights as a child advocate in local schools. And he finds that school personnel are often no more practiced than parents are at blending information (test scores, patterns, diagnoses, etc.) into an appropriate individual education plan for a learning-disabled child.

To devise such a plan, however, does not guarantee that it will be carried out. William Healey, Director of the American Speech and Hearing Association's School Services Program points out that, while the old maxim of education is to serve the individual child, "there isn't a state law or a state rule or regulation or funding pattern anywhere in the United States that will allow you to work with an individual child on a full-time basis. In most instances, everything is group-oriented." Like many others, Healey argues that "the system is part of the problem," in this case because, for a long time, educational specialists—in reading, speech and language pathology, etc.—have been told that they had to work with large numbers of children in order to generate funding for the school district. If the specialists wanted employment, Healey contends, and if the school districts wanted money, large caseloads—of 60 children or more—were the only option. "And what that did," Healey says, "was to force people for the most part to take children with the least severe problems and work with them. Children with severe problems, if they got help at all, had to be sent out of the system."

The same overloading phenomenon also accounts in part for the reluctance of many school systems to identify the problems in the first place. Ronald Spector, Director of the Beverly Center School in Los Angeles, tells the story of the school psychologist who, when asked why L.A. public schools had no mandatory screening procedures, answered: "Look, we don't have the classes. We don't want to get parents upset and have them banging on our doors when we can't help them." In Los Angeles, Spector says, there may be as many as 5,000 children on the waiting list for EH (Educationally Handicapped) classes, and "if you have this many children who are waiting to be served, there is not going to be a hell of a lot of motivation to keep identifying all the other kids that are out there." As one consequence of the difficulties inherent in screening and helping kids within the school system, Spector notes, oftentimes a learning-disabled person and his or her parents are not informed of the problem until the student is about to graduate from high school, which, from the point of view of remediation, is quite late in the game.

Mainstreaming

But if many parents are upset over the lack of services for their children, a large number of parents also seem to be growing distraught over the methods used by schools that do attempt to provide help. A particularly volatile issue at the moment is the question of "mainstreaming," trying to keep LD children in regular education classrooms, usually while giving them extra help in "resource rooms." The problem of labeling, and the stigma that often attaches to children who are assigned to remedial tracks—the "dummy classes"—are two related factors that give the mainstreaming concept some appeal; a third, of course, is economics: it is often less expensive for schools (as well as for parents) to educate a child in the standard manner than it is to call in specialists. A fourth influence favoring mainstreaming is that this approach is the method specified as most desirable by P.L. 94-142 which mandates that, whenever possible, a handicapped child must be educated in "the least restrictive environment," defined as the setting where a child "can function as comfortably as possible within as nonhandicapped a group of children as he can accommodate" (Kappelman and Ackerman 1977, p. 269).

Critics of mainstreaming do not necessarily oppose the concept per se. For instance, Sally Smith, Director of the Kingsbury Lab School in Washington, D.C., acknowledges the fact that mainstreaming spares many children the burden of carrying a label but argues that, "on the other hand, it's harming others who are not getting the chance to be out of the mainstream and get themselves together, and *then* go into the mainstream." But many opponents do contend that the concept has never really been carefully thought out. A typical argument along these lines is that, even when mainstreaming seems the best choice for a child with a learning disorder, it is not always the case that the remedial help provided in a resource room is as good as it ought to be. In Massachusetts, explains Charles Drake of the Landmark School, Chapter 766 has "wiped out" diagnostic criteria and, consequently, "any specificity in teaching to children with special needs." What the resource room teachers now must amount to, Drake comments sarcastically, "are absolute marvellous wizards. They can take any child with any disorder at any intensity and work with them in masses all day long."

Perhaps the most serious shortcoming of mainstreaming arises primarily as an outgrowth, or logical consequence, of the historic line of demarcation between special and regular education. Says Hofstra Reading Professor Harvey Alpert: "My wife is a resource room teacher, and I will see her send a youngster back to the classroom with recommendations, and the teacher will say 'I can't give this child only three arithmetic problems if the other kids are doing ten,' or 'If there's a paper that has to be written, this child must write the same paper as everyone else; I simply will not accept the fact that instead of doing a paper this week and a paper next week, this student can do one paper for both weeks.'" Many of these teachers, Alpert adds, insist that they are simply maintaining standards. Alan Orenstein, a Senior Research Associate with the Cambridge, Massachusetts-based Research Institute for Educational Problems, heard similar observations from parents he interviewed in the course of a study of the appeals system established under Chapter 766. A majority of the parents with whom Orenstein spoke had taken their children out of public schools and placed them in private day school facilities (and were retroactively appealing for financial aid on the grounds that the public school services were inadequate). In explaining why they thought their children's academic performance had improved so dramatically after the switch, a number of parents pointed to the lack of coordination between resource room programs and the regular classroom in public schools. The resource room teacher and the classroom teacher were doing completely different things, parents told Orenstein. Some also complained that their children, upon returning to their regular classroom after time spent away in the resource room, were scapegoated and rejected by their nonhandicapped peers, particularly as they got older.

What Should Be Special About Special Education?

As we suggested above, at the center of the challenge of educating dyslexic children lies the question asked by Michael Cole: where is the needle's eye, what should be threaded through it, and how? Increasingly, people in the LD field— and elsewhere, for that matter—are taking the position that a certain portion of what is being forced through that narrow opening, as well as some of the methods being used in the forcing process, has become outdated, and possibly useless. During his two-year hitch with the White House Conference on Handicapped Individuals, Paul Ackerman came to the conclusion that traditional education is littered with "obsolete things that are relics of our system," such as "certain facts about American history or geometry" that children will never use again once the course has ended. What disturbed Ackerman even more deeply was his growing awareness of the fact that, though "we can't get figures on it, it looks as if the hiring of handicapped people in schools is much below the average that we would allow in industry." In other words, there are no role models for handicapped children in a system that is, for the most part, "working from the basis of the person's being atypical, and trying to get them typical again." The creativity of many types of handicapped people—both children and adults—is being ignored, Ackerman says.

The same idea of making atypical people typical again is criticized by psychologist Barbara Keogh of UCLA in the context of instructional strategies. "A lot of educators talk about focusing on the child's deficit," she points out, "and say you've got to remediate the deficit in order to be successful." But Keogh contends that deficits are never cured; instead, she says, people must be taught to deal with them. How? Her model is based on the notion of "compensating mechanisms." She writes: "Simply stated, a compensatory model is based on the assumption that although school learning requires minimal levels of competence in a number of abilities, it is possible to compensate for less highly developed, even submarginal, skills in some areas by sound development in others." One of the implications of this model, Keogh observes, is that "emphasis upon a particular or single instructional strategy may contribute to learning problems for a number of children" (Keogh 1971, pp. 544-548).

It is only a matter of degree that separates Keogh's compensatory model from the concept of compensatory education elucidated by special educator and researcher Don Hammill in Austin, Texas. "If you've got a child with normal intelligence who's in 4th grade, and he is at the pre-primer level, and he has had the benefit of good teachers and the remedial reading people and the learning disabilities people, one must get about the business of making the child educated," Hammill says. "And reading is but a skill. So, we would move that child immediately to listening and talking. We would continue trying to teach him to read," Hammill adds, "but not at the expense of his education." Schools, however, are resistant to the idea of programs in which people could be educated without having to learn how to read, Hammill complains. What schools "tend to do is to keep recycling these children. They recycle them through LD, through remedial reading, through perception classes," and so on.

Occupational Training

Hammill's remedy may be extreme, but it is nevertheless typical of a trend of thought in the LD field today that might be best expressed—to rephrase the famous aphorism about Ireland—as "too much teaching, and too little education."* BEH State Plan Officer William Halloran argues not only that most curricula neglect the skills that both normal and LD people will need after they get out of school but also that even if occupational training were broadly established in the school system, it would be "the occupational training most like the normative." On the basis of poor reading, for instance, a school might decide that a dyslexic entering the automotive field would not be successful at anything above the level of gas station pump attendant. But, says Halloran, "if you were to study successful people working, you'd be amazed to find out that many of

---

*The aphorism we have in mind refers to Ireland's problem as "too much Christianity and too little religion."

them do not have—or do not need—the skills that other people assume to be absolutely necessary. So, the problem is that we're not looking at the demands of society and the demands of employers, and then taking them back to start teaching from them."

Both normal and LD people are thus put at a disadvantage, Halloran maintains, by the irrelevance of much of the education that is offered at the secondary level, as well as by the shaky assumption that "abstract learning can be automatically translated into concrete problem-solving." But LDs also face a third obstacle, which was briefly mentioned earlier in this report, namely, the idea that to establish occupational training for learning-disabled students is ipso facto to subscribe to the notion that the condition is incurable. And this third obstacle, Halloran concludes, owes its existence in large part to the tendency of many professionals to believe that they can reshape anyone's behavior using the behaviorist techniques that have recently enjoyed such a vogue among educators.

"We have so many kids that we keep asking to commit themselves to further pain in the traditional high school program," says Sylvia Richardson. For children who are truly learning (as opposed to teacher) disabled, Richardson suggests establishing "learning communities, where the high school kids could have an opportunity to learn all the different kinds of work that man can do. Stop putting the emphasis on reading, writing, and arithmetic. In order to build a building, you've got to know arithmetic, you've got to be able to read plans. So let the reading, writing, and arithmetic be secondary to the work. Give these children self-respect. Allow them to produce."

Private Schools

In the meantime, as Melvin Levine likes to ask, what about the kids? At the moment, with the practical benefits of P.L. 94–142 yet to be determined, the best education for LD children is that offered by private schools. The two schools discussed immediately below help explain why this is so.

In the course of preparing this report, the project director visited more than a score of private schools, many of them acknowledged leaders in this field. Space does not permit us to discuss the work of more than a few of these schools. The two schools discussed below were selected because they seemed to offer unique approaches to the education of learning-disabled children and because it was our subjective impression that they are doing their work very well. We do not mean to imply, by selecting these schools as illustrative examples, that other special schools are not also doing an excellent job. In fact, while everyone in the field is convinced that special programs are effective and that some schools are better than others, objective comparative data are almost completely lacking and are difficult to acquire. There is at present hardly any objective evidence that any special school is doing better work than any other or than the public schools; nor even that any special program is effective. We have had no choice but to rely on subjective impressions. One further consideration influenced our choice of these two schools: we believe that the needs of adolescent and adult LDs have been sadly neglected in a field that is dominated by concern for the early years of schooling. We have chosen, therefore, to emphasize the work of the few schools that deal with older children and adolescents. We shall return to this point when we state our conclusions.

The Landmark School, located about 25 miles from Boston in Prides Crossing, Massachusetts, is "looking for the young Tom Edisons, Niels Bohrs, and Hans Christian Andersens who were not very good at reading and writing in school, but who were among the great contributors of their time," says the school's brochure, reflecting the belief of Headmaster Charles Drake that dyslexics often develop superior conceptual and problem-solving abilities in order to cope with their environments. Landmark does not accept emotionally disturbed or retarded children or children with detectable brain injuries. The school has about 280 students of both sexes (girls make up 12 percent of the student body), ranging in age from 8 to 18. To minimize the embarrassment that its teenagers might feel, Landmark maintains separate campuses for students under and over 12. The staff-pupil ratio is 1 to 3. Tuition for the 1977–78 school year is $9,640 for residential and $5,375 for day students, for some or all of which parents are reimbursed, depending on their home state and the severity of the child's problem.

A nongraded school, Landmark does not attempt to teach its students what they would be learning in regular classrooms (the assumption being that all Landmark students are bright enough to catch up when they have gotten the basic skills under control). Instead, the main emphasis is placed on developing language skills—oral composition, reading, writing, and spelling. A varied athletic and physical education program, arts and crafts, square dancing, typing, a seven-week summer program in seamanship (using the school's 63-foot schooner, *When and If,* which once belonged to General George S. Patton, Jr.—a dyslexic), and other such activities are designed to help students improve their motor skills. Landmark carpentry students built a small gymnasium on the school's under-12 campus last year and are now erecting a library.

The key to Landmark's approach, explains Headmaster Drake, is "organization and structure." No effort is made to protect students from academic stress: work is hard, and, as a recent article about the school points out, "any excuse for neglect of homework, short of sudden death, is not likely to impress a teacher" (Sutton 1976). There is no magic in the Landmark program, although there is undoubtedly a large and intangible value in the example of success and accomplishment set for the students by Drake, who is dyslexic.

Students are very thoroughly evaluated, tested, and diagnosed when they come to the school, and the information gained from these procedures is used constantly by the school's faculty. "For example," says Drake, "[a] child has a severe auditory memory problem but is able to function if he can see while you are talking to him: his teachers will be advised of this fact and, whenever possible, there will always be a visual input while there's an auditory input, because that's how he works best." Classes at Landmark are small—the maximum size is six students—which allows teachers to develop a deep understanding of each child. In addition, every student spends at least one hour a day with a tutor. To round out its rigorous academic program, the school plans parties, special events, and other social activities, and also runs a work program in which every student must participate on a daily basis.

The average length of stay for the older students is about two years; the younger students tend to stay for two to three years, Drake says, before getting back into the mainstream. "Of course this whole concept of mainstreaming causes us some problems," Drake notes, "because it's our feeling that students are actually being mainstreamed here. For the first time in their lives, these youngsters feel as though they are a true part of a school system; they no longer are the outcasts and the children caught in the backwaters and stagnant pools of education. One of the things that happens to them at Landmark is that they feel that at last they have found a place in education."

Sally L. Smith, the mother of a former Landmark student, has been running a school of her own for nearly 11 years: the Lab School of the Kingsbury Center in Washington, D.C. The motives that led Smith, a former writer in the psychology/mental health field, to establish the school were initially parental rather than educational per se. School authorities had decided that Smith's then-young son should be placed in classes for the emotionally disturbed or the retarded, but Smith sensed that that was the wrong approach. "I knew he could learn through association and through drama, dance, music," Smith recalls. So, she broke reading down into component tasks and then sought out art forms that could be used to impart readiness to perform those tasks. She also looked for ways to involve her child's—and all children's—natural love of make-believe and play in the learning process.

The Kingsbury Lab School is affiliated with the Kingsbury Center, which has been functioning for nearly four decades as a diagnostic and tutoring center for children with learning problems. The Kingsbury Lab School admits children of both sexes between the ages of 6 and 13 who have primarily neurologically based learning disabilities. In the academic year 1976–77, there were 54 students in attendance at the school (48 boys and 6 girls), all on a day basis; tuition was $4,350 for students aged 6 to 12, and $4,550 for 13- to 15-year-olds (again, with reimbursement depending on the regulations in parents' home states). The average student attends the school for three to four years before returning to a regular school. Kingsbury Lab School plays an active role in the transition and often recommends that the child receive help from a Kingsbury Center tutor for the first year or so after leaving the school.

Smith believes that learning disabilities—or disorders, as she prefers to call them—are related to immaturity in the central nervous system. The primary problem faced by these children, Smith has said, is the inability to "filter out the sensations that are coming to the brain from the eyes or the ears, or through the body. This is the child," Smith says, "who is *over*stimulated—who is bombarded by sensations and cannot sort out that which is relevant or essential and that which is not."

Thus, as at Landmark, at the core of the Kingsbury approach is an emphasis on organization and structure. In each activity, teachers painstakingly explain what is to be done, step by step. If a child's chair is to be moved, for instance, the teacher tells the child where the chair will be moved and allows the student to go over and try out the new spot first—to reduce uncertainty and confusion. Sometimes strips of masking tape are used to help define each individual's place. Teachers almost never touch or rearrange a student's books or school materials, since even a simple act such as this can introduce a powerful and disruptive distraction.

The Kingsbury Lab School's curriculum is built around this basic ordered, and organized, environment. Its major thrust is to help children learn to "differentiate" and "integrate," words Smith uses to denote the ability to distinguish one thing from another and then file the information in the appropriate mental slot, and also to help children develop a knowledge of order and sequence— hence the emphasis on regular routines and the careful explanation of them to students. "Every part of our curriculum is geared to helping students organize themselves, their bodies, their minds, their *work*," reads the school's 1976-77 Factsheet.

In these aspects, the Kingsbury Lab School is not terribly different from many other institutions that educate primarily learning-disabled children; but what sets Kingsbury apart is the manner in which it uses creativity in both the teaching and learning process. Although students of all ages spend part of the day doing academic work in classrooms (in junior high, for instance, every student has tutoring in reading, spelling, and study skills daily, as well as math, geography or American History, and then either sex education, language arts, or "lifetime skills"), they also spend part of every day learning through the arts. In woodworking, for example, students practice eye-hand coordination or develop physical self-awareness by building a chair to fit their bodies. In music, Kingsbury students learn to link sound to color, shape, and, finally, to symbols—all to develop or reinforce readiness for reading. The Lab School also has a media center in which Library of Congress Talking Books, films, home-made tapes, and other products are used to help students understand, appreciate, and organize their thoughts about literature.

As part of the arts program, Kingsbury uses an "Academic Club Method" to involve students through drama and make-believe in various subjects and situations. Many of the Club teachers are artists; their creativity and problem-solving skills, Smith believes, are an asset, because "you've got to teach the same thing a hundred different ways" to learning-disabled (or -disordered) children. How does the Club method work? In the Secret Agent Club, for instance, students decode "secret" light and sound messages to strengthen visual and auditory perception;

in a Greek Gods Club, students learn about Athenian democracy by casting votes and about Spartan tyranny by being ordered about by a King; as members of the Renaissance Councillors Club, students examine great works of art, seeking signs of the use of perspective; a Keystone Cops Club helps students acquire decision-making skills by acting out the arrival of cops to break up a family quarrel.

Indeed, the content of the Kingsbury curriculum goes far beyond the purely academic. Speaking of her son, Smith says, "if he doesn't look at the difference between 'went,' 'want,' and 'won't' in a word, why do I expect him to look at a face and see what's sad, what's happy, what's angry?" In junior high school, Kingsbury students build self-knowledge by gathering once a week in small groups to meet with a trained group therapist-psychologist to explore, as the Factsheet says, "the general feelings of turbulence that accompany adolescence combined with the special feelings of inadequacy and fragmentation that accompany learning disabilities." Self-knowledge, coping skills, and socialization are also integral parts even of such courses as math, in which once a month each class plans, budgets, purchases, cooks, and serves a Friday lunch for the junior high school's students and teachers (and then calculates whether money was made or lost on the meal). An extension of this approach is the Lifetime Skills course, in which students form their own mock corporation, sell shares of stock to raise capital, manufacture a product, and then market it. The exercise helps students to understand such ideas as profit and loss, wholesale and retail, and interest; to develop telephone and record-keeping skills; to get information from newspapers; and to find their way around the Washington metropolitan area. The Kingsbury Lab School must do more than simply teach reading, writing, and math, Sally Smith has written; it must also "give our students the social tools that will allow them to utilize their learning effectively, to function in life independently and as useful members of society" (Smith, no date).

For all students, the working world is an ultimate mainstream. But close behind work, from an educational point of view, is the mainstream of college (and graduate school). Among the different types of LDs who pursue their education on the university or postgraduate level are (1) those who have received some remedial help earlier in their lives and who are aware of their problem and (2) those who have received no remedial help at all and either are or are not aware that they are learning disabled. Both groups, of course, continue to need help after high school, yet, on the university level, there are practically no programs available. (The Forman Schools—a secondary school in Litchfield, Connecticut—provided a list of two dozen colleges and universities that claim to offer special help of varied scope for dyslexics. In fact, only a few of them have serious programs.) On the graduate level, the paucity of programs is even more pronounced. One of the few exceptions seems to be a reading skills acquisition service recently established at the Harvard Medical School.

(Within the LD population, there appears to be a subgroup that is unusually gifted in three-dimensional skills. Their Wechsler Intelligence Scale for Children [WISC] profiles tend to be significantly higher on the performance than on the verbal part of the test. These individuals, many of them parents—and particularly fathers—of learning-disabled children, gravitate towards careers in certain branches of medicine, engineering, and architecture. Generally speaking, the high-performance LD person is better adapted to survival in the work world than his or her high-verbal counterpart. There is little data to support this observation, but the phenomenon was noted often enough by people we interviewed to merit mention.)

Why make a fuss about people who have made it to this elevated level of learning? If they can get into college, not to mention graduate school, how serious can their disabilities be? This is not an unfair question, but there is an answer. To achieve well enough in school to gain admission to college is enormously costly for a learning-disabled person: emotionally, physically, psychologically. This is as true for the person who is aware of his or her learning problem as it is for the person who only senses that something is wrong but cannot define the difficulty precisely.

Without help, LDs—who are, remember, of at least average and frequently better-than-average intelligence—cannot perform at full strength. They are intellectually handicapped. And their handicaps are invisible to all but themselves. For people in wheelchairs, architectural barriers are being torn down and ramps are being built—at an expense running well into the millions, and possibly billions, of dollars—all over the country. For LDs in higher education, the needs are simpler but every bit as urgent: intellectual barriers must be removed, and ramps for the mind must be built. In large college lecture courses, where a student must produce on paper in order to pass, many LDs simply don't stand a chance to get an education.

"We believe that a person's potential ability to develop newer and better ways of doing things, to improve his own situation, and even to improve the lot of humanity generally can and should be enhanced by a college education." So says the brochure for the seven-year-old Program of Assistance in Learning, otherwise known as P.A.L., operated by the Learning Center at Curry College in Milton, Massachusetts.

P.A.L. came into being in 1970. Gertrude Webb, a psychologist and LD specialist, had joined Curry in 1969 to design an undergraduate program for training teachers in the LD field (the program was the first of its kind in the country). "After I'd been here a little while and the faculty started to understand what we were doing," Webb recalls, "they started to send over students' papers and say 'Is this what you're talking about?' At that point I realized that there was a whole generation of people in their late teens who hadn't had the opportunity for identification and remediation." At its inception, the P.A.L. program consisted of four students; since then it has grown to 50—10 percent of Curry's student body.

The P.A.L. program is a kind of ERIN for college students. There is no labeling, and participants are totally integrated into the regular academic program. P.A.L. does not accept students whose test patterns suggest weaknesses in the area of abstract reasoning—which, says Webb, is a sine qua non of success in college—and there is, therefore, no need for Curry's faculty, which cooperates fully with the program, to conceptually "water down" material for P.A.L. students. The faculty is asked, however, to refrain from grading students' written assignments for at least a year.

The program is conceived of as a one-year program during which a student develops the skills needed to become an "independent learner," as the brochure says. One of the first things that happens after a student has been accepted into the program is that a member of the P.A.L. staff explains to the student what his or her testing profile actually means. Webb says the discussion sounds something like this: "Here are your strengths. You do not need our help here. We will expect you to take those and run with them. These are your areas that are giving you a curve ball in being an effective producer in the academic scene. These are where we will help you. We will build support, with the anticipation that in a year's time, you won't need us. That's what we're striving for. We want to get rid of you. We don't want to see you hanging around here next year, because there are other kids who need this kind of support." If they wish, P.A.L. students can remain in the program for an additional consultant half-semester in their sophomore year, in which they are no longer scheduled for regular tutorials but may come in once a week if they have a problem. At the beginning of the school year, P.A.L. students are also given a one-week course in testing and study skills: how to take an exam, how to organize one's time effectively.

For P.A.L. students, various volunteer groups, mostly local, put books and other written materials on tape (occasionally, professors arrange for material they plan to hand out in class to be taped as well). During the years she has spent working with such taped material, Webb has discovered that reading skill improves noticeably if the student follows the text visually while hearing it read. Using this method, students learn to correct their own habitual mistakes and to achieve an increasingly better match between the auditory and visual components of language which, Webb notes, "is all that reading is." Working in favor of this method, Webb observes, are the facts that the students are, first of all, bright, and, secondly, very anxious to learn. The books-on-tape aspect of the program is supplemented by a minimum of three hours weekly of individual tutoring and small group work to help students get more mileage out of their areas of strength while working to improve skills in their areas of weakness. The staff of the Curry Learning Center maintains communication with professors to foster understanding of each student's particular problems and, when it seems necessary, also administer exams to P.A.L. students in an untimed, supervised format at the Learning Center.

In addition to academic support, P.A.L. also offers help in the area of social skills. For instance, last year the program began offering a "group interaction experience" called "oral communication." Due to their problems with memory and with picking up cues—"in reading the unheard, unsaid expressions from people," as Webb says—some P.A.L. students have trouble in social relationships.

In "Oral Communication," Webb explains, students "are not only bringing out on the table their emotional hurts, they are also thinking through into the future and planning on that base. They challenge each other. They make each other stand up to the issues. And in order to do that, they're developing visual sequencing in relation to 'how did that affect Johnny when I said that?'"

P.A.L.'s hope is that students who go through the program will go on to feel that they are a part of the "normal" world, and that, as a result of having learned to use their strengths and work around their weaknesses, they will be able to make the significant contributions that Webb—and others—feel learning-disabled individuals are capable of making. But the program does not offer false hopes for cures or for the elimination of every problem a student might face. To sum up the philosophy behind P.A.L., Webb quotes an old Norwegian expression: "God, make me wise enough to know the difference: what I can change, I shall work at, and what I can't change, let me accept it."

Even if such programs eventually become widespread, they will not solve the problems many learning-disabled people encounter in coping with adult life. Again and again we heard from adult LDs who had graduated from college that the strategies that were successful in making their way through college were not working for them in the job world. Such people may need continued assistance even after they have graduated from college—assistance which may take the form of programs of adult education.

Adult Education

Educational obstacles do not vanish for the LD once he or she has become an adult. Increasingly, for instance, non-LD adults feel the need to return to school —to enrich their lives by satisfying a curiosity; to pick up practical or impractical skills, ranging from auto repair to decoupage; to advance in their jobs by gaining new knowledge; or to re-educate themselves for a new career. LDs need such opportunities no less than nonhandicapped people do, yet adult education remains, for the most part, inaccessible to LD adults, no matter how much schooling they may already have.

Particularly for the LD who struggled through high school and then quit—to get an unchallenging job, or, failing that, to go on welfare, or, unable to succeed at anything else, to turn to crime—adult education could spell the difference between a wasted life and a productive one. Yet, unlike other handicapped people for whom government agencies provide money, counseling, and even help in getting employment, LDs are offered very little in the way of government support once they have passed their 21st birthday (see pp. 37–38). And yet, observes Paul Ackerman of BEH, an educational structure almost perfectly suited to providing help is already operating in the United States: the system of junior and community colleges, which could offer not only courses for LD adults but also counseling and guidance as well.

One of the few community colleges that offers a program designed specifically for LD adults is Ventura College in Ventura, California. The need is clearly there, asserts Jeffrey Barsch, the architect of the program and himself a dyslexic: in Ventura County, he says, there are approximately 20,000 "labeled, diagnosed adults who before our program was developed could not receive services unless they were to go to a private agency and spend a great deal of money for assessment and programs." But even statistics like these do not speak for themselves. For when Barsch first approached the college's administration and told them of the many people in the community who needed help, he got a typical response: "'So where are they? Why don't they come here and tell us?' And we tried," says Barsch, "to say 'Well, many of these people have just given up. If they had an opportunity, they would come back.'" To its credit, Ventura College decided to take the gamble.

In September of 1976, the program began with no students and a professional staff of one—Barsch. His first job, quite clearly, was to find people to take part in the program. "We went on TV," he recalls, "we put advertisements in the newspaper; in many cases we took vocational rehabilitation records or old public school records and called people who had left high school but failed in vocational rehabilitation for academic reasons, and said 'We have a program. Are you interested in coming for an interview?' We actually recruited," says Barsch, "and I don't think that's a dirty word in our field." Dirty or not, the recruiting worked. By June of 1977, the program had already served 160 adults for an average of six hours a week per person. Barsch estimates that the program will serve 250 adults in its second year. None of those students had paid—or will pay —a penny for the education they received. The Ventura program is free, funded on a per-student basis by the California Assembly—under a bill guaranteeing equal rights in access to education for the handicapped—and also by the California State Chancellor's Office.

The adults who came to Ventura during the program's first nine months tended to be between 20 and 30 years of age and were, due to a very active women's center on the Ventura campus, twice as likely to be female as male. As more students came, both the program and its staff began to grow. As of June, 1977, the program offered assessment, information about learning disabilities, and remediation, based largely on the Barsch Movigenics Curriculum, a perceptual motor training technique developed by Jeffrey Barsch's father, Ray. Adults in the program have at their disposal a wide array of audiovisual equipment, including books on both video- and audiotape, and a language lab capable of playing 50 different tapes simultaneously for 50 different listeners. The program also offers a variety of physical activity programs. For adults whose social skills have never had a chance to mature, Barsch teaches a "polishing" course that concentrates on such matters as awareness of and relatedness to one's self and others and on more efficient self-presentation through a better vocabulary.

At the same time as it offers educational opportunities to adults, the Ventura program also endeavors to educate the community at large—particularly employers. One member of the Ventura staff is a full-time vocational specialist who makes contact with local businesses and talks to employers about learning-disabled people. The specialist also takes LD adults to sites where possible employment opportunities exist. "We feel that the most important thing is to get the employer to realize that these people are capable," says Barsch. And it is an uphill climb all the way. Barsch had bumper stickers printed that read, "The Disabled Are Capable"—when he went to call on various employers to ask them to put the stickers on their cars and also to think about hiring the handicapped, they would invariably respond: "Oh yes, we can employ the deaf," or "We'll be glad to employ someone in a wheelchair." After a year's effort, Barsch had placed two LDs in training positions with employers who were willing to hire LD adults on a permanent basis.

This is not to say, however, that the Ventura program is geared specifically to helping LD adults get jobs—or, for that matter, diplomas. "What I try and tell our students is that we're here for life," says Barsch. "You don't have to go for a degree. You can work all day and come at night for years if you want. You can take three credits a semester for 50 years. What we've tried to do in Ventura for the whole college is to get across the idea of continuing education for life. Even if you get a degree, you're going to come back."

Is it utopian to believe that the philosophy behind Ventura's fledgling program should guide education at all levels and for all ages, LD and normal alike? Probably. To look at it practically, the question of what pace and what environment are most conducive to high-quality learning could be—and already has been —the starting point for a library full of reports and dissertations. Still, the question must be pondered, for the most widely accepted answers—at least those most widely accepted in regular education—are held by many in the LD field to be at the root of innumerable learning disabilities. "Education is a process, not a product," asserts Larry Lieberman of Boston College. And so much of the research being done today, he says, "is oriented to a product: what grade level did he achieve on the basis of my intervention? Can he now read because he dealt with the Frostig materials for the last three months? Did he get a higher score in auditory reception because I trained him on the Milton/Bradley goal program for the ITPA [Illinois Test of Psycholinguistic Ability] ? All these things are product oriented now; but what does it mean when a person is 20 or 40? It's life. That's what the problem is—the problem of living."

Having examined the ways in which the educational system as a whole is serving and failing to serve the learning disabled, it is now time for us to look in detail at the techniques of special education. How are the learning disabled identified? What actually happens in the resource room? Does it actually work? These are questions we shall address in the chapter that follows.

Chapter 4
Evaluation and Remediation

"The strength of the arm . . ."

Ultimately, everything that is done in the LD field—by educators, by scientists, by politicians, and by parents—can be judged by one question: does it work? Although the riddles of learning disabilities have inspired many a theory, the roots of the LD movement, as we have seen, and the goal of most of the government spending that that movement has helped to bring about, derive from the practical concerns of identifying and helping learning-disabled individuals. And it is these two efforts that constitute the bulk of the activity in the LD field today.

Nobody questions the need for evaluation and remediation, but neither can anyone completely justify them. There has been hardly any cost-benefit analysis of remediation, but the cost component is all too clear. For both parents and children, remediation is costly, not only in terms of money, but in terms of time as well. Special teachers, schools, programs, and equipment are all expensive; medical and educational evaluations are expensive; and all these costs will rise as the demand for special services—which P.L. 94–142 will help to intensify—increases.

The benefits, on the other hand, are not clearly documented, as we will show in the pages that follow. Some children learn to read, write, spell, and calculate; others do not. It has not yet clearly been established how much the success or failure of any given remedial technique can be ascribed to the technique, and how much to the remediator; nor how long skills are retained by a learning-disabled person after the remediation ends; nor how valuable those skills are after that person has left school; nor to what extent special education can relieve the frustration that many learning disabled people face and can help them to become happy and productive members of society; nor to what extent special education, with its attendant labeling and stigmatization, increases frustration and leads a person to become an angry, and perhaps a deviant, member of society.

Although there is little hard evidence to show how or if remediation is effective, it is strongly felt that something must be done. The costs of school failure are high. James Kavanagh and Grace Yeni-Komshian, for instance, write:

> The educational cost of requiring children to repeat a grade due to a reading problem reaches nearly $2 billion a year. But more important than the dollar cost to the school system is the cost to the nation, and to the children themselves, of allowing students who cannot read to leave school and enter society without the basic skill they need to function in society. It is here that the statistics are truly alarming: about half of the nation's unemployed youths age 16–21 are functionally illiterate with virtually no prospects of obtaining good jobs. A recent study in a major Eastern city showed that 75% of juvenile offenders are two or more years behind in reading; other studies show a similar proportion of poor readers among adults convicted of criminal offenses [Kavanagh, Yeni-Komshian 1978, p. 1].

Evaluation and remediation activities range from the scientific to the educational, from the academic to the physical, from the cognitive to the affective. From within the field, two radically different perspectives emerge: the orthodox scientific view is summed up by Christy Ludlow, who writes that the poor results of remediation to date "are not surprising, since the basis for [learning] disorders, their characteristics and their symptomatology are not understood. Language pathologists and special educators," she continues, "can only attempt to apply general language teaching programs which are based on normal acquisition to the education of these children. Clearly some understanding of the problems these children have is needed before diagnosis, treatment, and prevention can improve" (Ludlow 1978).

The educational hard line is articulated by University of Texas (Austin) Associate Professor of Special Education Steven Larsen, who is currently President of the Division for Children with Learning Disabilities of The Council for Exceptional Children: "I would say by all means conduct all the neurological research you can. But the idea that so-called psychological abilities such as 'auditory sequential memory,' or 'visual sequential memory,' or 'auditory reception,' or 'figure-ground perception' are the manifestation of some type of neurological functioning is a very tenuous, unsupported proposition. For the teacher, remember that he or she is a teacher. You're there to transmit information, and nothing should stand in the way of doing that. Once you've ruled out ongoing neurological pathology, you're still faced with a child who's reading probably at the pre-primer 1 level and is resistant to all types of very excellent instruction. At that point, it just becomes the teacher and the child. The etiology is unimportant." As far as the actual carrying out of evaluation and remediation is concerned, both Ludlow and Larsen are saying the same thing: because so little is known about learning disorders at this point, the relationship between diagnosis and treatment is a weak one at best.

But that relationship is the key link in the learning disabilities field. It provides the connection between science and education. Public Law 94-142 attempts to provide "a free and appropriate education" to a large population of handicapped children, not through a massive investment in science or a reform of the public education system, but rather by influencing that relationship.

Diagnostic Techniques

There is, as we have seen, no single medical symptom that infallibly indicates a specific learning disability. The EEG, dichotic listening, and tachistoscopic vision tests all remain unreliable. Nor do neurological soft signs provide conclusive evidence: there are children with severe motor disturbances, left-right confusions, erratic eye movements, or other problems—including those stemming from documented cases of birth trauma or brain injury—who can read, write, and calculate perfectly well. "Almost every kind of neurological dysfunction that has been described in people with reading problems has also been described in people who read all right," observes psychiatrist Leon Eisenberg. "The signs and symptoms don't add up to a total picture—or at least to a total picture that makes sense."

Much the same is true on the education side. There is no surefire test or surefire way of interpreting a test. More often than not, the meaning of the test results is in the eye of the test-giver. "When we do a WISC [Wechsler Intelligence Scale for Children] on a kid, for example," says John Sikorski of the Reach for Learning Clinic, "we're not looking at the number. We're looking at how they deal with each individual task—how each subgroup uses different combinations of modalities." Sikorski uses the Illinois Test of Psycholinguistic Abilities in the same way: "you go through a whole battery of tests without ever adding up the numbers, you come to a learning profile for each kid, and out of that you generate your remedial program."

Gertrude Webb of the P.A.L. program at Curry College (who has recently helped to design a "learning ability-disability" clinic at Carney Hospital in Boston) says the same thing: "We try not to get excited about the final numbers. We're looking for strengths and weaknesses on which we can develop an appropriate educational program." During the three-hour evaluation of children at Carney Hospital, Webb and other members of the staff try to rely as much as they can on observation to learn about gross motor movement: "The people I use in testing can notice, for instance, a 5-year-old walking up a stairway and doubling his feet on each step. Or the gait of a 10-year-old walking across the room. Their own familiarity with physical development will point out to them irregularities. We do have formal tests, but, in a three-hour period of testing, we're trying to get in a tremendous amount. So we try to do as much as we can through observation of the behavior. You have to be skilled to do that."

In intellectual or mental testing, says Webb, "I'm inclined to use the Wechsler first because it gives us a breakdown between verbal and performance scores, as opposed to the Stanford-Binet, which is also a very good test, but you have to go fishing to find the same information. On the other hand, if we have a young, seemingly 'mentally retarded,' we'll move to the Stanford-Binet, because that seems to get us greater depth than the Wechsler Preschool and Primary Scale of Intelligence [known as the "WPPSI" for ages 4 to 6½].* But a test," says Webb, "is only a measure of the child's performance at the moment of testing, and although it gives us great insights, one must recognize that it's of that moment, and, therefore, I am very open to the teachers' experience with the children—to comments like, 'Gee, I'm surprised you got such a low measure on that, because in my classroom he does this, that, or the other thing,'—and to information from the parents like, 'Yeah, but there's something strange going on because he wakes up in the middle of the night screaming. So, we've got to look for something more. In the social and emotional areas we use the 'draw-a-person,' which is a classic test, and we also use the TED, which is Tasks of Emotional Development, devised here at Children's Hospital in Boston, and which correlates with the stages of development that Erik Erikson prescribed. We also ask the child for five of his likes and dislikes in the categories of home, school, friends, and his world, and we score that. And, we also have a self-concept measure that my students here at Curry College devised that we find rather effective for an elementary school-age child."

The types of tests used, and the meaning ascribed to them, will obviously vary from one evaluator to another. Some measure of the lack of consensus in the field as to which instruments are most reliable can be inferred from the fact that the BEH was forced to remove from P.L. 94–142 the requirement that the discrepancy between achievement and expectation be defined numerically. As some opponents of the discrepancy formula argued, "Sometimes, tests just don't work." "There's one youngster who I've tested who has an IQ of 80," says Hofstra Reading Professor Harvey Alpert. "And if you sat and talked with that youngster, you'd know he doesn't have an IQ of 80. He's probably superior but at least bright-normal. But he does not test well; it's a disaster to try to test him. He can't think, he gets frustrated, and he has a tendency to over-elaborate." And it is for this reason that many say that the notion of diagnosing a learning disa-

*Other Wechsler intelligence tests are the Wechsler Intelligence Scale for Children, the "WISC–Revised" 1974, for ages 6–16 years; and the Wechsler Adult Intelligence Scale, "WAIS," for 16 years–adult.

bility on the basis of a discrepancy between achievement and expectation really amounts to measuring the disability twice: an achievement test itself is a measure of the disorder, and, on an IQ test, a youngster with impaired verbal abilities, for instance, is going to have trouble in every part of the test that requires functional verbal skills.

But the fallibility of tests is only one factor that has an impact in the area of diagnosis; another is the fact that an evaluation will be influenced by the evaluator's own definition of a learning disability. For instance, John Sikorski argues that neurological factors alone cannot explain the tremendous range of figures reported in various incidence studies. "But when you start to look at differences in class, and the differences in urban/rural, and the differences in family communication styles, it becomes abundantly clear why the inner city ghettoes have the 25 percent of school age population being called 'learning disabled', while the more homogeneous areas of cities, suburbs, and small towns, where the value systems of parents are more coincident with the value systems of the teachers and school administrators, have a much lower incidence of learning disabilities —5, 6, 7 percent."

This is an abstract notion. How does it work in practice? Sikorski presents a case history that, while not dealing with learning disabilities per se, suggests the kinds of details that go into an accurate diagnosis:

A woman came into his clinic for an evaluation of her 11-year-old son, who was in a second grade class for educationally handicapped children. The boy was considered to be mentally retarded and hyperactive. "As I spent time with the parents and we began asking more questions about family patterns and styles," Sikorski, a psychiatrist by training, recalls, "I was struck with the kind of discontinuities in moving around the countryside, from one city to another, the father constantly changing jobs, the mother constantly doing things to get the family to move back closer to where her mother lived—and lots of contention."

Sikorski finally obtained a copy of the boy's birth record and found written thereon a note by the obstetrician to the effect that, even though the delivery was perfectly normal and the child was physically healthy at birth, he had asked the mother to spend an extra day in the hospital so that a pediatrician could look at the boy. The obstetrician, Sikorski says, "couldn't trust the mother to take proper care of the infant. He felt that . . . there was something too anxious about what was going on."

"It turns out," Sikorski continues, "that 11 years and two more sons later, the mother wants all of them evaluated for school problems." The oldest son, she told Sikorski, was mentally retarded; the second son had a behavioral disturbance; and the mother had been told that the third son would have to repeat kindergarten because he had missed too much school. "The mother said that he always had colds," Sikorski notes.

"It turned out that the mother is severely disturbed. Two of her brothers have been hospitalized much of their lives with severe mental illness, and she keeps the boys home from school when she gets lonely and depressed—a real psychiatric nightmare."

Strangely enough, Sikorski points out, all three boys had been seen and were being regularly followed by a pediatrician, and, aside from the hyperactivity diagnosed in all of them (for which they were all receiving Ritalin), the boys had excellent health records.

The situation had gone on as long as it did, Sikorski suspects, because the mother was adept at disguising her condition: "If you only have one interview with her, you'd think everything was fine. But when you start getting the records and piecing it together and sitting down and really looking at the issue, the kid's not mentally retarded—he's developing a severe childhood anxiety neurosis."

No less meticulous is the approach that Mel Levine uses in his clinic* at the Children's Hospital Medical Center in Boston. A pediatrician concerned with development, Levine is particularly interested in children between the ages of 5 and 13—a period that psychiatrists call "latency" but that, says Levine, "is anything but latent. I think it's a very active period and a crucial one."

In the past, Levine observes, the "life problems"—which include, of course, school problems—of the school-age child were attributed to emotional or psychosocial problems, parental fighting, a hard-working father, or some such cause. Today, however, Levine sees an increasing awareness all around the country that, for the school-age child, "living with his own head is one of the major challenges, and having to adjust to that particular profile of strengths and weaknesses that was dealt down to you and you didn't really ask for. So we are very interested in looking at the components of function in the school-age child."

The core of the full-day workup in Levine's clinic is the "pediatric neurodevelopmental examination," which takes about an hour and gives an indication of where problems might exist in a wide variety of specific parameters of function, among them: attention, motor function, receptive language, expressive language, output abilities in terms of speech and writing, memory, and a number of other basic aspects of functioning including social interaction. But the full evaluation also takes into account hearing and vision tests, a psychiatric assessment, and a thorough medical history, including the capacity to control one's body appropriately in terms of urine, stool, and other fundamental body functions. "We look for subtle dysfunctions in these areas," says Levine, "recognizing that many of these are intrinsic or constitutional in the child—that they're not caused by the environment, they're influenced by the environment—but that the underlying predispositions can be identified and worked with."

At Levine's clinic and others like it, it is becoming standard practice for evaluations to be conducted by multidisciplinary teams. "In our present state of knowledge," argues Barry Russman, Clinical Director of Neurology at Newington

---

*Levine is Chief of the Division of Ambulatory Pediatrics, Medical Outpatient Department. He is also Assistant Professor of Pediatrics at Harvard Medical School.

Children's Hospital, Newington, Connecticut, "it could hardly be otherwise. We don't have a blood test we can draw to show that this is the problem," he says. "So it must be a team of people knowledgeable in learning disabilities, in child development, and about growth in terms of social and emotional health, that has to sit down and arrive at programs for these children. I don't think it can be one person that can say, 'Yes, this child is learning disabled with perceptual problems,' and so on."

At the Child Development Center of the Children's Hospital in San Francisco, for instance, evaluations are conducted by teams consisting of at least four members: an occupational therapist, an educational psychologist, a social worker, and a pediatric neurologist. Medical Director Jerome Mednick notes that there are both advantages and disadvantages to the multidisciplinary approach: "I personally think the more disciplines you get involved, the more complicated it can become," he says. "But at the same time," he notes, "if there is mutual respect among team members, the procedure can work very well." Pediatric neurologist Mednick and his staff are not concerned with the "why" of the problems they see; when faced by a profoundly learning-disabled child with no history of a birth problem, on the one hand, and on the other hand by a perfectly normal child with a history of serious oxygen deprivation at birth, Mednick explains, "trying to define cause and effect is very difficult." So the team, Mednick says, "concentrates on looking at the 'what' and at what we can do to help treat the final common denominator, which is an educational problem."

Though unconcerned with causes and effects, Mednick also recognizes that learning disabilities are frequently accompanied by other types of problems. By the same token, the social worker tries "to get some insight into whether the family dynamics of the situation are contributing to the disorder. I personally feel," says Mednick, "that the individual who has been learning disabled for, say, a year already has some secondary emotional problems. So it's just a matter of time before the emotional problems become major problems, and in the final analysis—in my opinion—may become more severe than the primary disorder. And unless you look at the whole thing, you're not really going to get to home base." His role as the pediatric neurologist, he says, is to pick up some insight into the overall developmental history of the child: "I try to correlate what might have happened from the day of gestation to the time we see the child." And Mednick also attempts to "give the total evaluation some degree of respectability by having the family see that they're dealing with a board-certified physician who—it is hoped—knows what he's talking about but who readily admits that when he is giving them the final impression, it is not his impression alone but rather the impressions of the members of a team working closely together." In essence, says Mednick, "I put myself and my team in the position of being an advocate for the child and a protector of the parent, and in this day and age, we need both, because there are so many fly-by-night people who are coming up with this theory and that theory."

The approach developed by Susan Trout, Chairperson of the Department of

Learning Disabilities at the University of the Pacific, School of Medical Sciences in San Francisco, involves not so much the use of multidisciplinary teams as of multidisciplinary team members. The staffers who evaluate the children at Trout's clinic—a member of the clinic faculty, a neurologist, and both an advanced and a beginning clinician (other team members include a parent interviewer and a school visitor)—all have had previous professions or training in other disciplines. Trout, for instance, has a doctorate in learning disabilities and a master's in speech pathology and audiology; another team member has degrees in both learning disabilities and occupational therapy. Neurology and psychiatry residents, and psychology interns, also observe the work of the clinic. "Anyone involved in this field," says Trout, "must be multidisciplinary to be able to understand the multiple aspects of learning disabilities and to know when to refer or to consult or to call in another dimension." As a result, team members have a fairly deep understanding of one another's professions: "For example," says Trout, "the neurologist that we have knows just as much as I do about the diagnosis of learning disabilities, and I can speak about psychoneurology as much as he can."

Mel Levine insists, too, that the lines of communication between disciplines be kept open; he feels no reluctance in drawing up an educational prescription and is open to medical observation from the educators on his teams. Team members at the clinic include a pediatrician with a special interest in child development, a child psychiatrist, and an educator. Rather than "multidisciplinary," however, Levine likes to use the term "transdisciplinary" to describe his teams. By this he means not only that disciplines overlap, but also that "this is not a team where everybody agrees with each other all the time and where everything gets blamed on emotional problems; this is a team whose members don't like each other too much. On the teams that I organize here in the hospital, there's a certain amount of tension. If the team really gets along, then the kid isn't really seeing a team. It almost has to be like going to court. There almost has to be a kind of built-in adversary relationship among the team members instead of all of them patting each other on the back. One of the problems in this field is that you get the diagnosis that a place likes to sell. So you can almost tell by reading the letterhead what the report's going to say, and that's a real danger."

The final diagnosis that Levine's team reaches is never simply a label like "LD." "You've got to individualize," Levine says, and he admits that "one of the things that I love about evaluating these children is that they're so dissimilar. It would get boring if they were all alike; well, here's another visual-perceptual problem. No. Here's another visual-perceptual problem whose main difficulty is in whole-part relationships, but for whom relative position sets and figure-ground relationships and relative size, and the permanence of objects in different planes are intact, and who just has this one problem in whole-part relationships."

Many diagnosticians, then, are beginning to move away from the use of simple IQ tests in order to arrive at very specific characterizations of not only a child's deficiencies but also a child's abilities and of the "natural ecology," as

Levine puts it, of those strengths and weaknesses. As Steven Larsen argues, however, a diagnosis on this order of sophistication may be of little value to the educator who has to work with the child. In the Levine clinic, an educational specialist is part of the evaluating team, and the diagnosis includes an educational prescription. But it is more often the case, as pediatric neurologist Barry Russman points out, that a physician can only indicate the kind of treatment needed, e.g., special education, medication, or psychiatric care, and not the precise educational program called for. Beyond this is the fact that there are virtually no guidelines for precisely matching remedial techniques with particular types of specific learning disorders.

In the final analysis, the diagnosis of learning disabilities is, at the present time, more of an art than a science. In a report submitted to the Office of Juvenile Justice and Delinquency Prevention, Law Enforcement Assistance Administration (LEAA), Charles A. Murray, a political scientist and leader of the American Institutes for Research Team, writes that the complex nature of learning disabilities has raised the question whether LD can be diagnosed reliably even under the best of conditions (Murray et al. 1976A). "Among the consultants interviewed for this study, there was a broad consensus," Murray reports, "that reliable diagnosis is possible, if a skilled diagnostician is in charge. By determining patterns of behavior, combining the results of a variety of tests, and running these data through the mind of an experienced observer of LD children, a learning disability can be distinguished from general retardation, emotional disturbance, and (in non-clinical language) ordinary contrariness or lack of motivation.

"But," continues Murray, "it was strongly and widely agreed that reliable diagnosis cannot yet be conducted by nonspecialists using standardized instruments. . . . No test battery which has learning disabilities as its construct has achieved wide acceptance among professionals in the field." According to the Murray report, this lack of a standardized diagnostic instrument is a cause of some concern in the field because, "as it happens, a great many people and institutions are currently conducting diagnosis of LD. In many states, entire school populations are supposedly being screened. To put it very simply, the amount of diagnosis which is being attempted is far out of proportion to the number of competent diagnosticians" (Murray et al., 1976B, p. A3).

The Politics of Diagnosis

Over the next few years, under the impetus of Public Law 94–142, activity in the area of diagnosis and evaluation will increase considerably. But at the same time, as we saw in chapter 3 on education, there is a conspicuous shortage of LD specialists in the educational system. In tacit recognition of this fact, the regulations prepared by the Bureau of Education for the Handicapped (BEH) require that public agencies responsible for determining whether a child has a learning disability must use a team to evaluate each child. The evaluating team, according to the regulations, must consist of the child's regular classroom teacher, or, if the child has no regular teacher, a regular classroom teacher qualified to teach a child of his or her age; and "at least one person qualified to conduct individual diagnostic examinations of children, such as a school psychologist, speech-language pathologist, or remedial reading teacher" (P.L. 94–142 Regulations 1977A, Section 121a.540).

A number of groups and individuals have strong misgivings about the mechanics of this procedure. For one thing, even with federal funds from P.L. 94–142, states and local school districts will still be carrying most of the costs of educating handicapped children—and those costs are as much as four to five times higher than the expense of educating a normal child. Roy Lasky, Executive Director of the New York Association for the Learning Disabled, points out that in New York State, which did not recognize LD as a handicap until well after the passage of P.L. 94–142, the cost of recognizing the condition could amount to $45 million (based on an estimate—perhaps conservative—that 2 percent of all the children in the state public education system have a learning disorder and are thus entitled to some $700 apiece in aid to cover the additional costs of their schooling). Until recently, Lasky continues, the state was receiving about $70 in federal aid for every LD child, an amount that it split evenly with local school districts—"and of course," says Lasky, "$35 is not a lot of incentive." This is particularly true because P.L. 94–142 does not provide funds for the evaluation procedures themselves.

Another disincentive, as we suggested above, is the lack of trained personnel to work with LD children. In New York City, according to an article in *The New York Times,* there are 9,000 handicapped pupils on waiting lists for evaluation (and about 53,000 currently being served). Former City School Chancellor Irving Anker estimated that these children could add $19 million to the city's education bill—at a time when rising costs have already forced a reduction of some 17 percent in supervisory and administrative positions in special education in the city (Goldman 1977). Other communities offer similar complaints. As we noted earlier, there are already 5,000 or so children on waiting lists for educationally handicapped classes in Los Angeles; and in Michigan, a regional superintendent for special education told *The New York Times,* "We are finding kids faster than we can find competent staff" (Maeroff 1978).

Personnel shortages and financial constraints such as these, plus the mandate in P.L. 94–142 that students be educated in "the least restrictive environment," make mainstreaming an attractive alternative to many school districts. This is not, however, an attractive alternative to many regular classroom teachers, few of whom have received adequate training in working with handicapped youngsters.*

---

*Teacher's unions in various parts of the country such as Wisconsin, New York, and Minnesota have taken positions that P.L. 94–142 is irresponsible because it mandates costly pro-

Mel Levine argues that "children who are failing are entitled to an evaluation that is outside the political system, and that is outside the major monetary systems. If you get evaluated in your school, mixed into the evaluation is going to be the school budget, considerations of what services they can offer and what services they can't offer. If you have a receptive language problem and they don't have a language therapist, they're going to play down your receptive language problem because they have this wonderful woman who's great at motor training. The process is loaded with hidden agendas." Similarly, William Healey of the American Speech and Hearing Association, is concerned that "once you call a child learning disabled, it seems to serve as excuse enough to provide some special services for him, but it may not provide for an in-depth analysis of what the real problems seem to be."

Parents and children are not, however, entirely at the mercy of the local school district where evaluation is concerned. Decisions made at the local level can be appealed. But as Roy Lasky notes, few parents are informed or articulate enough to take advantage of the appeals mechanisms; in small communities, cultural factors work against parents' arguing with school officials. Moreover, there are few lawyers available anywhere who are familiar with the intricacies of appeal at the higher levels where the process can become expensive.

Appeals aren't the only potential expense for parents. A private evaluation also can be expensive: the cost of a full workup, according to pediatric neurologist Barry Russman, can be $500. Under certain circumstances, explains Russman, third-party payers—insurance companies and the like—will reimburse parents for the cost of an evaluation. "An evaluation of children with learning disabilities that involves not just educational testing but a total evaluation of a child—his growth and development, his social and emotional health, how all these relate to the child's ability or inability to learn—is considered part of a medical evaluation and will be reimbursed depending, of course, on the parents' insurance policies," says Russman. But as a rule, straight educational evaluations will not be reimbursed.

Nor do insurance companies, at present, provide reimbursement for remediation under any circumstances. Nor, argues Russman, are they ever likely to. "If you were going to start to look to the insurance industry to start covering the 'treatment' of these children, the costs would be so incredibly mind-boggling that the insurance companies would say, 'Fine, we quit.'"

It would be hard to blame them. The National Institute of Neurological and Communicative Disorders and Stroke estimates that the annual cost of care for 8 million children and adolescents with reading disabilities is $8 billion.

---

grams without providing for the requisite funding. In addition, some unions are unhappy with the law because of the added burden on teachers who must draw up lengthy individualized education programs (known as "IEPs") for each handicapped student. In fact, the inordinate time a teacher must spend on the IEPs has become an item in collective bargaining in some areas.

Remediation

For the learning disabled, care primarily takes the form of remediation. This does not mean "cure"—few believe that the word will have a meaning in the field for a long time to come, if ever. Rather, remediation is a means of helping a person to strengthen weak skills, or to acquire, or develop, the ability to function in spite of his or her handicaps. Most efforts in the remediation area are aimed at one or some of the following goals:

1. *Academic skills.* Some of the best-established remediational programs, such as the Orton-Gillingham, attempt primarily to instill academic skills such as reading and writing, which are considered to be essential to a person's ability to cope with modern society.

2. *Sensorimotor readiness.* Other programs such as the "sensory integrative therapy" of occupational therapist and psychologist Jean Ayres and "developmental optometrics" attempt to strengthen supposedly fundamental perceptual and motor skills which are considered to be components of academic performance. It is thought that by strengthening these component processes, a solid foundation can be laid, upon which the more specialized and elaborate academic skills can be constructed.

3. *Social and emotional adjustment.* Learning-disabled people are often handicapped as much by a lack of ability to send and receive conventional social signals as they are by the lack of formal academic skills like reading. Some programs attempt to strengthen the ability to read and to express body language and other arts of social communication. It is also argued that a child suffering from a learning disability will almost inevitably have concomitant psychological problems or secondary psychological problems brought on by his troubles in school and in life and that these problems will require psychotherapy.

4. *Occupational training.* Some programs attempt to equip learning-disabled adolescents to be economically self-supporting.

5. *Holistic approaches.* Some remediators see learning disabilities as global disorders that affect many realms of thought, emotion, movement, and feeling. They consider remediation to encompass education, training, and socialization in the broadest sense.

6. *Juvenile delinquency.* There is some evidence of a link—perhaps causal—between learning disabilities and juvenile delinquency. A disproportionate number of incarcerated youths appear to be deficient in reading or other academic or perceptual skills. Only now are strict incidence studies being undertaken (see pp. 122–126). If the link is firmly established, it would suggest that remediation should be made an integral part of rehabilitation for many juvenile delinquents and also that it might have some potential as a means to prevent such delinquency from developing in the first place.

In the same way that approaches to evaluating learning disabilities vary widely from one professional or clinic to the next, methods of remediation tend to be influenced by a variety of personal and clinical factors. "It's hard to find any systematic data anywhere in the remedial reading literature," says psychiatrist Leon Eisenberg, "that shows in fact that teaching kids on their heads or lying on their sides is any better than teaching them standing up, although there are people that will swear to you that this method or that method is the only way to teach them."

Eisenberg suggests, in effect, that the key to successful remediation may have less to do with the method used than with the teacher. Dyslexic children, he has observed, tend to be helped most not by teachers who are committed to a theory, but by those "who aren't fixed on any one way of doing it, who know how to relate to a child, to get the child's confidence and then play around with various approaches to teaching the child until they see what works."

How does remediation work? There are so many methods currently in use, and so many individual styles of using them, that it is impossible to characterize the process in any general way. But Reading Professor Harvey Alpert's description of his work with one learning-disabled student illustrates something of the pace and the challenge involved.

I was working with a youngster on the Fernald technique. He picks the word he wants to learn, and I write the word out for him on a card. Now he's going to trace the word over and over again while he says it aloud, usually breaking it into syllables. So he's saying the word over and over again and tracing it as he says it—which is the way the Fernald system works. I say to him "When you have traced the word enough times, and when you think you can write the word without looking at it, you tell me." And then you turn the card over and give him a crayon and he writes the word.

All right: he's traced the word twelve times, and finally he says to me he can write the word. He turns it over, and he successfully writes the word. (Sometimes, by the way, they don't. If they don't, you let them go back and trace the word some more, and then when he says he can do it, you give him another piece of paper and he can write the word. If worse comes to worst, you can let him compare letter by letter and see where he made the mistake, then go back and trace some more. In Fernald, you're not supposed to point out the error: I won't point it out, but I'll say to him "let's look at it." We'll do it letter by letter, and I'll say "Do you see any difference?" And he says "Yes, I left this letter out"; I say, "good," and then I'll give him the word to trace some more.)

So he's traced the word twelve times, he's written the word successfully. "What's the word?" He tells me.

The next day, I said to him "Do you remember the word we learned yesterday?" He said "yes." "What was the word?" And he tells me. And I said "can you write the word for me?" He can't.

But I can show you another youngster who, the next day, when you say "Do you remember the word we learned yesterday?" will say "no." "Can you write the word you learned yesterday?" And he'll write the word he learned yesterday. You say "Do you remember what that word was?" "No."

What remediation boils down to, notes veteran remediator Margaret Rawson, is matching a treatment to a problem with "pedagogic skill." And this does not mean, says Alpert, following a program to the "nth degree." Many teachers, he fears, "see that something isn't working, and instead of saying, 'with this minor change, it will work,' they conclude that the program is no good and they throw it out." Thus, as Eisenberg has argued, the reason that "it has been so difficult to document the superiority of one teaching 'method' over another" is that the teacher, not the method, is the key variable. Special educator Don Hammill, among a number of others, goes so far as to suggest that even the successes enjoyed by the creators of widely used remedial therapies have more to do with their clinical skill than with their theories or, in his words, with "the strength of the arm, not the sharpness of the blade."

This is not to say that there is no rational basis for remediation. One scheme in which the connection between diagnosis and treatment is easy to see has been developed by Elena Boder (see p. 13). In the subgroup of dyslexics that she calls "dysphonetic," for instance, the problem is interpreted primarily as a deficit in the auditory channel. The initial remedial approach to take with these children, Boder argues, should be a "whole-word" (or "look-say") method, taking advantage of the child's intact visual channel. After the child has built up a sufficient sight vocabulary (with tactile-kinesthetic reinforcement such as tracing, or touching letters cut out of textured materials like sandpaper), the teaching of remedial phonics should be undertaken. In the "dyseidetic" category, where the primary deficit is thought to be in the visual channel, the approach could be reversed; if the child has already learned to identify and write the letters of the alphabet, treatment would start with remedial phonics. (If a child has not learned the alphabet, Boder prescribes a tactile-kinesthetic technique.) Implicit in these strategies is the belief that emphasizing a learning-disabled child's areas of strength will automatically bring about some improvement in the areas of weakness; working to the strength also helps to develop and maintain motivation in the child.

This, however, is only one approach. Some favor working directly with the deficit. Others believe that, rather than remedial techniques, what is most needed is intensive regular classroom-type instruction on an individual basis. Going a step further, some argue that, as Marcel Kinsbourne, Professor of Pediatrics and Psychology at the University of Toronto, says, "the nature of the instruction is not as important as the fact that it's individual. The reason is that in an individual instruction setting, the child will often tell the teacher how to teach." Some remediators try to get at the root of the academic problem by working on so-called basic abilities like memory or spatial relations or eye-hand coordination. Some work on the body alone, leaving academics out of the process entirely. Other types of remediation include the use of medication, counseling, or psychotherapy.

"The problem is," says Mel Levine, "that everybody gets a little bit better. There isn't a single treatment program you can find around the country that isn't working. No matter what you do, it helps." For instance, Levine notes that some children seem to be helped by the elimination of food dyes from their diets. "And," says Levine, "this is what we're going to keep on finding: little small groups. Because what we're talking about is the development of the school-age child. That's very broad: on this development can impinge thousands of variables. And deviations in development can have multiple etiologies."

In practice, many remediators do not hold grudges against specific approaches. "All techniques have a place," says Kinsbourne. "In children with dyslexia, each one has a different problem, and each problem is best suited for a different approach. The remediator should know them all to be able to select intelligently among them for the purposes of any given child. Anybody who uses one technique for every child must be doing it wrong." Similarly, Susan Trout of the University of the Pacific explains that "our philosophy is that, once we uncover the learning style—how the child can effectively process information— then an individual program is set up. We're not 'one-method' oriented, but 'all-methods' oriented, because methods can be adapted for particular children, or new ones can be devised."

The debates in the field about the superiority of one method over another tend to involve theoretical—and conceivably testable—issues rather than practical ones. For example, does it make sense, some wonder, to talk about "getting the body ready to learn," or to say that eye-muscle training leads to improved academic performance? These issues are complicated, however, by two relatively down-to-earth problems: one is that many professionals feel that the proponents of various remediation techniques are making exaggerated claims about the success and applicability of their programs; the other is that many of these proponents feel that their work—and their claims—are widely misunderstood. A number of factors seems to be responsible for this situation:

1. There has been up to now a lack of rigorous conceptual and methodological standards in research on remediation (for instance, populations being studied have been inadequately characterized; procedures used have not been described in sufficiently explicit detail; follow-up data is sparse).

2. The various disorders that fall under the LD rubric are still not well defined.

3. To keep their jobs under P.L. 94-142, a number of professions—speech and language pathologists and reading specialists, for example—are adapting remedial techniques for use with LD children that have not been so used in the past.

4. Many professionals fear that some people doing remedial work in the field are motivated more by financial than by humanitarian considerations.

5. Because they are anxious and worried about their children, many parents have a tendency to accept uncritically any treatment that promises improvement.

Techniques for Remediation

Remediation techniques can be arranged (somewhat arbitrarily) along a continuum: at one end are the strictly academic or cognitive methods, and at the other end are the strictly somatic or physical therapies. As the foregoing discussion has suggested, remediations are modified, combined, or otherwise adapted for use in specific instances as often as, if not more often than, they are used in an "undiluted" form. It is not our intention to evaluate these techniques, or even to describe them all. Rather, in order to put some of the issues in the field into a clearer perspective, the following is intended merely to suggest the range of techniques currently being used to treat LD and to explain in a general way some of the philosophies or theories involved.

It is important to remember that no remediation is in and of itself a cure, no matter how sound or appropriate a method may be. Drake Duane observes that, in severe cases of dyslexia, remediation may be required throughout a person's lifetime. Doris Johnson, head of the Program in Learning Disabilities at Northwestern University (Evanston) reports that, typically, while LD people may retain skills they acquired through remediation, they do not move forward without additional help. To be sure, there are success stories, but as we have seen, it is difficult to explain these successes solely in terms of the technique used.

Indeed, what cannot be described, but must once again be mentioned, is the factor of the remediator's skill: "the strength of the arm." It is one of the ironies of the LD field today that the immense pressures to be "scientific"—pressures that originate both inside the field and at its periphery (from Congress, for instance)—have tended to elevate the importance of theory while obscuring the importance of practice. There is some reason to believe, in fact, that, in the rush to gain acceptance for a theory, the creators of various remedial methods have in the past occasionally overlooked the importance of their own clinical procedures. H. Wayne Johnson, the Director of the Southwest Regional Resource Center in Salt Lake City, recalls that in the 1960s the techniques developed by Marianne Frostig and the late Newall Kephart—both of whom ultimately sought to strengthen perceptual functions through various kinds of motor training—were very popular. "Everyone was walking on the balance beam and doing 'angels in the snow' and that kind of thing," Johnson says. "The bad part, though, was that Newell and Marianne didn't take the time along the way to do the research and establish the validity of their systems. They just said, 'Look at what it does and let it exhibit itself'—and both of those techniques became prostituted in a lot of ways because people started doing a lot of other things with them." Jean Ayres finds the same thing happening today with sensory-integrative therapy, a nonacademic remedial technique of which she is a leading practitioner. What worries Ayres is that the method, which is a physical therapy that seeks to increase the efficiency with which the brain organizes sensory input, is being used by nonspecialists who have had little or no training in occupational therapy. Ayres suggests, in fact, that one of the reasons sensory-integrative therapy has become so controversial is that "so many educators have been doing it in such a lousy way."

That clinical factors can play an important role in the success or failure of a student on any given day is suggested by the observations of a number of remediators. Jeffrey Barsch, among others, finds that his students read and listen better when they are lying down. Sister Eileen Marie Cronin of the Ellen K. Raskob Learning Institute in Oakland, California, recalls that, in the days when the members of her order still wore habits, she would have to put the large crucifix she wore over her shoulder so that it would not distract the students. And by the same token, Harvey Alpert says, "When I work with these kids, I take my rings off, I don't wear my watch—because it's metal—and I use a pair of horn-rimmed glasses that I keep in the car and bring in if I'll be seeing the kids that day. Still, I can see them staring at the glasses, which isn't so bad, because at least they're looking at your face; but I've seen women with lockets and bracelets, and that's what the kids are looking at." Alpert also observes that remediation is more effective in the morning than in the afternoon, and that during a 45-minute lesson, many kids need to spend at least 15 minutes relaxing—doing body movements, looking at pictures, listening to music, etc.

Of the straight academic approaches to remediation, among the oldest (and least controversial) are those clustered around the Orton-Gillingham method. Originally developed by Samuel T. Orton and subsequently refined by teacher Anna Gillingham, the Orton-Gillingham method places a relatively heavy emphasis on phonics. The method, according to Reading Consultant and former Orton Society President Margaret Rawson, focuses on "the problem that learners have in mastering the forms of language; mastering linguistic items in sequence; remembering them; and being able to analyze and synthesize." This is not so much of a perceptual problem, Drake Duane, current President of the Orton Society explains, i.e., an inability to see the letter, as it is a matter of not being able to remember the configuration of letters or to recognize their symbolic content. Thus, the Orton-Gillingham approaches concentrate on the alphabetic-phonetic structure of the English language and provide a system for remembering the correspondences between graphemes (written language units) and phonemes (spoken language units). All "channels" are used, so that the student will, as Rawson says, "overlearn": information is presented in the visual, auditory, and tactile-kinesthetic form (work is also done with the motor or muscle activities involved in speaking and writing), and then, it is hoped, the channels can be made to work together.

A related approach is the technique devised by Grace Fernald. It, too, is multisensory, but, rather than phonics, the Fernald system involves more of a "whole-word" approach. Instead of breaking words down into letters, students using Fernald break words into units no smaller than syllables. The rationale behind whole-word approaches derives in part from linguistic studies. It is argued, for instance, that the sounds of speech do not bear a simple one-to-one relationship to letters. In formal terms, "the segmentation of the acoustic signal does not correspond directly or in any easily determined way to the segmenta-tion at the phonemic level" (Liberman et al. 1977A). When children are taught to break words up into sounds of letters, they are being taught to pronounce, for example, c-a-t not as "cat" but as "kuh-a-tuh." And, Liberman notes, studies of LD children show that, no matter how quickly these children speak, or "blend," those sounds, they are rarely able to derive "cat" from its three phonemic seg-ments. A much less artificial relationship exists, according to one line of thought, between the sounds of words and the syllables that make up the words. Studies show, in fact, that the ability to segment words into syllables develops earlier than the ability to segment words into letters, and that this may be par-ticularly true for learning-disabled children (Liberman et al. 1977A).

An example of an approach located approximately in between the alphabetic-phonetic and the whole-word approaches is a relatively new, but increasingly used, technique developed by Professor Gerald G. Glass, Director of Adelphi University's Reading/LD Center. "Glass-Analysis," as the system is called, is based on the observation that written English consists in part of letter clusters. For instance, the consonants /pl/ are almost always followed by a vowel. By the same token, there are certain combinations that almost never appear (such as /hs/) or almost never appear in certain places in a word (such as /wr/ at the end of a word). Normal children seem able to recognize these letter clusters and consonant combinations, whereas learning-disabled children do not seem to recognize the existence of these clusters. In developing his system, Professor Glass went through basal readers to find the most common clusters and then organized them in terms of their difficulty to learn. The actual instructional technique used in Glass-Analysis is a form of perceptual conditioning: through both the auditory and visual channels, children are taught to recognize in whole words the 119 common clusters, 117 beginning with vowels and 2 with consonants.*

The general philosophy behind the types of approaches outlined above is straightforward: if you want the child to read, teach the child to read. This means concentrating on the structures and usages of language, and conveying them to the child in the manner best suited to the type of problem or disorder involved. But a number of remedial techniques eschew this approach and focus instead on strengthening or developing the skills thought to form the basis of reading (and writing), such as memory, eye-hand coordination, eye movements, the recognition of forms in space, body rhythm, and so on.

Most of these methods fall into the category of "perceptual-motor" training. According to Daniel P. Hallahan and William M. Cruickshank (1973), one of the theorists most responsible for the growth of interest in the treatment of percep-tual-motor problems was Newell C. Kephart. At the core of Kephart's theory is the notion that perceptual activities and motor activities are not two different items—

---

*A list of the clusters is available, free of charge, from the Adelphi Reading/LD Center, Garden City, N.Y. 11530.

hence the term perceptual-motor. Kephart believed that, in the child, motor development begins earlier than perceptual development. Thus, in order to distinguish left from right in the world around him, a child must first be able to distinguish the left side of his body from the right and to be able to control each side individually as well as simultaneously. Without this so-called laterality, Kephart explained, "the child . . . will not develop directionality, and therefore, will not, for example, recognize the difference between 'b' and 'd.'" (Hallahan and Cruickshank 1973, p. 75). The educational programs developed by Kephart, therefore, sought to bring about a better match between perceptual information and motor information.

Implicit in this approach is the notion that human beings (as well as other living organisms) require learning opportunities in order to develop to their full potential and that the perceptual problems seen in some learning-disabled children can be traced back to improper or insufficient motor development. Sharing this view are three other influential perceptual-motor theorists: optometrist Gerald Getman, who argued that "the visual system is the most accurate human processing system and the one most basic to school learning tasks" (Hallahan and Cruickshank 1973, p. 81); Ray H. Barsch, originator of "Movigenics," which Hallahan and Cruickshank describe as "the study of the development of spatial movement patterns that are the physiological bases of learning" (p. 83); and Marianne Frostig, founder of the Marianne Frostig Center of Educational Therapy in Los Angeles (she is presently Executive Director Emeritus of the Center) and creator of a remediation program that is chiefly concerned with the role in learning of visual and visual-motor abilities that are held to be independent and are classified as "(a) eye-motor coordination, (b) visual figure-ground discrimination, (c) form constancy, (d) position in space, and (e) spatial relations" (Hallahan and Cruickshank 1973, p. 86).

In *The Physiology of Readiness: An Action Program for the Development of Perception for Children,* some of the concepts described above are spelled out in operational terms (Getman et al. 1964). After noting that academic performance in school depends heavily upon "form and symbol recognition and interpretation," and stating plainly that "there are perceptual skills which can be developed and trained," the authors explain that "the development of perceptual skills is related to the levels of coordination of the body systems, i.e., the better the coordinations of the body parts and body system the better the prospects are for developing perception of forms and symbols." To bring about the development of these perceptual motor skills, Getman et al. specified a number of specific programs, among them "Practice in General Coordination . . . Practice in Balance (Walking Beam) . . . Practice in Eye-Hand Coordination . . . [and] Practice in Eye Movements."

Beyond the perceptual-motor programs are those approaches that—in their pure form—work almost exclusively with the body and not at all with aspects of cognition or academic performance. Sensory-integrative therapy is one such approach.

The theoretical underpinnings of sensory-integrative therapy derive from the argument that many children with learning disabilities suffer from disorders of the vestibular system. The vestibular system is a part of the brain that is responsible for regulating balance and body-in-space awareness. The vestibular system seems to create, in the first year or two of life, a "spatial map," in the words of Bob Thatcher, Research Associate Professor, Department of Psychiatry at NYU Medical Center, that is crucial to the development of "all other sensory maps, such as the auditory and visual and touch."

One of the more ambitious, but speculative, theories of the causative role of vestibular disorders in learning disabilities has been set forth by Julio B. de Quiros, Director of the Research Medical Center at the University of the Museum in Buenos Aires, Argentina. In very simple terms, the impact of the disorder, as de Quiros explains it, is as follows: the vestibular system is responsible for the automatic maintenance of balance and posture, as well as for the control of purposeful motor acts. In normally developing children, as body information is integrated and spatial relationships are established, the control of purposeful motor acts becomes specialized in one hemisphere of the brain, while the other hemisphere becomes dominant over the control of automatic motor skills. De Quiros writes that "to the extent that voluntary control is needed to maintain posture, equilibrium, and purposeful motor acts, there will be a corresponding delay in the development of symbolic skills controlled by the dominant hemisphere" (1976).

The diagnostic importance of this theory, de Quiros argues, is that disorders of the vestibular system can be identified within hours of birth. For that matter, vestibular disorders can be diagnosed in people of any age through relatively straightforward tests that analyze a reflex called caloric nystagmus—the back-and-forth movement of the eyes in response to such stimuli as the irrigation of the ear canals with hot and cold water.

De Quiros also observes what he calls "exigency responses." These are studied by placing the child in an environment that can be modified in a controlled manner. For instance, de Quiros uses a device called a "changing consistency board," which is a plank of wood with a nylon section in the middle, all wrapped in a woodlike cover to give the appearance of a uniform surface. The child walks along the board, and when he or she hits the soft part, the diagnostician can observe whether the response is "adaptive," which is characteristic of normal children, or "non-adaptive," which is characteristic of LD children with vestibular disorders. When the child reaches the soft part of the board, de Quiros points out, he or she must use all available systems of postural compensations (e.g., the proprioceptive [muscle and joint] system, kinesthesis, vision, etc.), and the exigency response gives the diagnostician an opportunity to observe specific pathologies in functional systems (such as how the arms or legs move, or what the eyes do).

Jean Ayres, an occupational therapist and psychologist in Los Angeles county, calls her approach to the treatment of vestibular disorders "sensory-integrative therapy." The key to her program is the stimulation of the vestibular system through various types of body movement and, in some instances, through vibration applied to muscles. "The vestibular system is quite malleable," according to Ayres. What she aims to do in her clinic (she needs about 500 square feet per child) is to elicit "somatosensory input"—from the body, the skin, the proprioceptors (muscles and joints) and from the body's gravity and movement receptors. The ultimate goal is to make automatic, through repeated stimulation, certain sensory or muscular processes so that the brain no longer need concern itself with the control of those processes or with the constant organization or integration of incoming sensory stimuli.

Ayres works mostly with young children, and she observes, as does de Quiros, that many of them cannot, for instance, hold their heads up without "a constant motor command going out to the [neck] muscles to hold the head up." In a classroom situation, children with this sort of vestibular disorder become fatigued simply by sitting upright at a desk. The problem, she says, is not that sensory information is not getting through; rather, it reaches the brain in a disorganized manner. And, she argues, "If the brain is disorganized as far as sensory input is concerned, it's apt to have trouble organizing the rest of life." In terms of learning disabilities per se, Ayres finds vestibular disorders most typically associated with reading, letter-sequencing, and math problems. She estimates, on the basis of her most recent research, that vestibular disorders are involved in about 50 percent of the LD cases in her area of Southern California.

Ayres is not trying to improve coordination or motor skills in the children with whom she works. Rather, she says she is trying to get the brain to work more efficiently in organizing sensory inputs. A common type of problem that she sees is in children in whom neither the tactile nor the proprioceptive systems are working well: children may be tactually defensive, for instance, becoming uncomfortable or threatened when touched under certain circumstances; or they may be physically awkward or unable to lie in a prone or supine position. Other children show signs of "postural insecurity," a fear of movement that can create anxiety and restlessness.

The actual treatment depends upon the problem at hand. In some cases, she will place children in certain positions—such as lying on a semi-inflated ball while hanging on to overhead ropes—to elicit sensory input that will "modify" the vestibular system; or she may use procedures aimed at creating better interaction between the vestibular and muscles and joints or at establishing fairly automatic patterns of muscle activity. Occasionally, Ayres uses one of her diagnostic instruments to provide vestibular stimulation. Colloquially referred to as "the spinner," this rotating device consists of two flat, connected boards that are mounted on a swivel so as to resemble a "lazy susan." Ayres uses "the spinner" diagnostically to examine postrotatory nystagmus.

In a young child, sensory-integrative therapy can produce lasting benefits, Ayres reports, and, "in some children, we make an enormous difference in their lives." Ayres insists, however, that she does not get "dramatic" results and that she would never use the word "cure." Nor does Ayres contend that sensory-integrative therapy itself improves academic performance. "The best I'm going to do is to ameliorate the situation," she explains: "the child will still profit from special education; I simply make the special education easier."

Drugs

A number of treatments now being used in the LD field seek to correct the learning disorder through biochemical manipulations of one sort or another. In cases of true hyperactivity, as we have seen, psychostimulant drugs are often prescribed. The consensus among members of the medical profession is that these medications do not improve learning per se but, by calming children down and increasing their attention span, make the child "more available" for learning. A relatively new drug approach to certain kinds of learning disorders has been developed by Harold Levinson, a Queens, N.Y., psychiatrist. He has described a "dysmetric dyslexia" that results from a dysfunction in the inner ear and is diagnosed by measuring caloric nystagmus. Levinson claims that over-the-counter "seasick" medicines such as Dramamine and Marazine can bring about a marked and rapid improvement in a child's school performance. Levinson claims that his therapy succeeds with over 50 percent of the cases he treats, provided the children are properly selected.

Although there is solid evidence that drugs can contribute to the management of hyperactivity and distractibility in some children, their use remains problematical for a number of reasons. For one thing, as Drake Duane notes, "if someone prescribes medication for a kid, I think it's oftentimes done helter-skelter. We don't have a good predictor as to whether or not the child will respond favorably to medication. It's also hard to know when to stop; that's done by guesswork." Another problem, according to Elena Boder, is that "when the hyperkinetic syndrome is associated with a specific learning disability, psychostimulants may be successful initially in modifying the child's school behavior, only to be followed by a recurrence of hyperkinesis, the neurogenic hyperactivity being replaced by anxiety-based hyperactivity." Drugs can also adversely affect a child's motivation, it is argued. In this context, Barbara Keogh, Education Professor at UCLA, cites the work of her colleague, psychologist Barbara Henker, who has applied an "attributional analysis" to the study of children receiving medication for hyperactivity. "The hyperactive kids who are on medication," explains Keogh, "talk about 'my good pill,' or 'the pill that makes me good.' The attribution is not to the child's ability to change or control the behavior, but to an external agent that brings about some change. The teacher will say to the kid, 'You're really bad today. You didn't take your pill.' Or the parents will say, 'You'd better be sure to take your pill so you'll be good.'" Indeed, as Peter Schweich, Executive Director of the Archway School, points out, parents of children on medication frequently make matters worse for the child than they already are by administering drugs to suit their own needs. At Archway, Schweich says, Mondays are always the worst days for his students because their drug regimen has been tampered with over the weekend by parents: a guest is coming for dinner on Saturday night, for instance, and the parents want the child to be on best behavior. So they give him or her an extra dose of drugs. Then, fearing that the child may have already had as much medication as he or she should take, they don't give any more medication for the rest of the weekend. And, in this regard, there is some disagreement among physicians as to how often, or under what circumstances, medication should be taken. Harold Levinson argues, for example, that the drug therapy he administers is effective when taken five days a week, and that medication is not needed on weekends or during summer vacations. On the other hand, Jerome Mednick argues that, since children have to do homework and deal with their parents on the weekends, and since so much of the problem is often related to the interaction of the child with the environment, "going up and down like a yo-yo can only complicate the problem. My feeling," he says, "is that once a kid is going on a drug, it's got to be monitored very carefully, and he's on it seven days a week, 12 months a year, as long as he seems to need it."

Diet

Two other therapies in the biochemical area are dietary manipulation and orthomolecular medicine. The former, primarily associated with the work of Ben Feingold, a Calfornia allergist, involves putting children on diets free of such substances as synthetic food additives, dyes, and salicylates, a class of chemicals found in many fresh fruits. Among many parents of learning-disabled children, diet therapy is particularly popular at the moment. Feingold's initial research indicates that 50 percent of the time, hyperactivity disappears when additives are removed from the diet; although other studies have shown that some children do in fact improve when the diet is changed, it is regarded as unlikely by many that the diet alone could be responsible for all learning disorders.

Carefully controlled studies by C. Keith Conners, Professor of Psychiatry and Psychology at the University of Pittsburgh, have partially supported Feingold's claims. Conners found that the disabilities of some of the children he tested were exacerbated by the ingestion of certain food colorings. Conners believes that allergies to foods or food additives do cause or exacerbate some learning disabilities, but he doubts that such allergies can account for the disabilities of more than 5 to 10 percent of all learning-disabled children.

Orthomolecular medicine has been defined by Linus Pauling as "the treatment of mental disorders by the provision of the optimum molecular environment for the mind, especially the optimum concentrations of substances normally present in the human body" (Silver 1979). In the LD field, orthomolecular therapy involves primarily the use of massive doses of vitamins. New York psychiatrist Allan Cott, a leading exponent of this form of treatment, has found that vitamin B_3 improves the sleep patterns of many learning-disabled children, and that large doses of vitamin B_6 have a calming effect. In his treatment program, Cott also puts children on additive-free diets, prescribes certain agents, such as "kupramine," to remove toxic substances, particularly lead, from the body, and, he says, refers about 90 percent of the children he sees to a developmental optometrist for work with "undeveloped visual functions."

Technology

In a situation in which one skilled teacher is dealing with one learning-disabled student, the teacher can adjust his teaching methods from moment to moment to fit the specific needs of the student—at least to the extent that the teacher can understand them. If current estimates of the prevalence of learning disabilities are even approximately correct, the cost of providing individual instruction to each learning-disabled student would at least double or triple the entire cost of public education. Since the cost of education is already the major part of state and local budgets, it is clear that individual instruction on this scale will not be available. However, it may soon be economical for each learning-disabled student to have his own interactive computer terminal. If teaching programs of sufficient subtlety and complexity can be written, this may provide an economical means of giving each student instructional help tailored to his individual needs and learning style.

We do not now foresee a time when the computer will replace the teacher. As far as we know, we do not even have the beginnings of a technology that could allow computers to read and interpret the student's body language and facial expressions as a skilled teacher can; however, a computer can take over many time-consuming and repetitious teaching tasks. Computers need not be programmed to become weary or irascible or impatient. Their responses can be utterly reliable and consistent, virtues which have been shown to be of considerable value in teaching. The pertinent technology is evolving rapidly. Today, some computers can respond correctly to a few words of human speech. It is to be expected that computers that can respond to a wide variety of verbal commands are only a few years in the offing. Such machines could, for example, take dictation. Machines are already available for use by the blind which can scan printed material and read it aloud.

So rapid and extensive are the technological changes affecting teaching and communication that it is conceivable that reading disabilities as a major social problem will turn out to have been a phenomenon confined to a century or two —from the time when literacy became almost universal and the key to information flow in a complex society to the time when the printed word may be replaced by electronic devices as a means of disseminating information. Technology will not make learning disabilities go away, but it may transform their roles in a technological society. Literacy is itself part of our current technology for preserving and sharing information, and, as a technology, is in principle subject to obsolescence and replacement.

At present, we have a long way to go to this imagined future. Let us look, however, at some of the current technological approaches to learning disabilities. They range from educational materials, such as textbooks and flashcards, to equipment and games, to the latest advances in large-scale computers and consumer electronics. We shall mention only a few: two innovative approaches based on large-scale computers now being developed specifically to help dyslexics; some devices for the consumer market which may ultimately replace them; and a technology originally developed for the blind which makes it possible for LD individuals who find reading difficult to obtain books and magazines in audio format.

The two learning systems are Prentice-Hall's "Oralographic Reading Program" and Control Data Corporation's "Minnesota Learning Disabilities Consortium."

The Oralographic Reading Program, which has been studied at eight schools across the country and field-tested in an additional thirteen schools, is a multisensory phonetic decoding program that uses a specially designed curriculum and two pieces of computer hardware known as the "Talking Page" and the "Voice Mirror." The Talking Page is a compact table-top unit that employs sound and text in a coordinated manner: a specially constructed disc in the back of the machine gives commentary or instructions while an educational task is presented in written form on a piece of paper placed on top of the machine. "Unlike other hardware, the Talking Page in itself is *responsive*. The user can repeat, skip or practice in any fashion he wishes. Further, the pupil can write on the sheet according to instructions given by the voice on the disc or indicated by the printed word on the page" (Steg and Schenk 1977).

The Voice Mirror resembles a cassette tape recorder. It is capable of instant playback, so there is no need to wait for the tape to rewind. The Voice Mirror can also be prerecorded, so that a student can match his or her voice with a good speech model.

The Oralographic Reading Program presents letter sounds and symbols that a student learns to associate and then blend into words. These words are then used in sentences that the student sees, hears, writes, reads, and records—comparing them with the machine model. The Oralographic curriculum contains 60 lessons (plus five reviews) and is designed to assist an LD child to advance to a level where he or she can read a third grade vocabulary with a good measure of fluency and comprehension in eight to ten months' time.

Both the Talking Page and the Voice Mirror are second generation descendants of an ambitious piece of machinery developed during the early 1960s called the "Talking Typewriter," or, in technical jargon, "The Edison Responsive

Environment [E.R.E.]." The E.R.E., explain Steg and Schenk, "consists of a unique electric typewriter with jumbo-size type; voice units, including microphones, speakers, and a magnetic recorder; an exhibitor on which typed or printed words appear; and an automatic projection unit for the presentation of pictorial material. The components are tied together by a compact special-purpose computer to respond to the students' actions in a continuous multi-sensory dialogue. Hence, 'responsive environment'" (1977).

For the severely handicapped student, all three pieces of hardware can be used together. Prentice-Hall is most actively involved, however, in developing the Talking Page and the Voice Mirror. The Talking Typewriter, Schenk points out, "is incredibly expensive—on a direct sale basis, almost $40,000. The Talking Page and Voice Mirror system is a lot more economical: we can service 12 kids for about $1,300 including service, training and consumables."

The Control Data Corporation learning disabilities system is an offshoot of their PLATO program developed for use in regular education. The LD system is actually a joint effort by Control Data and the Minnesota Department of Education, with funding for design and demonstration coming from a three-year, $360,000 BEH grant.

The unit used consists of an audio device, a keyboard, and a TV-like screen that is laminated to be touch-sensitive. The program, based on a wide selection of junior high school special education curricula, contains an on-line dictionary whose 5,000 words have been cross-referenced in a variety of ways.

In using the program, a student is first given a pretest that measures his or her deficits and indicates the direction in which remediation should proceed. The precise content of each lesson can be determined by the teacher. All of the lessons in the program, however, are designed to help students develop concept formation abilities—generalizing rules of language from specific instances—rather than memory skills. The computer uses a multisensory approach: for instance, the display screen might show three similar words, like "stretch," "stritch," and "strutch." The computer will then ask the student to touch the word "stretch" (or the word that has the letter e in it), and the touch-sensitive screen will register the correct (or incorrect) answer. For each child participating in the program, the computer keeps a comprehensive, up-to-date learning profile that allows the teacher to monitor the student's progress and also to plan the best lesson for any given day.

The Control Data learning disabilities system—formally known as the "Minnesota Learning Disabilities Consortium"—is presently being used at one site in Minnesota (the demonstration phase began in January 1978). Control Data and the Minnesota Department of Education have now located another site in the state (where a project will start September 1978, and run until June 1979), and there are also plans to install a program at the John F. Kennedy School in Baltimore, Maryland.

Interestingly, one of the original participants in the project (but no longer involved) was the Minnesota Department of Corrections; an early plan called for the use of an LD computer with a juvenile delinquent population. Administrative complexities forced that plan to be dropped, but a number of PLATO terminals are being used in correctional facilities around the state, reports Susan Schilling, Learning Disabilities Project Manager, Control Data Corporation, and it is conceivable that LD terminals might be used in such facilities in the future.

The development of large-scale integrated electronic circuits is proceeding so rapidly that teaching systems of this kind that are now based on large computers will soon be available inexpensively on the consumer market. Several manufacturers are marketing calculator-like devices that present practice arithmetic problems and give instant feedback. They will indicate whether the operator's answer is right or wrong, and also exhibit the correct answer. Such teaching calculators can now be had for less than $15. Texas Instruments Co. has recently introduced a children's toy called *Speak & Spell* which will perform many of the functions of large computer-based teaching systems. It will ask a child aloud, in a male voice, how to spell a word. The child keys in a spelling on a typewriter-like keyboard, and this spelling appears on an illuminated display. The toy will then tell the child (speaking aloud in a synthetic male voice) whether his spelling is correct, and if it is incorrect, the toy will both pronounce the correct spelling aloud and display it in illuminated letters. This toy is about the size of a transistor radio, and sells for under $60. Evidently, such devices are the vanguard of a range of teaching machines that will be inexpensive, portable, and available for mass consumption. These devices are made possible by the same developments in electronic technology that have created mass markets for pocket calculators and video games, and by the results of two decades of research on machine processing of language.

The Talking Books program of the Library of Congress, Division for the Blind and Physically Handicapped, was originally developed for the blind, but is now available to individuals with other physical handicaps as well. With money appropriated by Congress, the Library of Congress produces specially designed record players and cassette machines and distributes them at no cost on an indefinite loan basis through 156 regional and subregional libraries around the country.* (Similar machines are available from the American Printing House for the Blind, according to Frank Cylke, Chief of the Division for the Blind and Physically Handicapped of the Library of Congress, but these are not free.)

Talking Book subscribers get a bimonthly bulletin (in print or in recorded form) that lists books—including children's literature—and magazines that are available from participating libraries. The books and magazines (some on records and others on cassette tapes) are commercially produced for the library primarily by nonprofit organizations throughout the United States, says Cylke. To date, the Library of Congress has not sought to advertise the Talking Books program to learning-disabled people. The reason, says Cylke, is that, to be

---

*Fiscal 1978 budget, including allocations for the Library of Congress, the states, and the Post Office (which mails materials, free of charge, to subscribers) is about $50 million.

eligible to receive a cassette machine or phonograph, a person must present a letter from a physician certifying a neurological impairment. It has become evident, Cylke explains, that learning-disabled people are not aware of this requirement, and that not all are able to qualify; thus, advertising the program, he explains, "is like waving a red flag."*

Controversies

Many professionals in the field view remediation techniques such as perceptual motor training, sensory integrative therapy, developmental optometry, diet treatments, orthomolecular medicine, and newer drug approaches such as Levinson's with skepticism because they require expenditures of both time and money that might better be spent on treatments aimed at teaching children to read. Numerous professional organizations have issued strong statements critical of these approaches. The American Academy of Pediatrics, Committee on Nutrition, for example, issued a statement that megavitamin therapy as a treatment for learning disabilities and psychoses in children is not justified on the basis of documented clinical results.** A task force of The American Psychiatric Association has come to a similar conclusion regarding the use of megavitamins in treating mental disorders.†

Concerning the educational and sensory-motor-perceptual training techniques used by developmental optometrists—based on the concept that visual-perceptual processes are related to sensory-motor coordination—The American Academy of Pediatrics, the American Academy of Ophthalmology and Otolaryngology, and the American Association of Ophthalmology issued a joint communique warning that there are no peripheral eye defects that can cause dyslexia or associated learning disabilities and criticizing the remedial methods of the developmental optometrists (American Academy of Pediatrics, 1972).

We can discern several underlying themes in these controversies:

1. Objective standards for the efficacy and efficiency of remediation are almost completely lacking, and the consumer is therefore ill-equipped to choose among competing suppliers of remediation.

2. Some remediators may be sound and effective practitioners but unsound and ineffective theorists. They may do well with children but explain their methods poorly.

3. Consequently, competing schools of remediation that use similar methods in practice may bitterly attack each other's theories.

---

*It should also be noted, however, that not all learning-disabled people who do qualify find the system easy to use. Long periods of passive listening can produce a tiring sensory strain.
**American Academy of Pediatrics Committee on Nutrition 1976, pp. 910–912.
†American Psychiatric Association Task Force 1973.

4. Jurisdictional disputes abound. Many groups are competing for a piece of the remediational pie.

To take the dispute over developmental optometrics as an example, the three professional societies that issued the statement critical of developmental optometrics (cited above) may be correct that dyslexia is not explained by a defect in the eye. They may also resent the attempt of optometrists to expand the practice of optometry to include the treatment of learning disabilities. (Ophthalmologists and optometrists have been struggling for years to carve up the eye-treatment territory.) They may be correct in arguing that optometric training per se does not qualify an optometrist to treat learning disabilities, but some optometrists, like some ophthalmologists, special educators, psychologists, and speech therapists, may be helping learning-disabled children. Others may be helping the learning disabled waste their time.

Optometrists such as Gerald Getman have indeed contributed many techniques and approaches that are widely used in the field. It may not matter whether or not these contributions depend upon their optometric training. Their interest in learning disabilities, experience, and clinical skill may be more important than their theories or professional training.

Perhaps the most heated debate to date in the learning disabilities field has arisen over the Doman-Delacato theory and associated procedures for treatment of neurologically handicapped children. In 1968, the controversy over this method led several prestigious professional organizations, such as the American Academy for Cerebral Palsy, the American Academy of Physical Medicine and Rehabilitation, the American Congress of Rehabilitation, the Canadian Association for Children with Learning Disabilities, and others, to adopt an official statement highly critical of the Doman-Delacato approach.

For background, the Doman-Delacato method, also known as "patterning," is essentially a technique for redeveloping the organization of the brain in neurologically impaired children by manipulating the children through certain remedial developmental patterns. Hallahan and Cruickshank describe the five basic elements of patterning as follows: "(a) placing the child on the floor for training activities in order to remediate damaged areas of the brain, (b) externally manipulating the child into body patterns characteristic of the level of the damaged brain, (c) imposing hemispheric dominance and unilaterality, (d) administering carbon dioxide therapy [based on the hypothesis that carbon dioxide increases the size of the small vessels of the brain and results in better blood circulation], and (e) stimulating the senses to improve body awareness" (1973, p. 92).

The official joint statement issued listed several concerns about this approach:

1. Promotional methods appear to put parents in a position where they cannot refuse such treatment without calling into question their adequacy and motivation as parents;
2. The regimens prescribed are so demanding and inflexible that they may lead to neglect of other family members' needs;

3. It is asserted that if therapy is not carried out as rigidly prescribed, the child's potential will be damaged, and that anything less than 100% effort is useless;

4. Restrictions are often placed upon age-appropriate activities of which the child is capable, such as walking or listening to music, though unwarranted by any supportive data and knowledge of long-term results published to date;

5. Claims are made for rapid and conclusive diagnosis according to a "Developmental Profile" of no known validity. No data on which construction of the Profile has been based have ever been published, nor do we know of any attempt to cross-validate it against any accepted methods;

6. Undocumented claims are made for cures in a substantial number of cases, extending even beyond disease states to making normal children superior, easing world tensions, and possibly "hastening the evolutionary process";

7. Without supporting data, Doman and Delacato have indicted many typical child-rearing practices as limiting a child's potential, increasing thereby the anxiety of already burdened and confused parents [American Academy of Physical Medicine and Rehabilitation 1967].

We quote these comments, not to support their accuracy or to endorse the truth of the criticism made, but rather to suggest the intensity of the controversies that can arise where remediation is concerned. Many professionals fear that, because the field of remediation is still relatively wide open, there are abundant opportunities for incompetent or self-serving individuals to move in and take advantage of the situation.

Ron Spector, Director of the Beverly Center School in Los Angeles, points out that "one of the dangers in the field of learning disabilities is that when you have a field that is uncharted, you have open territory for people who are professionally qualified and financially motivated to stretch their own professions into this area. . . . So all these things eventually become therapies and become very expensive to parents. And so the therapies have raced way ahead of the scientific knowledge. . . ."

Similarly, Jerome Mednick notes that the problem is "that some people may have a sound idea, but, once they try to become famous and make money, they become entrepreneurs. From what I am seeing," he says, "there are many people who are in the field simply for the financial return." Mel Levine sketches a scenario:

> I would like to call Doubleday and have them come over here, tell them I'm a Harvard professor and that I've found out, from seeing lots and lots of patients, that air pollution causes learning disabilities and that I'd like to write a book about it. I could have that book done in a few months' time, full of anecdotal evidence about how it hits the kid nearest the city, or tell stories about a kid who lived near a factory and when he moved there his schoolwork got worse, and when he moved away it got better and how that got me thinking. . . .
>
> This book would sell a million copies.

I would then go to Arthur D. Little, which is a consulting firm, to see what they could do about designing me a mask for kids to wear that will filter the air they breathe. Let them design that mask for me, put activated charcoal in the mask so they'll breathe pure air, and then sell these for $15.95 each—you can send away for them—to parents of LD children.

I'll say have them wear the mask at least eight hours a day; kids will go to school with their masks on. I'll have a following around the country—the "Levine Dyslexia Society." It will be extraordinary, with parents who can provide abundant testimony as to how their child's whole life was changed when they started using the Levine method. I'll be famous; I'll get on the "Today" show with my mask; and I'll continue to make money because we'll patent it and sell replacement cartridges that you have to get for $6.95 every six months.

No problem. It will be antitechnological, which is in the spirit of the times; antiauthoritarian (it's those big boards of directors that are poisoning our kids' brains). . . . I'll guarantee you that my air pollution idea will come up within the next three or four years.

Cost and Benefits

The situation which Levine satirizes cannot really be understood apart from the phenomenon of what we referred to earlier as "the consumerization of LD." Many parents, as we have seen, tend to shy away from evaluations or diagnostic procedures that may come up with findings of a psychological or psychiatric nature, such as emotional disturbance. This, plus the high prices of many medical evaluations and the uncertainties associated with diagnoses and remediations offered in the public school system, may serve to increase the attractiveness of other types of therapies, particularly those that claim—either directly or by reputation—to work wonders in short periods of time. The two most significant factors may be, first, the lack of reliable information about which remediations are likely to bring about the best results for different kinds of problems, and second, as Mednick observes, the fact that "a lot of these people are desperate. Their kids have had problems for many years and suddenly they hear of somebody who is offering them some help. And this is why we have charlatans—because they see that the prey is ready, so to speak." And because the LD field is "leaderless professionally," says Spector, "what happens is that parents get on a bandwagon. Parents have often been in the vanguard of chasing educators and other people to get help for their kids," he notes, "and so parents are often soaking in the new fads and developing clubs and all kinds of groups to popularize this therapy or that therapy."

The larger question—and the question that many parents fail to ask—is not whether a given remediation works, but what it is good for. In the case of sensory-motor integration, for instance, Mednick notes that "in some instances, it can definitely be of help—not so much in helping a child to read per se, but many children with what could be called dyslexia have associated motor dysfunction of one degree or another." At the Child Development Center, Mednick and his staff go to great pains to define the need for specific therapies "in terms the consumer can understand," which does not mean, he insists, saying "because you've got this problem you need our form of therapy." Some children will have motor dysfunctions all their lives, he points out. "So the question is, at $20 an hour, four times a week, what's reasonable, and for how long?"

Professionals complain that, without this precision in the prescription of one form of therapy or another, parents find themselves in the position of paying high prices for a treatment that may not be producing the results they expect. In the eyes of many in the field, the most desirable result is having taught a child to read. Thus claims are constantly made that motor or psychological abilities, important though they may be in their own right, do not transfer to reading.

But no matter how valid these claims may be, they do not really answer the question of whether a form of treatment is, in fact, necessary or not. And it is in this context that the problem of defining the subgroups within the learning disability population becomes of paramount importance, because, without it, a precise match between diagnosis and treatment can never be made. Hallahan and Cruickshank (1973) argue, for instance, that the roots of the perceptual-motor training being used in the LD field can be traced very directly back to work done during the 1930s, particularly by Alfred Strauss and Heinz Werner, on perceptual-motor dysfunctions in mentally retarded and brain damaged children. A therapy of this sort, then, might be best suited to LD children whose syndrome includes certain specific symptoms. By the same token, orthomolecular medicine, though it remains unvalidated, has produced its strongest results in experiments involving psychosis. And, as psychiatrist Larry Silver notes, Allan Cott's theory of megavitamins is based on his studies of 500 children who were for the most part autistic and schizophrenic, rather than MBD (Silver 1979).

One of the most striking aspects of the area of evaluation and remediation, in fact, is the wide range of characteristics that professionals report seeing among LD children—characteristics whose significance or relationship to specific learning disabilities remains undetermined. These "bits and pieces" include: a disproportionate number of blond, light-eyed people in the white dyslexic population; susceptibility to allergies; zinc deficiencies; a white "chalk spot" on one cheek or a patch of light hair double the thumb size on the back of a child's head; stiff neck muscles; weak eye muscles; an inability to tolerate certain kinds of music; an inability to sustain effort (the quality of the effort notwithstanding); the need to read and watch television lying supine; a propensity for junk food or foods high in sugar; youthful appearance; various physical abnormalities; and behavior patterns and certain clinical signs (i.e., measurements of the diameter of pupils) resembling those of sleep-deprived adults.

Added to the problem of what groups or subgroups are likely to respond best to different treatments is widespread confusion over what the practitioners of those treatments—as opposed to the theorists—claim are the benefits. Practitioners of nonacademic remediations do not generally claim that their treatments lead directly to an improvement in academic performance. A typical comment is made by Larry Jebrock, developmental optometrist in Novato, California, who works with learning-disabled children: he does not concentrate on academics in any way in his program, he says. "I'm not trained in it. My philosophy is simply to get their eyes working well. I'm not going to guarantee that they'll read, but it will give them a chance. People usually do better no matter what you do," he observes, "if you give them some attention. But what I find of greater importance is that the kids come out of therapy and they feel like they can survive in the world. They have a better self-image."

Social and Emotional Problems

There is abundant evidence to suggest that self-image problems are a common feature of learning disabilities at any age. How long it takes the problems to develop is a matter of debate: some say only a year; others say not until 4th, 5th, or 6th grade. But most agree that, sooner or later, psychological or emotional problems are sure to appear. "The 'inevitability' of psychiatric disturbance in the poor reader," argues Leon Eisenberg, "stems from the pivotal role of success at school for the self-concept of the child. Schooling is, in the first instance, reading . . . . In the school environment, reading is being. An inadequate reader is, in his mind's eye, an inadequate (that is, bad or stupid) person—and all too often, in the eyes of his teachers, his parents, and his peers as well . . . . To the degree that a remedial reading teacher is able to assist a child in task mastery, she is an effective therapist for his psychiatric symptoms" (Eisenberg 1975). Indeed, Elena Boder notes that the most common presenting complaint of children referred to her for school failure is a behavior problem (Boder 1976). And these behavior problems can interfere significantly, of course, with learning and with every other aspect of life. Harvey Alpert notes, for example, that many LD children develop refusal or avoidance syndromes: they simply refuse to learn, or they go to great and reportedly cunning lengths to distract the remediator with (sometimes tall) tales of problems at home or of other matters geared to catch the interest or sympathy of the instructor. By the time a child gets to be 16 or 17 years old—a time, incidentally, when services become less available—the so-called "emotional overlay" and the learning problem have become so entangled that remediation is extremely difficult. This is even more true of adults, as we will see below.

Nor is the LD child the only one affected; his or her poor image is carried from school to home. Particularly with manipulative children, Alpert notes, there is never enough parental affection; and, eventually, the parents will tire of giving affection and become hostile—"which feeds," Alpert says, "right into the youngster's system, because he's saying they really didn't like me anyway." Eisenberg reports that quite often, in fact, a learning-disabled child's parents will themselves need psychotherapy to deal with the feelings of guilt they often experience.

In many cases, of course, these psychological and family-dynamics problems arise for no apparent reason, which is to say, before a child's learning problem has been identified. It is not surprising, then, that Elena Boder writes that "the psychotherapeutic impact of a correct diagnosis, particularly of developmental dyslexia, can be quite dramatic. Leading to an improved self-image for the child and to better parent-child and teacher-child relationships, the diagnosis itself often proves to be a turning point in the child's emotional development and school adjustment, even when remedial facilities are not immediately available" (Boder 1976).

But, even when facilities are at hand, the remediation is often hampered or obstructed by the kinds of secondary emotional problems that many LD people develop. One of the most widely noted of these problems is the phenomenon of "secondary gains" or "secondary benefits" of having or retaining a learning disability. Susan Trout notes that "our children tend to get colds when they're getting better, as if they feel that there's something within them fighting. What's at stake is more responsibility, more participation in life." Similarly, Ron Spector observes that "many times we see a youngster who loses motivation when he's getting close to getting rid of the problem so that his actual unconscious needs can hold onto it." LD children, Spector finds, derive certain "payoffs" from their condition. "A parent may do all kinds of things for the youngster, give special dispensations to the child, and the child may get certain breaks along the line that then create the feeling that even though this condition is terrible in some ways, at the same time, this is a sort of special status that the child doesn't want to give up."

Looking at the situation from another angle, Eisenberg notes that, "however generated, reading problems often interlock with parental psychopathology," with the result that a change in the child might threaten the equilibrium of the family. For example, Eisenberg writes, "Remedial reading instruction will almost certainly be doomed to failure for the teacher struggling to help a child who dares not abandon his position as the scapegoat lest a worse emotional cataclysm engulf him." Or, says Eisenberg, in a certain group of children, "reading becomes the arena in which parent-child conflicts are fought out. For parents with a high stake in their child's school success, his almost deliberate sabotage of their inordinate expectations is a dramatic mode of retaliation against their demands" (Eisenberg 1975, pp. 225–226).

Even so, Eisenberg suggests, the type of symptom presented may not represent psychodynamic factors alone, "but may reflect a 'point of least resistance' because of an associated language learning handicap" (p. 225).

Experiments conducted by UCLA Professor of Education and Psychology Norma D. Feshbach suggest that, in certain cases of reading disability, there may be a correlation between a child's school performance and the types of interactions he or she has with parents. Feshbach designed a number of simple experimental tasks that mothers could teach to children. Using a sample of young children divided into "readers" and "nonreaders" groups, Feshbach then divided the parent group into mothers of readers and mothers of nonreaders. Each mother taught the tasks to three children: a reader, a nonreader, and her own child. Feshbach found significant differences in the "teaching styles" of the mothers—she classified these behaviors as "nondirective positive" and "negative intrusive"—and also found that, regardless of whether a child was a reader or a nonreader, he or she learned the tasks better if taught by the mother of a reader. "I didn't look at mothers teaching kids the task as a paradigm of mothers training children," Feshbach explains. "But mothers are constantly teaching children how to tie their shoes, how to take a bath, how to go to bed at night—so you can conjecture that, if you can have this effect in a 7 to 15-minute experimental task, what might be the effect of prolonged exposure?"*

To what extent environmental influences affect the outcome of a child's development, or, to put it another way, to what extent the emotional problems associated with specific learning disabilities are endemic to the condition or secondary to it, remains an unanswered and, perhaps—in the final analysis—an unimportant question. To Elena Boder, this is a chicken-and-egg problem: "I take it for granted that every child with school failure will have an emotional problem," she says, and what is important is not to decide whether that problem is primary or secondary, but whether it is severe enough to warrant psychotherapy.

From a diagnostic point of view, however, the question does have some import, because the label a child receives—and hence the type of treatment—will depend largely on whether the diagnosis is "LD" or "ED" (that is, "emotionally disturbed"). Parents in the middle class are generally more able to seek out and pay for the type of evaluation that would result in a LD classification, while poor people, particularly the members of minority groups living in inner cities, are generally unable to afford such services. This may be one reason that LD is thought of as a white middle class condition, and that blacks tend to be labeled emotionally or mentally retarded more often than whites.

Whatever their genesis, some argue that the emotional problems associated with learning disorders constitute a compelling reason for early screening and identification programs. Desirable as these may be, there are two major problems associated with early screening: there is no generally acceptable way to carry it out (and there is thus the risk of mislabeling); there is no generally accepted treatment at this point for young children found to be at risk for LD. In addition, Doris Johnson, head of the Program in Learning Disabilities at Northwestern University, points out, there is a danger that, "with the press to get early

---

*One might speculate that a significant number of the mothers of LD children are themselves LD, and that their teaching styles might reflect their own disabilities.

identification and to get children in and out of a program, people are simply not going to recognize the need for long-term special services."

Juvenile Delinquency

Still, it is increasingly suspected that, the longer LD goes undetected, the more severe do the emotional problems become. These problems, moreover, may be associated with, and possibly responsible for, deviant, antisocial, or psycho-pathological behavior in adolescents and adults. Over the past few years, for instance, many have come to believe that there is a link between learning disabil-ities and juvenile delinquency.

According to the report prepared for the Office of Juvenile Justice and De-linquency Prevention, Law Enforcement Assistance Administration, by Murray et al. (1976A), there are two broad hypotheses linking LD and JD in a causal relationship. In the first scenario, a child gets a reputation with parents, teachers, and peers for being a slow learner, a disciplinary problem, an undesirable play-mate. In the next stage, a child so labeled develops a negative self-image "and is thrown together (informally, or through class assignments) with other problem students." The student then develops a felt need "to compensate for continued school failure" and develops a tendency towards absenteeism, suspension, or drop-out from school. "At the fourth stage," Murray writes, "immediately preceding delinquent behavior, the child has the psychological incentives, the economic incentives, and increased opportunity (in the form of time on his hands) to commit delinquent acts."

The second and more direct line of argument linking LD and JD posits "that certain types and combinations of LD are associated with behavioral tendencies that facilitate delinquency." According to this so-called "susceptibility" ra-tionale, certain types of LD children are generally impulsive, limited in their ability to learn from experience, and also limited in their ability to decipher social cues. "Together," Murray explains, "characteristics like these point to a child who is not wholly responsive to the usual systems of sanctions and re-wards. Messages do not get through to him in quite the way they were intended, with the result that some of the factors which might restrain a normal child from committing a delinquent act might not restrain the learning disabled child. In short, this type of child starts out with one strike against him when exposed to opportunities for committing delinquent acts."

A number of objections have been raised in regard to the concept of a causal link between LD and JD. Numerous "causes" for delinquency have already been identified, such as poverty, broken homes, cultural alienation, social disadvan-tages, and so on, so that, as Murray notes, "the argument that LD is a primary cause of a major part of the delinquency problem is extremely dubious on its face—we are accumulating more 'primary causes' than the number of delinquents will bear."

The difficulty of disentangling cause and effect is illustrated by a study cited by psychiatrist Leon Eisenberg. In a high delinquency area of Chicago, male youths who were in trouble with the law were compared with those who were not in trouble. A major difference between the two groups was that the trouble makers "were much more pessimistic about the likelihood of finishing high school, and they expected to hold jobs with low status and little prestige when they grew up. Particularly noteworthy," Eisenberg observes, "was the discovery that pessimistic attitudes toward completion of high school were as prevalent at the age of ten as they were in later years. Thus pessimism about the future appeared to precede later law-breaking." And if it is the case, as Eisenberg concludes, that both "poor reading and delinquency reflect antecedent factors that contribute to each," some wonder how much difference it would make to treat delinquents' learning disabilities (Eisenberg 1975, pp. 223–224).

The question is almost academic at this point because of the lack of reliable quantitative data on the incidence of learning disabilities among delinquency populations. A survey commissioned by the General Accounting Office (GAO) in 1977 found that 26 percent of the juvenile delinquents tested by the survey's educational consultants in Connecticut and Virginia institutions had "primary learning problems" or learning disabilities (Comptroller General of the U.S. 1977, p. 40). A "primary learning problem" as defined by the GAO study is "a demonstrated inability to perform a specific task normally found within the capability range of individuals of comparable mental capacity. It involves deficits in essential learning processes having to do with perception, integration, and verbal and nonverbal expression" (p. 7).

The GAO Report notes that, "overall, the results of the testing in Connecticut and Virginia substantiate similar studies conducted in other states which also showed considerable academic underachievement in their delinquent populations," pointing out that, in a study conducted by the State of Colorado's Division of Youth Services, 90 percent of adjudicated delinquents tested "were diagnosed as having learning problems" and, in a Rhode Island study, 70 percent of the delinquent youths tested "were found to have measurable disabilities significant enough to warrant professional attention" (p. 15). No doubt these much higher Colorado and Rhode Island incidence figures indicate that, not only were "primary learning problems" measured and included, but also "secondary learning problems" such as truancy, familial and social problems, and emotional and behavioral difficulties, some or all of which can interfere with successful acquisition of academic skills (Comptroller General of the U.S. 1977, p. 7).

In response to the recommendations of Murray et al. (1976A), the first strict incidence study aimed at detecting a link between LD and JD is now being carried out in three cities (Phoenix, Arizona; Baltimore, Maryland; and Indianapolis, Indiana) under the auspices of the Office of Juvenile Justice and Delinquency Prevention (OJJDP) of the Law Enforcement Assistance Administration. The project consists of two separate grants: one is a two-year grant to Creighton University's Institute for Business, Law, and Social Research in Omaha, Nebraska; the other a two-year grant to the Association for Children with Learning

Disabilities (ACLD). Creighton is responsible for determining the incidence of LD among male youths, aged 12 to 15, in public school systems in the three cities and also among "adjudicated" male youths (those in institutions, on probation, or on parole) in the same three locations. The actual testing is being carried out under subcontract to the Creighton Institute by the Educational Testing Service, Princeton, New Jersey. Preliminary results of testing show a 32 percent incidence rate of LD among the adjudicated populations and 16 percent incidence among the school-age populations. Results further indicate that LD youngsters are more likely than non-LD youngsters to be adjudicated delinquents. However, there was no clear evidence (based on self-reports) that LD children engage in more delinquent behavior than those who are not LD. The OJJDP is taking a cautious approach to these findings, noting that one reasonable interpretation is that, while LD youngsters are no more likely than the general school-age population to commit delinquent acts, they are likely to be handled differently by the juvenile justice system.

The point of the comparison between the two (normal and JD) groups, explains Research Branch Chief Bonnie Lewin of the OJJDP, is that "what's important is to find out how many kids who aren't in trouble with the law are also LD. If it seems as if the incidence rates are the same, then you're on much weaker ground in saying there's any kind of causal connection between LD and delinquency."

The ACLD's role in the project is to provide up to two years of remediation (dealing only with academic, as opposed to social or emotional, problems) to 100 randomly selected adjudicated youths in the three cities.* Although females will not be included in the testing, they will be included in the remediation, partly to insure that the groups receiving remediation will be large enough to support statistical inferences. Following the two-year remediation program, Creighton will compare outcomes of the groups that received help from the ACLD with those of the adjudicated groups that received traditional kinds of services offered by institutions.

The implications of the study are reasonably clear: if a link is established, and if remediation is shown to reduce delinquency, then there would be a strong indication, Lewin suggests, that the diagnosis and treatment of learning disabilities should be made an integral part of the rehabilitation programs offered in correctional institutions. But what if a link is not found? What if the incidence of LD in both normal and JD populations turns out to be the same? "Regardless of LD's causal role," Murray points out, "the populations of the nation's juvenile facilities can be presumed to include at least as many seriously learning-disabled youth as the population at large" (Murray et al. 1976A). Moreover, he notes, there are indications "that strange patterns of learning handicaps exist among institutionalized delinquents, even if they are not learning disabilities

*Upon termination in the fall of 1978, the remediation grant was extended for one year and the research grant continued for another two years.

strictly defined." These handicaps include hearing loss, ocular impairments, and motor dysfunctions, "problems that share with LD (strictly defined) a clinical meaning and a susceptibility to solutions either through direct treatment or through classroom methods that work around the deficit," and that differ, Murray says, from "the all-embracing set of 'learning problems' which undoubtedly characterize virtually all delinquents but which call for the much more elusive solutions of better teachers, better schools, and more supportive parents" (Murray et al. 1976B).

Although P.L. 94-142 provides funds for the remediation of juvenile delinquents found to have specific learning disabilities, most of the nation's correctional institutions seem ill-prepared to provide such services at the present time. As the GAO report explains, these institutions are, to begin with, more concerned with changing the behavior patterns that got the child into trouble than with addressing the child's educational needs. But, even if these institutions were to place greater emphasis on education, "including the remediation of learning problems as opposed to behavior modification," correction officials told the GAO that the effort would be inhibited by a number of factors. Two interrelated obstacles are: (1) the extent and severity of the delinquent's learning problem and (2) the relatively short period of time the child is institutionalized" (Comptroller General of the U.S. 1977, pp. 17-18). By the time a youth reaches an institution, several years of frustration and failure have promoted negative attitudes towards self and learning. In addition, these youths are "significantly behind academically in relation to their age and ability levels."

And because the average period of confinement of these youths is relatively brief—the GAO study of institutions in California, Colorado, Connecticut, Texas, and Virginia showed a range of confinement of 4.3 to 13 months—the GAO's consultants "believed that total remediation of the types and seriousness of the learning problems evidenced by the tested children was not likely . . ." (p. 18). As for other constraints, the GAO reports that, "although state correctional institutions attempted to meet the delinquents' educational needs, we were told that either the necessary detailed diagnostic evaluations needed to determine a child's specific problems were not performed or, if they were, the prescribed recommendations were not received by the teachers, or the teaching staffs were not adequately trained to implement or interpret recommendations" (p. 19).

While it is widely agreed that, in Bonnie Lewin's words, LD is "a problem, and whatever it leads to, kids should be taken care of," the implicit—and by no means inappropriate—goal of the OJJDP lies ultimately in reducing delinquency and not in establishing effective remediation programs in correctional institutions; if the current study fails to demonstrate a link, Lewin suspects the OJJDP will have little reason to pursue the problem any further. In this connection, Roy Lasky, Executive Director of the New York Association for the Learning Disabled, argues that "there is a danger in taking the approach: pay for this program now, or this person is going to victimize you later on. I don't think society is terribly sympathetic to that, and the danger is that is puts the learning disabled in the position of making other people victims. Our experience has been that the LD children are the victims, and so are the LD adults the victims—usually passive victims—and they go through their entire lives suffering, victimized, brow-beaten by society. The revenge is never there."

Life After School

Lasky's statement is a strong one, but it does make the point that a learning disability is a life-long burden, regardless of whether it produces a conscious desire for revenge or not. Psychiatrist Paul Wender has suggested that the minimal brain dysfunction (MBD) syndrome—which he attributes to a biochemical imbalance—evolves as a person matures, and that, in adults, it produces a number of relatively severe psychiatric disturbances such as alcoholism or hysteria. Psychiatrist Larry Silver suspects, on the other hand, that those adult disturbances are not the expression of the syndrome itself, but rather the outcome of untreated learning disabilities. In any event, those problems, which become increasingly difficult to detect and treat as a person grows older, persist.

As we have already mentioned, the availability of services for LD people decreases steadily after elementary school. Yet professionals all over the country report that, increasingly, handicapped adults are beginning to seek help. Harvey Alpert reports that there has been a noticeable change in the type of adult who comes to the Hofstra University Reading-Learning Center. "We used to get adults who came from foreign language situations or who had been misdiagnosed in school and just plain never learned to read. We're now getting adults who have been through school—through normal classes—and their reading is so far below what it should be that they just can't function on the job. They come to the realization that promotion and everything else depends on their learning to read."

But, in fact, it is not only poor reading that stands in the way of job success for LD adults. Both pediatrician Sylvia Richardson and John Arena, Executive Director of the Arena School and Learning Center in San Rafael, California, tell almost identical stories about bright young women who got jobs with state agencies (one in North Carolina, one in California), performed their duties with intelligence and energy, and yet, because one could not write a neat report, and because the other could not sit at a desk for a long period of time, lost their jobs. For some LD adults, simply getting into the mainstream of life is sometimes an insurmountable hurdle. "There are students I had when they were kids," Arena says, "who are now 26, 28, 30, and they're calling here with problems: they want to get out of the home—particularly the girls—they want to make the step, but there's no halfway house to help them make the transition."

The simple mechanics of living a life—getting an apartment, finding a roommate, caring for one's own health, making friends, eating properly, dealing with problems—may be far from simple for LD people. Peter Schweich, Director of the Archway School in New York City, has proposed a plan which is worth a brief mention here even though it is unlikely that the plan will be realized in the near future. The core of the plan is professional, social, and vocational support. The program would consist of 48 two-hour meetings per year, to be conducted by qualified professionals; the meetings would address job-related problems, family and social relationships, budgets, leisure time activities, and other aspects of daily living. The meetings would also give participants a weekly opportunity for social contact with others whose problems are similar. Among the other services and benefits that the program would offer are low-cost insurance and discounts on retail goods and vacations (acquired through group purchasing plans); trust-fund management, no matter how large or small the trust may be; help in finding apartments and roommates; financial planning; and a 24-hour emergency service.

The overall picture in terms of adolescent and adult services is a barren one. This may be due in part to the confusion that still surrounds the symptoms of specific learning disabilities. Where other disorders are concerned, individuals who can demonstrate concrete handicaps are often able to get help from a number of different state or federal agencies. Harvey Alpert, for example, recalls working with a youngster who had "a reasonably high IQ," a reading retardation of four to five years—and an 80-decibel hearing loss in one ear. That handicap made the student eligible for funds from the New York State Education Department Office of Vocational Rehabilitation that paid, not only for his reading remediation, but also for his college education. By the same token, Peter Schweich observes, "there's camp for mentally retarded, stipends for the mentally retarded, after-school programs for the mentally retarded, residential programs for the mentally retarded—anything you want for the retarded you can get. But if you're brain injured, you've got to pound every door. Even if you can find a program for the brain injured, then you have to start looking for an appropriate program for the particular disability caused by the particular neurological impairment."

At the moment, there are few, if any, laws on the books or programs run by the government that offer services to LD people over the age of 21—which is where the responsibility of P.L. 94–142 ends.

At the present time, then, what is the range of services available to the learning-disabled adult? Roy Lasky sums it up: "there is no range."

Most remediational programs for the learning disabled are run by schools, and their aims are mostly to attain success in school. But success in school does not assure success in life. Some remediators, like Charles Drake, Headmaster of the Landmark School in Prides Crossing, Massachusetts, mention former students who have gone to college, earned advanced degrees, and are successfully pursuing professions. But, for the majority, the success of remediation as a preparation for autonomous adult life is open to question.

Susan Trout has been following 500 learning-disabled clients in a longitudinal study that is now in its tenth year. She has been dismayed to see how many are failing in life: "The problem does not seem to go away. Either the adult functions on a job relatively well despite the fact that he still can't read or write or spell, or he turns to crime or develops a social problem or significant emotional difficulties. The main thing is, the problem doesn't go away. It can transform itself—take a different form—from an academic to a social problem or from an academic to an emotional problem. I would say that between 50 to 75 percent of our clients from all sectors of society are not making it. Not many of ours are going to college. A couple of ours, like the Harvard example—I am very worried about him. I am worried whether he is going to hold himself together emotionally. Some of ours have dropped out of college because they just couldn't handle the stresses of it. I think my profession is truly the profession of delayed gratification. You can't expect immediate rewards. I spend most of my awareness in my job on my failures. There are successes. But what is a success? I don't know. Remediation is not the answer."

What might the answer be? There is hope that scientific research may provide answers. At this moment, however, the scientific study of learning disabilities is in a crude and primitive state, as we shall see in the next chapter.

Chapter 5
Science

"When reality came . . ."

Grace Yeni-Komshian had already made a number of contributions to the scientific literature on dyslexia when she was offered an opportunity to switch hats for a while: to administer science rather than practice it. As a researcher, experimental psychologist Yeni-Komshian had been trying to elucidate the specific type of brain dysfunction that might lead to a disorder in language or reading. Now, as a Health Scientist Administrator in the Human Learning and Behavior Branch of the National Institute of Child Health and Human Development (NICHD), Yeni-Komshian was going to try to spotlight some of the areas of difficulty in scientific research on reading disabilities and to spur progress in the field by offering contracts to researchers for work on specific problems.

In many ways, Yeni-Komshian's story is a variation on the Frank King theme, if not a repetition of it. She began her career as a science bureaucrat by reviewing the literature. "The first thing that struck me," Yeni-Komshian recalls, "were the inconsistencies in the findings of what could be the matter with people who are called dyslexics, or developmental dyslexics, or, to use a neutral term, poor readers. There is no way in which we can find even a tiny bit of evidence that everybody agrees to, other than some notion that children are not achieving at some level that you expect of them. I use the word 'notion' because if you look at how they decide this is the case, it's very confusing: sometimes it's kids who

129

were sent to a clinic, and sometimes it's through a test that measures reading achievement at the same time as it measures all sorts of other things."

So, Yeni-Komshian concluded that she might be most helpful by working to develop a standard methodology for selecting and labeling people with dyslexia. "I felt," she explains, "that too many times, researchers do not pay enough attention to the reading deficit, to quantifying in what way the poor reader is a poor reader. You can be a poor reader if you can't decode the words properly," she points out, "or you can be a poor reader if you can't decode multisyllabic words; or you can be a poor reader if you can't comprehend what you have read. And it seemed to me that if we're interested in poor readers, we have to spend more time finding out in what ways they are actually poor."

To this end, Yeni-Komshian decided to hold a workshop that would focus on the question of "how to measure reading achievement and therefore lack of reading achievement," and would consider whether any test already in existence could be put into use throughout the field as a standard instrument. Participants at the workshop consisted chiefly of two groups: those doing research on developmental dyslexia, and those doing research on reading mechanisms. After two days of discussion, it became clear that no test was without its problems; but the workshop group agreed that the time was clearly ripe for the NICHD to issue a Request for Proposals (RFP) asking people to bid for contracts to develop a standardized test for subject selection.

An RFP asking for two separate tests went out in March, 1977. A realistic goal, Yeni-Komshian thought, would be to develop a test of decoding skills (e.g., translating print into sound) and a different test of reading comprehension (including oral comprehension). By looking separately at the components of reading, she hoped, the two tests might make it possible to acquire data systematically over a period of several years that might eventually bear out the widely held assumption that there are many different types of reading disabilities, and not just one.

The RFP drew 350 responses. Out of that original group, 17 finally applied for contracts: ten for the decoding skill test, the remainder for the comprehension part. Overall, Yeni-Komshian reported in late June, 1977, the proposals were not very good. She hoped to be able to issue a contract for the decoding skills test, since in that area there is some solid conceptual ground-work to build on. But in comprehension, major obstacles remained. "Although the workshop said we were ready," Yeni-Komshian observes, "when reality came, it seemed as if maybe we were not ready. I keep on hearing that yes, this field needs something like this desperately. We must have a tool that is workable, and that everybody can use. But when it comes to comprehension, when you sit down and think about how you might measure it, there are many aspects: Do we mean literal comprehension? Inference? Gist? How are we going to control the reader's knowledge of the world? Because, if you know about something already, then reading about it is easier than if you don't know about it. Maybe I'll have to retract the statement," Yeni-Komshian concludes, "and say that the field is not ready to tackle comprehension yet."

James Kavanagh, Chief of the Human Learning and Behavior Branch, NICHD, reports on the outcome of the process Yeni-Komshian set in motion. "We awarded two contracts for the decoding process and none for comprehension," he reports. "The reason for no contracts in comprehension is that, in the judgment of our reviewers, none of the applications were acceptable: not a person in the United States who had been willing to apply could satisfactorily evaluate comprehension, which is an incredible thing. We were very surprised."

To Albert Einstein is attributed the aphorism: "As far as the laws of mathematics refer to reality, they are uncertain; and as far as they are certain, they do not refer to reality." And so it was with Yeni-Komshian, to whom the "laws" of psychology suggested that comprehension ought to be measured as an aspect of reading achievement; but, as she herself noted, "when reality came," comprehension proved ephemeral. The same Einsteinian aphorism can be invoked in many of the other branches of science that are involved in work on dyslexia: no matter how coherent the theory, no matter how sound the concept, science has not yet managed to account for the palpable reality of the condition.

The dilemma, by most accounts, has two major and interrelated horns: for one thing, as Yeni-Komshian notes, there is no standardized method for measuring the phenomena of learning disabilities, either in terms of their prevalence among populations (large and small), their differing manifestations, or their extent and severity among individuals. The conditions, by whatever name, simply have not been defined precisely enough to satisfy anyone.

In 1967, according to Careth Ellingson, author of *The Shadow Children* (1967), the clinical literature on dyslexia amounted to more than 20,000 professional articles. Recent interviews with scientists have made it plain, however, that, despite the increases in the size of that huge stack of papers, science in the field is still, for the most part, in its formative stages.

Why? Some of the more frequently heard explanations include the following: research on reading, note Kavanagh and Yeni-Komshian, has long been hampered by confusion arising from the term "dyslexia." Some researchers, they write, used the term broadly; others used it narrowly; while still others rejected the term altogether and substituted vocabulary of their own. As a result, "vast amounts of data were collected which proved to be of little use in advancing the knowledge of dyslexia. Differing testing methods, experimental procedures, control groups, and research objectives were due in large part to different interpretations of dyslexia. And because the early research varied so greatly, much of it was [non]-comparable; one piece of evidence could not be used as a stepping stone for further research" (Kavanagh and Yeni-Komshian, 1978, pp. 89 to 90).

As recently as the late 1960s, according to Christy Ludlow, a speech pathologist at the National Institute of Neurological and Communicative Disorders and Stroke (NINCDS), the tools and methodologies available for use in research in the LD area "were very poor, and our ability to make interpretations from the results of research were very limited. In fact, many times things happened and nobody knew why, or things didn't happen and nobody knew why, and, in general, the rigor of research in this area was questionable when you compare it to other areas."

Ludlow goes on to suggest that another factor responsible for the slow movement of the scientific study of learning disabilities is the fact that researchers were working with an excessively simplistic view of the phenomenon. "We were looking for single causes before, for one problem, and for *a* population. Our ideas have changed: we realize that there are several populations, several possible causes, and that there are several types of syndromes and problems. Now we're trying to identify small problems and understand those better than to look for a whole problem that we could solve in one fell swoop—we're aware of the complexity of the area much more so than before." Norman Geschwind, Professor of Neurology at Harvard Medical School, observed that it has probably been only in the past 25 years that the full scope of the problem has become clear and researchers have begun to realize that a definitive characterization of the issues is still out of reach (Geschwind 1978).

Addressing the World Congress on Mental Health, neurologist Drake Duane, President of the Orton Society, defined the present state of science in the LD field in a gentle manner:

> The common denominator in the dyslexic population is the retardation in reading skills in relation to age and assessed intelligence. Investigation of genetic, neuropsychologic, and neurophysiologic factors have thus far not demonstrated a solitary factor that is also universal in this population. Either our technology and ingenuity are not as yet sufficiently discriminating or there are multiple physical, physiologic, and social factors that contribute to the disparity in written language skills (Duane 1977).

In contrast, Johns Hopkins University School of Medicine pediatrics professor Barton Childs, who specializes in human genetics, offers a down-to-earth assessment: "This field is a bloomin' bog. It's like quicksand: when you try to read around in the field, you feel as if you've disappeared into a never-never land. It's so unscientific—and I'm accustomed to science—that when I first got into this, I wondered whether I hadn't made a mistake."

The Prepared Mind

As Grace Yeni-Komshian's experience shows, it is often easier to see what scientific problems need to be solved than it is to solve them. The difficulties may be conceptual, methodological, economic, ethical, or a lack of prerequisite knowledge; but in many cases scientific progress waits for accidental events that are sometimes called "experiments of nature." Experiments of nature, not experiments planned in a laboratory, showed that the left cerebral hemisphere plays a special role in speech. This is the observation that gave root to all subsequent thinking about the lateralization of cerebral function. In the nineteenth century, Paul Pierre Broca, a French surgeon, reported a series of patients who has acquired speech defects following injury or disease of the brain. All of them had lesions extending into an area of the left frontal lobe (now called Broca's area) above and in front of the ear. Only experiments of nature could have furnished this insight. It could not ethically have been obtained by destroying Broca's area in healthy volunteers, nor could it have been obtained from experimental animals, which lack the power of speech.

Broca's interest had been directed to this question by the speculations of phrenologists and by the reports of other surgeons. While he had to rely on accidents to provide his subjects, it was no accident that he was on the alert to find them. Equally vivid experiments of nature go to waste daily. Unless they are seen by an alert observer who appreciates their significance and can follow them up, they contribute nothing to the advancement of science. "Chance favors only the mind that is prepared," said Louis Pasteur.

An amusing, but perhaps apocryphal, story will illustrate how experiments of nature can be wasted by observers who have not been alerted by their prior interests, questions, or hypotheses. Wilhelm Roentgen was experimenting with a device called a Crookes tube when he happened to notice that a fluorescent screen glowed while the Crookes tube was in operation. Roentgen deduced that something traveled from the Crookes tube to the screen. Within a few weeks he had demonstrated that the Crookes tube emitted a form of electromagnetic radiation (now called X-rays), a discovery for which he was awarded the Nobel Prize. The possibly apocryphal part of the story is this: another scientist had had as good an opportunity as Roentgen to make this discovery, but he had wasted it. He had noticed that photographic plates left near his Crookes tube were unaccountably fogged, but he had concluded only that he shouldn't leave the plates there.

The field of learning disabilities lacks neither interesting phenomena nor interested observers. Rather it is in the structure of its questions, hypotheses, and theories that it is deficient. It lacks, not data, but good theories. These alone can give data a meaning and guide the collection of new data that will not merely pile up but also advance knowledge. The field lacks accepted procedures for testing its hypotheses and theories and a sufficient corps of researchers trained in the investigative techniques that have proved themselves in mature scientific disciplines.

Perhaps we can appreciate what good questions, theories, and accepted procedures ought to do for the science of learning disabilities by likening it to the science of infectious diseases. Imagine a historian of science in the year 2178 looking back on the growth of these two disciplines:

"By the last quarter of the twentieth century," he might say, "it was widely recognized that learning disabilities were phenomena of great importance, but scientists were uncertain how many kinds there were, how one kind should be distinguished from another, what caused them, and what could be done about them. In all respects, the late-twentieth-century science of learning disabilities resembled the science of infectious diseases prior to the advent of the germ theory. It was not that either lacked theories. Learning disabilities had, among many others, the theory of incomplete cerebral dominance. Infectious diseases were thought by some to be divine punishments for wickedness. Both of these theories claimed great generality, and both suggested practical remedies—in the one case, forcing a child to achieve dominance of one hemisphere, in the other case, prayer. No, it was not that either field lacked general theories having practical consequences, but rather that they lacked theories that gave their adherents power to control the natural world.

"In neither case was there objective evidence that the remedies these theories suggested actually worked, although each theory was supported by many enthusiastic testimonials. Neither theory was designed to be tested by accepted objective procedures.

"Pasteur's germ theory revolutionized its field, bringing about, in the sense of the philosopher of science, Thomas Kuhn, a shift of paradigm. Not only did the germ theory explain infectious diseases, offer a means of classifying them, and suggest how they might be prevented or cured, but it offered explicit procedures for testing its validity. These were soon widely accepted. Scientists could use them to test whether a disease was caused by bacterial infection and could agree in principle upon the result. When viral, auto-immune, and hereditary diseases were discovered, these procedures also could be invoked as part of the proof that *these* diseases were not caused by bacterial infection."

Can we expect a similar revolutionary paradigm shift in the science of learning disabilities? It is too early to tell. As we pointed out above, "learning disabilities" is a general term like "illness" or "problem." It may be unreasonable to suppose that any one theory can give rational order to these diverse phenomena. Meanwhile, although scientists in the front lines may seem to be thrashing around with little direction, their efforts are guided by some standard questions and some widely accepted hypotheses. We can understand their enterprise better if we list some of their questions, hypotheses, and theories—many of which are analogous to questions scientists have raised about infectious diseases.

Questions About Learning Disabilities

1. The most difficult question about learning disabilities is how people who are *not* disabled can spell, read, speak, calculate, and carry out the many other intellectual tasks most people can do.
2. What are the causes of learning disabilities?

3. What makes learning disabilities selective? How is it, for example, that a person of otherwise superior intelligence can be unable to read?

4. What syndromes can be recognized? How many of them can we and should we distinguish? (A syndrome is a collection of symptoms that tend to occur together—for example, fever, cough, and runny nose.)

5. How well can we predict the future manifestations of a learning disability from its present symptoms?

6. Can we identify children who are likely to manifest learning disabilities before they actually do so? Can we identify them before they enter school? Can we identify them *in utero*?

7. What is the epidemiology of learning disabilities? How prevalent are they? What accounts for variations in their incidence?

8. Are remediational techniques effective? Which techniques are effective for which types of disabilities? Is one better than another? Are they safe? Are other (for example, medical or dietary) treatments safe and effective?

9. How can we explain from the perspective of the theory of evolution why learning disabilities have survived the process of natural selection?

Hypotheses and Theories About Learning Disabilities

Hypotheses and theories can give rational order to scientific investigation in two different ways: (1) When our hypotheses and theories are generally accepted and seem to give a good account of the phenomena of interest, we can go about the business of working out their consequences. This is what Thomas Kuhn has called *normal science.* (2) When our hypotheses and theories are controversial or of doubtful validity, it is a good practice to play several competing hypotheses off against each other. Ideally, we try to design experiments so that each competing hypothesis predicts a different outcome. Such an experiment can eliminate one or more of the competitors. Even in normal science, this is a good practice. Love being blind, entertaining several competing hypotheses helps us to avoid being blinded by excessive enthusiasm for any one of them.

Since the field of learning disabilities has ample controversy but no fully satisfactory theories, this second way of using theories ought to be its norm. Unfortunately, it has not been. Too much work on learning disabilities has been based on one theory alone—usually one that was espoused by one of the pioneers in the field or one that has become the pet of vested political, institutional, or economic interests. To show that theories are cheap, the lists below have deliberately been made longer than many lists published elsewhere. No investigator of learning disabilities need entertain only a single theory for want of alternatives —nor need these theories be mutually exclusive. Some of the phenomena might correctly be explained by one theory; others by another.

THEORIES OF NORMAL BRAIN FUNCTION

In contrast to research on learning disabilities proper, research on normal brain function is vigorous, healthy, and flourishing. For the science of learning disabilities, this is good fortune, for it is tied to the study of normal brain function like an alpinist roped to a climbing party—in some places it can range a bit ahead of the other climbers or it can stumble and fall behind, but it cannot safely go far on its own without being tied to the rest of the party. When the study of the disabled brain explores new ground, as in the case of Broca's studies of damage to the left frontal lobe, the sciences of normal brain function will soon follow the same route to gain their own ends.

It is beyond the scope of this book to review current theories of normal brain function. Almost all theories of learning disabilities imply theories of the way normal brains work. Here it is appropriate to mention only a few recent ideas about the way experience can influence the anatomical structure of the brain. They are of special importance for interpreting the causes of learning disabilities.

Mind and Brain

Modern psychology assumes that intellectual activities and emotions are functions of the brain; that changes in brain structure or function can affect the intellect and the emotions; and that, conversely, a person's sensory, intellectual, and emotional experience can affect the structure of the brain. Long-term memories, for example, are believed to be stored in the form of subtle changes in brain structure or chemistry.

It is only recently that there has been direct experimental evidence that experience can change the structure of the brain. To cite just one of the best-established examples, let us consider the deprivation amblyopia (the Greek roots mean "weak eye") that can be caused by closing one eye early in life. If a 6-month-old child should close one eye for a week, leaving the other eye open, the closed eye would become amblyopic. Timely treatment can restore normal visual acuity to the amblyopic eye, but, if it is not treated in time, it will suffer a permanent loss of vision. This loss can be severe enough for the amblyopic eye to be legally blind. It does not seem to matter why the eye is closed—the effects would presumably be the same if the eye were closed by an infected eyelid as they would be if the child simply decided to close one eye for several days. What does matter is the age of the child—susceptibility to deprivation amblyopia decreases with age. An adult would not become amblyopic even after having kept one eye closed for years.

Amblyopia can also be produced in experimental animals by raising the young animals with one eye closed. Neurophysiologists David Hubel and Torsten Wiesel of Harvard Medical School, among others, have shown that such eye closure in animals causes parts of the brain to shrink and certain cells in the brain to lose their connections to other cells. Many of these changes, which can be permanent, are gross enough to be seen without a microscope. They are believed to cause the loss of vision in deprivation amblyopia.

Competition

The cerebral cortex is the thin outer layer of cells, about two millimeters thick, covering the cerebral hemispheres. When one of an animal's eyes is closed early in life so that it becomes amblyopic, the territory in the cerebral cortex receiving input from the amblyopic eye shrinks. At the same time, the territory receiving input from the good eye seems to expand; that is, the connections from the good eye seem to expand into territory vacated by connections from the amblyopic eye. It turns out that the two eyes are in competition for control of some cortical cells. Closing one eye puts it at a competitive disadvantage, so that it loses cortical territory to the other eye. In this instance, it has been shown that a region of an animal's cortex with particular anatomical characteristics can be made to expand or contract by changing the animal's experience. One of these anatomical regions expands at the expense of another.

So far, such effects of experience on the anatomical structure of the cortex have most clearly been demonstrated in the striate cortex, a part of the cortex at the back of the head that is especially concerned with vision. It is tempting to guess that similar effects occur elsewhere in the cortex. For a century, anatomists have recognized that the cortex can be divided into a variety of regions, some primarily concerned with moving the limbs, some primarily concerned with vision, some with hearing, some especially involved in speech. It is conceivable that experience might influence the apportionment of the cortex into such regions and that one region might grow at the expense of another. Cortical "speech areas" might shrink in people who have difficulty speaking because their difficulties might deprive them of experience with spoken language.

Anatomists have usually been inclined to guess that the causal chain runs in the other direction. They have tended to assume that a person has difficulty speaking because he was born with a small cortical "speech area." There is no reason why both hypotheses might not be correct. Behavior and experience could influence the apportionment of the cortex into regions subserving different intellectual functions, while that apportionment could, in turn, influence behavior.

Stimulus Specificities of Cortical Cells

In the part of the cortex devoted to hearing, most cells will respond to appropriate stimulation by sound—but not just by any sound. For example, a cell that will not respond at all to most sounds might respond vigorously to a sound coming from the left side of the body that starts at middle C and rises through half an octave. It has been reported that in certain monkeys there are cells that respond especially well to some of the monkey's natural calls. Unfortunately, it is

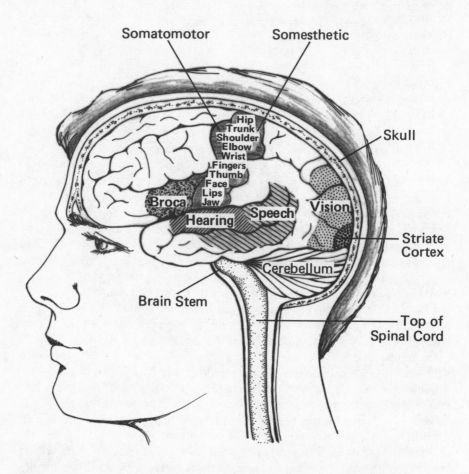

CORTICAL LOCALIZATION. The figure shows the approximate locations of some of the regions of cerebral cortex that are especially involved in visual, auditory, and somesthetic sensation, in the understanding and production of speech, and in the control of movement. The primary somesthetic cortex is separated from the primary somatomotor cortex by a deep fissure called the Fissure of Rolando (which in this diagram is largely obscured by the labels). Broca's speech area is located just in front of the confluence of the region of the left primary somatomotor cortex devoted to control of the lips and tongue and the region on the upper margin of the left temporal lobe of the brain which is the primary cortical receiving area for hearing. As a rule, relatively large areas of cortex are devoted to the control of fine movements such as those of the fingers and tongue, and relatively small areas are devoted to the control of coarse movements such as those of the hip. The same principle applies to the reception of sensations. The left hemisphere of the cortex (illustrated in the figure) is primarily concerned with receiving sensations from and controlling movements of the right side of the body.

not often possible to observe the behavior of individual cells in the human auditory cortex. They are likely to have a number of specialized properties reflecting the importance of human speech. It is plausible to guess that the innate specificities of cells in the human auditory cortex might account for our apparently inborn tendency to divide the sounds of speech into individual *phonemes*. (Phonemes are the basic units of sound out of which speech is constructed. They correspond roughly to the sounds represented by the letters of the alphabet.)

In the visual cortex, also, cells will respond only to stimuli having appropriate special features. They will not respond just to anything that is seen. Experiments with vision have shown that the stimulus requirements of cells in the visual cortex can be altered permanently by experience. These alterations go hand in hand with alterations in visual perception. What if the same would be true of the auditory cortex? That might explain why, for example, people raised speaking Japanese seem to hear the sounds /r/ and /l/ differently from the way they are heard by native English speakers and continue to have trouble distinguishing these phonemes even after years of subsequent exposure to English.

HYPOTHETICAL CAUSES OF LEARNING DISABILITIES

The distinction between learning difficulties that result from emotional, psychological, or educational factors and those that are caused by abnormalities in brain structure is blurred by evidence that behavior and experience can permanently modify the structure of the brain. As well founded as this distinction is in common sense and in the law, it is becoming more and more difficult to make scientific sense of it. Rather than thinking of these two kinds of explanations of learning disabilities as being mutually exclusive, we should think of them as potentially compatible explanations that operate at different levels.

Because they have been committed to the hypothesis that behavioral abnormalities express abnormalities of brain structure or function, diagnosticians have often described learning disabilities in terms that reflect fanciful theories and speculative notions of brain function—a practice sometimes called "neurologizing." A common example of neurologizing is the use of the term "brain injured" to describe children who exhibit learning disabilities in the absence of any direct evidence of injury to their brains. It reflects a commitment, in the absence of evidence, to a theory of learning disabilities—a theory that seems no more plausible than several others to be listed below. There is added pressure for diagnosticians to neurologize now that their clients can receive benefits for "neurologically based" learning disabilities that are not available if the disabilities are thought to have an emotional or psychological basis. This is an instance where law and administrative practice are at odds with good science.

In fact, the causes of learning disabilities are unknown. If we knew what caused a learning disability, we would call it by another name. "The term [dyslexia] means, quite simply, the inability to learn to read because of some unknown or undetermined cause . . . . As the causes of dyslexia are identified, they will probably be eliminated from the category of dyslexia and termed specific reading disorders. In this way, the term dyslexia should become increasingly narrow in scope until there won't be a need for the term because the causes of reading disorders will have been identified" (Kavanagh and Yeni-Komshian 1978). These remarks could be applied to learning disabilities generally, not just reading disorders.

It follows that none of the possible causes to be listed can be both well understood and well substantiated by empirical evidence. The list of theories that follows is representative of theories that are either plausible or popular, but there is no intention that it be complete.

Variations in Cognitive Style versus Rigid Expectations

Some children may be labeled "learning disabled" who would better be labeled merely "different." Their only disability may be an inability to fit a procrustean bed laid out for them by a rigid scheme of social expectations. We might be able to do some of our social business better if we learned how to take advantage of differences in cognitive style that we now label as disabilities.

To illustrate how "disabilities" of the individual can work to the advantage of society as a whole, let us take the example of red-green color blindness. In World War II, it was found advantageous to staff spotter planes with both a "normal" and a "color blind" observer, because camouflage that fooled the "normal" observer often would not fool the one who was "color blind" (and vice versa). *Because* of their differences in color vision, the team was more effective than either observer alone could have been. Similarly, a hunting party might be more effective in finding game if one of the hunters were "color blind" than it would be if all the hunters had "normal" color vision.

This reflects a general principle in biology: a species, especially a social and cooperative species like our own, is better equipped to survive in a variety of environments if the characteristics of its individuals vary from one individual to another. Variability in cognitive style is likely to be both normal and necessary for human survival. It may be that this variability can be achieved only by having people be good at some cognitive tasks at the cost of being poor at others. Only when society puts a unique and rigid emphasis on one kind of cognitive task may some of these biological variations be seen as disabilities.

Asynchrony Between a Child's Development and Social Demands and Expectations: Developmental Lag and Critical Periods

The Swiss psychologist Jean Piaget and other theorists have suggested that the growth of a child's intellect, like the growth of his body, passes through well-defined states. Just as a woman cannot bear children before puberty, a child may not be ready to master certain cognitive skills until he has reached the appropriate stage of development.

The rate of a child's cognitive development depends, not only on his education, but also on the physical maturation of his brain which, in turn, depends on heredity, nutrition, hormones, and other factors. Brain cells continue to grow after birth and form new connections with each other. Some nerve fibers in the brain do not have complete myelin sheaths until 3 years of age. (Myelin is a fatty substance that electrically insulates a nerve fiber from the surrounding brain tissue. An unmyelinated nerve fiber conducts nerve impulses much more slowly than a myelinated fiber of the same size. It is believed that major nerve tracts in the brain only become fully functional once they are myelinated.) The rate at which brain growth takes place must surely vary from one child to another.

A number of observations have suggested that there may be "critical periods" for cognitive development. A child may have great difficulty mastering certain skills unless appropriate experiences are available during the corresponding critical periods. Deprivation of these experiences may even lead to degenerative changes in the brain. One such observation was mentioned above: there is a critical period from birth through the early school years during which closure of one eye can cause amblyopia. Deprivation of vision during the critical period causes certain parts of the brain to shrink and causes certain cells in the brain to lose their connections to other cells. Other evidence suggests that there are critical periods for the acquisition of linguistic skills, particularly for the recognition of phonemes.

The schools may be trying to teach some children to read before they are developmentally ready. By the time these children are ready for beginning reading lessons, their classmates have gone on to something else. Their poor reading may be due to a *developmental lag* relative to the norm established by the schools.

Disturbances of Memory

Some learning-disabled people have unusual difficulty recalling information from memory. They may have difficulty recalling the names of objects, holding a telephone number in mind long enough to carry it from the telephone book to the telephone dial, or recalling what happened in the first act of a play while the second act is in progress. Often it happens that they can recall at some later time the information that was temporarily unavailable. In such a case, the difficulty must not have been due to a failure to store information in memory, but rather to difficulty recalling information from storage. It might be possible to explain many of the difficulties learning-disabled people encounter on the basis of deficits in memory or recall. Since memory is itself a mystery, despite decades of active research, explaining learning disabilities in terms of memory deficits is, at present, merely to replace one mystery with another.

Miswiring

The brain is a very complex and precisely organized structure—not at all like an undifferentiated bowl of porridge as it was once imagined to be. It contains billions of individual cells, connected to each other with remarkable specificity and precision. If some of the components of a radio are missing, misplaced, or improperly connected to one another, its function will be impaired. So it is with the brain.

There are many reasons why the brain might be miswired. Experiments on vision have shown that miswirings in the striate cortex can be caused by visual deprivation during certain critical periods. Miswirings can also be hereditary. Some strains of laboratory mice lack some of the kinds of brain cells that are present in wild mice. In other mutant strains of mice with bizarre behavior, the cerebral cortex grows upside down. One of the most striking forms of inherited miswiring is associated with albinism. In every species of albino that has been studied, from rabbits to humans, some of the fibers in the optic nerves grow toward the wrong side of the brain. This seems to account for the observation that albinos are frequently cross-eyed. Miswirings also can be caused during embryonic development by poisoning or by trauma. It is reasonable to suppose that miswiring of the brain might be responsible for some learning disabilities.

Incomplete Dominance

Samuel Orton, one of the pioneer students of dyslexia, was aware of Broca's localization of speech in the left cerebral hemisphere. He also noted that many of his dyslexic patients were left-handed or ambidextrous and that one of their common errors in reading was to reverse or permute individual letters or entire words. Based on these observations, he proposed the theory that dominance of linguistic function by one of the cerebral hemispheres is required for good reading. He imagined that the two cerebral hemispheres compete to control linguistic behavior and that confusion will result unless one competitor is dominant. He explained his patients' frequent errors of reversal by supposing that the right hemisphere represents the visual world in a mirror image of the left hemisphere's representation (Orton 1937, pp. 144–156, 199–200).

In its original form, this theory has not stood the test of time, but it has influenced many workers in the field. Orton set the stage for much current investigation by contributing the notion that "acquired" reading disorders, such as those caused by penetrating wounds of the left cerebral hemisphere, may have different causes from the "specific" reading disorders seen in apparently uninjured children. Neuroanatomical and neurophysiological evidence does not support Orton's notion that the cerebral hemispheres maintain mirror-symmetrical representations of information obtained from the same part of space. Rather, the left hemisphere is concerned primarily with events on a person's right side, while the right hemisphere is concerned primarily with events on his left side. Orton was aware that mixed lateralization is not always associated with reading trouble. Recent work also casts doubt on the idea that reversal errors are more common in dyslexic children than other kinds of errors (Shankweiler and Liberman 1972).

Neurochemical Theories

In order for the brain to go about its business, it must manufacture, take up, store, transport, release, and eliminate hundreds of chemical substances which perform special roles in brain function. Some, such as oxygen and glucose, are required by almost all brain cells. Others, like norepinephrine—the messenger for the "fight-or-flight" reaction—are involved in the control of specific forms of behavior. Some conditions that disrupt the chemical economy of the brain are known to cause behavioral disorders. Parkinson's disease is one of the best-known examples. It selectively affects brain cells that release the neurohormone dopamine, and it can be treated by administering L-dopa, a chemical that the brain transforms into dopamine.

A number of clues have suggested that some learning disabilities are associated with disruptions of the brain's chemical economy. Earlier in this century, there was an epidemic of a viral disease known as von Economo's encephalitis. In adults, it produced symptoms resembling those of Parkinson's disease, suggesting that it affected dopamine-releasing cells. In children, it produced symptoms resembling those of the MBD syndrome (minimal brain dysfunction). The fact that MBD responds to drugs that influence the brain's dopamine economy adds further weight to the idea that the MBD syndrome may result from a chemical imbalance. Experiments in animals have suggested that both dopamine and norepinephrine can control learning, at least under some circumstances. There is recent evidence from the laboratory of John Pettigrew, a neurophysiologist at the California Institute of Technology, that dopamine and norepinephrine can control the effects of monocular eye closure on the development of the striate cortex (Pettigrew and Kasamatsu 1978).

Brain chemistry can be affected by viral infection, by heredity, by poisoning, and also by diet. Some constituents of food serve as raw materials for the brain's chemical economy. Among them, some such as choline (one of the B vitamins found in eggs and meat), pass quickly into the brain. Indeed, dietary choline administration has recently been used successfully to treat a nervous disorder called tardive dyskinesia. If certain raw materials are not available during critical periods of development, irreversible brain damage may ensue. The development of a fetus can also be impaired by drugs ingested by its mother.

Some people are unusually sensitive to some of the natural and artificial constituents of food. Benjamin Feingold, a California allergist, has popularized the theory that some kinds of learning disabilities can be caused, or at least exacerbated, by reactions to food colorings and other constituents of the diet (Feingold 1975). The question whether these reactions are truly allergic reactions or whether they might be hypersensitivities of some other kind seems to involve difficult technical questions in immunology. Nonetheless, this is one of the few theories of learning disabilities that lends itself to direct experimental testing. It has received some support from such tests.

Brain Damage

Overt injuries to the brain by penetrating wounds, infections, tumors, and blood clots have been known since before Broca's time to cause a variety of disorders of the intellect, some of which resemble learning disabilities. It has been suggested that learning disabilities might be caused by "subclinical" brain injuries—injuries so subtle that they cannot be detected by the usual clinical diagnostic procedures. They might be caused by birth trauma, high fever, infection, intrauterine poisoning, or a variety of other causes. One of the principle difficulties with this theory is that people often read perfectly well after gross damage to the brain (such as concussion or even surgical removal of an entire cerebral hemisphere). Likewise, gross brain damage does not reliably cause hyperactivity or any other specific learning disability. When quite severe injuries of the brain fail to cause learning disabilities, it is not obvious why subclinical injuries should do so.

THEORIES OF THE SELECTIVITY OF LEARNING DISABILITIES

One of the most striking characteristics of learning disabilities is that they can coexist with a good general intelligence. Attempts to explain why intelligent people can be severely disabled in special fields of intellectual behavior tend to focus on one of four levels of organization: the organization of society, of an individual's experience, of the task to be performed, or of the brain.

Organization of Society

Reading is a highly stereotyped behavior. It is useful just because social conventions tend to ensure that everyone will read a printed page in the same way. Mass teaching of reading further limits individual variability. Not only are all readers supposed to read a text in the same way, but they are expected to learn to do so on a common schedule using common materials and teaching methods. The apparent specificity of dyslexia may lie, not in the nature of the underlying disorder of the brain, but in the limited range of behaviors that our society fosters, rewards, schedules, and evaluates. A disorder which impaired both reading and dancing might appear to us as a specific disorder of reading, for reading is central to our way of life, but dancing is not. In another society, the same underlying disorder of the brain might appear to be a specific disorder of dancing.

Norman Geschwind offers a somewhat different point of view (Geschwind 1978). Instead of imagining that a single underlying disorder may be seen by different societies to affect different functions, he suggests that there may be multiple disorders, only some of which are noticed in each society. His view is that everyone has a variety of strengths and weaknesses as a result of normal biological variation. Some people may have weaknesses in reading, others in carrying a tune. We pay special attention to the weaknesses that affect stereotyped behaviors highly valued by our society. In an illiterate but highly musical society, no one need be disabled by a reading disorder, but people might be severely disabled by the inability to carry a tune. In our society, it is the other way around.

Organization of Experience

Individual experience may be responsible for inabilities to perform certain kinds of tasks that are sometimes, perhaps erroneously, described as learning disabilities. Some academic subjects may be taught better than others. Children may miss critical lessons due to illness. Often they are taught to expect certain subjects to be difficult and these teachings may become self-fulfilling prophecies. For example, it is suggested that children are subtly taught at home (and by their peers, television, and other socializing institutions) that girls are expected to have trouble with math, while boys are expected to have little interest in poetry.

Organization of the Task

Reading is a complex and demanding task—one of the most demanding intellectual tasks required by our society. Many other intellectual tasks may be easy enough that they leave a substantial margin for error. General defects of the intellect that affect many cognitive functions may affect reading most severely because it leaves the least margin for error.

Most children do not have to be taught to talk—they teach themselves if they are exposed to speech. Reading is another matter; very few children teach themselves to read. Chimpanzees, by contrast, can be taught certain forms of reading, but no one has ever taught a chimp to speak. Even newborn human infants seem to be equipped with some of the perceptual abilities required to understand human speech. They can distinguish phonemes much as adults can. One demand that reading makes but speech does not (especially reading a language with an alphabet) is that the reader must become consciously aware of the divisions between phonemes in order to recognize the relation between the spelling of a word and its sound (Liberman et al. 1977B). We should not be surprised that it is much more difficult to achieve conscious awareness of phonetic segmentation than it is merely to use it in speech. A large part of the monitoring of our own bodies by our internal senses is ordinarily unconscious. Most people, for example, are not aware of their heart rates. Although people can be taught to achieve conscious control of their heart rates using biofeedback or yoga, this is a much more difficult and less common achievement than it is for people to control their heart rates unconsciously. Everyone does that.

Organization of the Brain

Since the various parts of the brain play differing roles in mental function, it is natural to suppose that learning disabilities might affect special cognitive functions because their underlying causes affect limited regions of the brain. Alternatively, the causes of learning disabilities might affect primarily certain types of brain cells or certain parts of the brain's chemical economy. These causes need not be brain *pathologies;* there appears to be considerable variation from one normal individual to another in the amounts of cerebral cortex devoted to various mental functions. Normal biological variation alone may result in allocations of limited resources of brain tissue that differ from one individual to another.

HYPOTHESES ABOUT THE EPIDEMIOLOGY OF LEARNING DISABILITIES

Familial Clustering

Since learning disabilities tend to cluster in families, it is natural to suspect that they are genetically inherited. There does not seem to be any one simple pattern of inheritance that accounts for the distributions of learning disabilities in families. This is true even of more narrowly defined kinds of learning disabilities such as trouble with reading. Either there must be several different kinds of inherited reading disabilities, or else they must be controlled by several genes. The hypothetical genes controlling hereditary reading disabilities may also interact with other predisposing factors, such as sex and diet, that do not by themselves cause reading disabilities.

Behavioral traits that run in families need not be transmitted by the genes. The tendencies to speak English and to vote for the Democratic Party also tend to run in families. Some familial traits are transmitted by viral infection. For example, in some strains of mice, the young mice are infected by cancer-causing viruses transmitted in the mother's milk.

Higher Incidence in Males than in Females

Learning disabilities seem to be much more common in boys than in girls. To a large extent, this may be due to a difference in social role expectations. It is also possible that some genes causing a predisposition to learning disabilities are recessive and located on the X chromosome. All X-linked recessive characteristics are expressed much more frequently in males than in females. However, the patterns of familial occurrences of learning disabilities are not consistent with the hypothesis that they are transmitted by any one X-linked recessive gene. Sex is known to affect brain structure and function in many ways; for example, men's brains are on the average larger than women's. Sex also affects the rate of maturation, so it may affect the relation between a child's experience and his or her stage of cognitive development.

Socioeconomic Status (SES)

There is an inverse relation between the incidence of learning disabilities and SES. Learning disabilities may be more common among children of low SES, because they are transmitted culturally, because they are caused by poor nutrition, or because they can be brought on by birth trauma or poor perinatal health care. They might be due to deprivation of appropriate experience during critical developmental periods. Diagnosticians may be biased—they might label a child learning disabled if they believe his SES to be low, whereas the same child might be given a different label by a diagnostician who believes his SES to be high. It is also probable that the chain of causation can run in the opposite direction: some people may have low SES because they are learning disabled.

Increasing Incidence

Much of the recent increase in the number of children labeled learning disabled may be due in part to the novelty of the category. Three decades ago this term was not even in use. Publicly financed programs to identify the learning disabled and financial incentives to use this label may also contribute to the tendency for the number of reported cases of learning disabilities to increase. Some people suspect that, in addition to these phenomena, there is also a real increase in the number of learning-disabled children. It might be occurring because advances in neonatal care are allowing children to survive birth injuries and hereditary defects that once would have killed them. It has also been suggested that increasing environmental pollution may be responsible for an increase in the incidence of learning disabilities.

There is a growing body of evidence that drugs administered to pregnant women can cause behavioral abnormalities in their offspring. Some, such as thalidomide, also cause physical deformities; others do not. For example, Yvonne Brackbill of the University of Florida and Sarah Broman of NINCDS have found evidence from the Collaborative Perinatal Project that obstetric medications commonly used in many hospitals can have long-lasting deleterious effects on the behavior of children born to the medicated mothers. There is also evidence suggesting that children of mothers addicted to narcotics suffer from behavior abnormalities that may have been induced by the narcotics. These tentative findings suggest that learning disabilities may be seen more often now than in the past, in part because increasing numbers of mothers are being exposed to drugs during pregnancy and childbirth (Kolata 1978).

Dyslexia and Native Language

Reports from Japan have indicated that reading disabilities are much less common in Japan than they are in English-speaking countries. Reading disabilities may also be less common in other countries where spelling is more regular than in English. The Japanese have suggested that reading disabilities are relatively uncommon among their children because Japanese Kana script represents words by syllables rather than by phonemes. The reported difference in incidence might also be due to genetic differences between the populations or to differences in teaching methods, but it is at least as likely that they are due to differences in techniques of measurement, diagnostic criteria, and social expectations.

THEORIES ABOUT THE INFLUENCE OF NATURAL SELECTION ON THE INCIDENCE OF LEARNING DISABILITIES

According to the theory of evolution, people suffering from a condition that is both hereditary and disabling will tend to have fewer descendants than people who are not so affected. Actually, the condition need not even be hereditary. It need only be transmitted to the descendants, whether by the genes, by learning, by viral infection, or by some other means. From this point of view, it is puzzling that there are so many learning-disabled people among us. Why hasn't natural selection eliminated these disabilities?

One possible answer is that learning disabilities are not actually passed on to the descendants of a learning-disabled person. This answer is probably false. A second possibility might be that learning disabilities are not actually disabling, or at least that they have become disabling only in the last few generations when society has become increasingly complex and technological. During most of human evolutionary history, the inability to read or to calculate would have been no handicap. It is less clear that our ancestors would not have been handicapped by the kinds of learning disabilities that interfere with verbal communication, orientation in space, and graceful movement.

A third possibility is that learning disabilities may represent trade-offs that confer both advantages and disadvantages in the struggle for survival. We have suggested above that many learning disabilities may be the consequences of normal biological variation. Here it should be pointed out that some kinds of biological variations that harm individuals may, nonetheless, contribute to the survival of the species. Sickle-cell anemia is a good example. It is a recessive trait, so that a person has the sickle-cell disease only if he has received one sickle-cell gene from each parent. People who are heterozygous for the sickle-cell trait—who received a sickle-cell gene from only one parent—have enhanced resistance to malaria. In a region like Africa where malaria is endemic, it actually favors the survival of the human population as a whole to have a large number of people who are heterozygous for the sickle-cell trait, even at the expense of having a high incidence of sickle-cell anemia. That may explain why the incidence of sickle-cell anemia is so high among people of African descent. Perhaps people who are heterozygous for some recessive genes controlling learning disabilities also have survival advantages.

This concludes our brief survey of some of the questions, hypotheses, and theories that scientists have, or ought to have, in mind as they study learning disabilities. It should be evident that some of these questions lend themselves to experimental attack better than others and that some of these hypotheses and theories can more easily be tested than others. The best hypotheses are those that lead to testable conclusions. We began this chapter by claiming that the science of learning disabilities had a plentitude of data and interesting phenomena, but that it lacked good hypotheses and theories. What is lacking in the latter department is evidently not numbers, but quality. Too few of the theories listed above lend themselves to experimental verification or refutation. Of those that do, too few have been tested. Some of the necessary empirical work is now under way. In the remainder of this chapter, we shall discuss some representative empirical studies and describe some of the problems that have been encountered in finding well-trained scientists to staff them.

Studies of Normal Language

Lucy Temerlin is a bright, active youngster who is into everything. She can unscrew electric outlets with a screwdriver or dismantle a tape recorder with her fingers. Although Lucy understands spoken language, she can't speak, so she has been learning the American Sign Language for the Deaf (ASL). Her adoptive father, Maurice Temerlin, a psychotherapist and former chairman of a university psychology department,* has written a book about Lucy's upbringing. At the time he was writing, Lucy's ASL vocabulary was more than 100 words. He quotes a typical conversation between Lucy, using ASL, and himself, speaking English.

L: Tickle Lucy.
M: No, I'm busy.
L: Chase Lucy.
M: Not now.
L: Hug Lucy, hurry, hurry.
M: In just a minute.
L: (*laughing*) Hurry, hurry, hug Lucy, tickle Lucy, chase Lucy [Temerlin 1977, p. 111].

It would not have been a remarkable exchange between a father and a daughter wanting his attention, except that Lucy was using ASL instead of speaking. Lucy Temerlin is a chimpanzee.

No one has succeeded in teaching a chimp to say more than four or five spoken words, despite years of effort; but several chimps have learned to con-

*For reasons explained in his book, he doesn't say which one.

verse in ASL, and at least one has been taught to read and express itself in a formal language based on arbitrary visual symbols. In the wild, reports Jane Goodall, a pioneer student of chimpanzee behavior, chimps communicate by a variety of grunts, calls, gestures and facial expressions (Temerlin, 1977, pp. 100-101).

Lucy Temerlin can understand and act appropriately in response to spoken sentences like, "Get the ball," "Let's play chase," or "Get a cup and I'll fix you some tea" (Temerlin 1977, p. 102). The fact that she can understand spoken language and express herself in ASL, but cannot talk, must reflect some hereditary differences between the organization of a chimpanzee's brain and our own; but it cannot merely be due to a lack of intelligence or a general inability of chimpanzees to use symbolic expression. Chimpanzees, in a sense, have a specific speaking disability.

To put the same observation the other way around, we can say that humans seem to have a specific hereditary speaking ability. Since the pioneering work of Allen and Beatrice Gardner, Psychologists at the University of Nevada who first taught ASL to a chimp, it has been apparent that humans are not unique among primates in their ability to use a language. We are, however, unique in our use of spoken language. Reading is widely believed to be a more difficult task than speaking and to depend, in most cases, on the development of speech. In this light, it appears paradoxical that chimps can learn to "read" but not to speak. Perhaps reading seems to us more difficult than speaking because we have special brain structures devoted to speech, but no special brain regions devoted to reading.

Noam Chomsky, Professor of Linguistics at MIT, argues that there must be principles of "universal grammar" common to all natural human languages that are based on the innate organization of the human brain (Chomsky 1976). There has not yet been much progress in analyzing the brain circuitry that could be responsible for universal grammar. Indeed, we have only the beginnings of an understanding of where to look for such circuitry in the brain. Neither has there been much progress in identifying the circuitry responsible for dividing up the flow of spoken language into individual words, nor for decoding their meanings. We are beginning, however, to get some insight into the means by which the brain could decode phonemes.

The distinction between one phoneme and another is not clearly marked by the physical characteristics of the auditory stimulus—the sound waves in the air. It is possible, for example, to make the vowel sound /ah/ grade continuously into the vowel sound /oo/ (as in "hoot"). To hear this gradation, pronounce the word "out" very slowly. No physical characteristic of the pattern of sound waves in the air makes a sharp distinction between an /oo/ sound and an /ah/ sound. Yet, to decode speech, we must make a clear distinction (to hear, for example, the difference between the words "hoot" and "hot"). (You will find it very difficult to pronounce a word that sounds a bit like "hot" and a bit like "hoot." Almost anything you can say will sound like one or the other, but not both.)

We have already mentioned that individual cells in the primary auditory cortex (that part of the cerebral cortex that receives the most direct input from the ears) will respond selectively to complex patterns of sound. It has been suggested that these cells may serve as "feature detectors" for the features of sound that characterize phonemes. Some of them may be wired up in such a way that they respond selectively to the sounds of individual phonemes. According to this view, the boundaries between phonemes might be determined by the feature-detecting properties of individual cells in the auditory cortex. To oversimplify: one cell might be an /oo/-detecting cell and another might be an /ah/-detecting cell. We would then hear /oo/ when the cortical /oo/-cells were active, and hear /ah/ when the cortical /ah/-cells were active. The distinctiveness of phonemes would depend, not on the distinctness of the acoustic stimuli, but on our having distinct populations of cortical cells with different feature-detecting properties.

Workers at the Haskins Laboratories in New Haven, Connecticut, an independent speech laboratory, have found some support for this view in experiments that show that very young infants distinguish between some pairs of phonemes in the same way as adults. These infants are so young that it is believed that they have not yet had a chance to *learn* to make these distinctions. Therefore, it is argued that they are relying on innate brain circuitry.

The methods used by the Haskins workers are typically used by a number of workers studying infant perception (Schubert 1975, p. 112). They judged the effect of auditory stimulation on the infant's spontaneous behavior—in this case, sucking. The infant is given the opportunity to suck a device that produces an artificial phoneme when he sucks on it. After a few minutes, the infant's sucking will decrease if the same sound continues monotonously. If the sound is replaced by another that the infant does not distinguish from the first, his sucking will continue to diminish. However, if a sound is introduced that the infant hears as novel, his interest will be reawakened, and he will resume rapid and vigorous sucking.

Isabelle Liberman and Donald Shankweiler, also at the Haskins Laboratories, found a strong correlation between a child's ability to segment speech consciously into phonemes and his reading achievement in the second grade (Liberman and Shankweiler 1976). They suggest that, at this stage of reading development, a child's ability or lack of ability to recognize phonemes consciously is likely to be crucial in determining whether he will be a good or a poor reader.

Localizing Functions in the Brain

In order to analyze the hypothetical brain circuitry that is presumably responsible for the innate human ability to learn languages, researchers first have to find it. In doing so, they have had to rely largely on experiments of nature. The injuries that Paul Broca studied are notable examples. However, the largest series of patients were obtained from soldiers who had received head injuries during the two world wars and from patients undergoing brain surgery for the removal of tumors, cysts, or focal regions of the brain that trigger epileptic seizures.

From such studies, and from numerous studies of experimental animals, we are beginning to get a picture of the functional specializations of different parts of the brain (see figure on page 138). At the back of the head are several brain regions specialized for vision. The visual regions on the right side of the head get information from both eyes about visual events on the left side of the body, and, similarly, the visual regions on the left side of the brain look through both eyes toward the right side of the body. The two sides communicate through several bundles of nerve fivers that cross from one side to the other, the largest of which is the *corpus callosum*. Within each of the regions involved in vision, visual space is represented in an orderly way, so that adjacent parts of the brain "see" adjacent parts of space.

Similarly, nearer to the front of the head are several regions of cerebral cortex concerned with hearing and several others concerned with skin, muscle, and joint sensations. Once again, as a general rule, the left half of the brain is concerned with the right side of the body, and vice versa; and the two halves of the brain communicate via the *corpus callosum*. The auditory regions of the cortex are laid out in such a way that cells in adjacent parts of the auditory cortex respond selectively to sounds of similar pitch. Each side of the brain gets input from both ears, but the left ear seems to provide the dominant input to the right half of the brain, and the right ear to the left half of the brain. The body-sensation (somesthetic) parts of the cortex are laid out so that adjacent portions of the cortex receive their sensations from adjacent parts of the body. Just in front of the primary region of somesthetic cortex is a band of cortex concerned with the control of body movement (somatomotor cortex). Once again, the left side of the brain controls movements of the right side of the body, and vice versa; and adjacent portions of cortex control movements of adjacent muscle groups. Broca's speech area lies at the confluence of the auditory cortex and the region of primary somatomotor cortex controlling movements of the mouth and tongue. Other speech areas have been identified nearer to the back of the head, lying between the auditory and visual regions of the cortex.

Much of our understanding of human cerebral localization comes from the work of Wilder Penfield, a neurosurgeon at the Montreal Neurological Institute, and his colleagues. In addition to removing diseased brain tissue, Penfield, using electrical currents, often stimulated the surface of the exposed brain in conscious patients as an aid to determining the functional specialization of the regions of cortex that he might have to remove. Such stimulation would frequently cause an interruption of function. For example, electrical stimulation of Broca's area can compel a patient to stop speaking. On other occasions, electrical stimulation of the cortex would produce body movement or even hallucinations or stereotyped emotional states, especially in epileptic patients.

Caution must be exercised in interpreting such observations. For one thing, Penfield was typically working with diseased brains. His observations need not tell us how normal brains work. For another, the brain is a complex organ, with many parts cooperating to perform each function. If destruction of a part of the brain interrupts speech, for example, that shows only that the damaged part was involved in speech. It does not show that the entire speech mechanism was contained in the part that was damaged. All parts of a complex mechanism may have to work together for it to function. Destruction of any one part may prevent it from working, even though the other parts are intact.

One can say with greater confidence that a function is performed by some part of the brain if it can be carried out with the remainder of the brain disabled. A technique for localizing functions in this way was developed by the Japanese scientist Juhn Wada and used extensively at the Montreal Neurological Institute by Brenda Milner. A rapidly acting anesthetic, amobarbital, is injected into one of the carotid arteries, the major arteries in the neck that supply the brain. Because the period of anesthesia is very brief, and because each carotid artery supplies blood primarily to one side of the brain, the anesthetic affects primarily the side of the brain on which it was injected.

Most people, both right-handed and left-handed, can talk when the right side of the brain is anesthetized by amobarbital injection. This provides a convincing demonstration that the left side of the brain is sufficient for speech. In most of these people, anesthesia of the left side of the brain will prevent the patient from speaking, although the right half of the brain remains conscious and can respond to spoken commands. Milner could be sure that the anesthetic was effective because the side of the body opposite to the injection (the side controlled by the anesthetized half of the brain) would be paralyzed while the anesthetic was acting.

Not everyone has speech localized in the left half of the brain. Seven percent of Milner's right-handed subjects and 13 percent of her left-handed subjects had their speech controlled by the right side of the brain. In addition, 1 percent of her right-handers and 10 percent of her left-handers could speak with either half of the brain (Milner 1972, pp. 421–446). These figures are not necessarily typical of the population as a whole, since they were obtained from patients being prepared for neurosurgery, but they should serve as a caution against too great a readiness to ascribe functions to one or the other side of the brain.

The right half of the brain also seems to have its specialties. There is evidence that the right half of the brain usually plays the dominant role in memorizing and recognizing faces, recognizing objects by touch, and orienting oneself in space. This evidence is less clear-cut and convincing than the evidence for localization of speech in the left hemisphere.

Further reason for caution in assigning functions to the two halves of the brain comes from observations on children who suffered brain injuries early in life. When Broca's area on the left side is injured early in life, the resulting loss of speech is temporary. Eventually, speech is recovered, but it is then localized in the right half of the brain. The critical period for recovering speech after a left-hemisphere lesion lasts at least through age 6. The ability of the brain to shift functional specialization from one side to the other needs to be taken into account by theorists who imagine that learning disabilities may be due to unequal development of the two halves of the brain. (For a review of hemispheric specialization, the reader may see Schmitt and Worden, 1974. The first eight chapters are devoted to this subject.)

Nonetheless, an increasing number of attempts are being made to detect differences between normal and LD individuals in the extent of hemispheric specialization. Some of these experiments can be viewed as tests of Orton's theory of incomplete cerebral dominance. For example, Sandra Witelson, a psychologist at McMaster University Medical Center in Ontario, has reported evidence that dyslexic boys show less of an advantage for the right hemisphere than normal boys in certain visual recognition tasks. She also reports that boys show a right-hemisphere advantage for certain visual tasks earlier in life than girls do (Witelson 1976, pp. 425-427 and Witelson 1977, pp. 309-311). Although these results are suggestive, the methods Witelson used for assessing hemispheric dominance are much more subject than Wada's amobarbital technique to interference by factors that can complicate the interpretation of her results (see, for example, the chapter by C. J. Darwin in Schmitt and Worden 1974). In relation to Orton's theory, it is interesting that Witelson reports mixed lateralization for visual recognition in dyslexics, but not for language. This is actually the opposite of Orton's hypothesis.

Since experience can influence brain structure, and brain injuries can influence lateralization of speech, it is an interesting question whether hemispheric dominance is the result of experience or is genetically determined. There has been considerable controversy whether handedness is inherited or acquired. A recent paper by Robert Hicks of the University of Lethbridge in Alberta and Marcel Kinsbourne of the University of Toronto, shows that a person's handedness is related to that of his natural parents, but not to that of his adopted parents, thus coming down on the side of a hereditary basis for handedness (Hicks and Kinsbourne 1976, pp. 908-910). This is almost certainly not the last word on the subject. Anatomical studies have revealed gross asymmetries in human brains that seem to be correlated with lateralization of function. For example, Norman Geschwind and W. Levitsky reported that a portion of the temporal lobe that seems to be associated with speech is usually, but not always, larger on the left side than on the right (Geschwind and Levitsky 1968, pp. 186-187). It is important to note that this portion of the brain was actually larger on the right side in 11 percent of their cases and of equal size on both sides in 24 percent. Thus, in order to interpret similar measurements on dyslexic brains, it will be necessary to measure quite a few of them to be sure that any differences that appear between normal and dyslexic brains are not merely accidental. At present, only a very small number of dyslexic brains have been measured, so it is not known whether they differ from normal brains more than normal brains differ from one another. The observations of Geschwind and Levitsky have by now been repeated by several other workers. Wada has shown that asymmetries of this kind are present in the brains of normal infants. This strongly suggests that they are hereditary. It has also been shown that such asymmetries can be detected in X-ray photos of living brains, a result that promises a rapid increase in our knowledge of this subject.

Future studies addressed to finding an anatomical basis for learning disabilities will require the availability of dyslexic brains. Because there is so much variability in normal brains, large numbers of dyslexic brains will be needed in order for the results to be significant. At McMaster University, Sandra Witelson and Wazir Pallie are trying to collect such brains from a population of terminally ill cancer patients who have agreed to donate their brains to scientific research. In the meantime, Witelson and Pallie are administering a wide range of psychometric tests to the patients which they hope to be able to correlate with their anatomical findings. The Orton Society is also planning an International Brain Research Project to gather such information. In broad outline, the project will seek to gather information on people who agree to will their brains to science. In consultation with neurologists and anatomists, the Orton Society plans to specify uniform dissection strategies so that the results of one dissection can be comparable with those of another. The crucial problem in this work is one that we have emphasized above: to know in advance what to look for. Until scientists have sufficiently good questions and hypotheses to guide the planning of such projects, the chances are great that they will make the wrong plans. Only later will they discover that they had failed to ask the right questions of their brain donors while the donors were alive or failed to use the right anatomical techniques. We must expect the studies being planned today not to be definitive. Future studies will be required as our questions and hypotheses change. They will almost certainly change as a result of the studies planned now.

Biochemical Studies

Most work on the theory that learning disabilities could be due to a disruption of the brain's chemical economy has been addressed to the MBD syndrome.* As discussed earlier, there is reason to suspect that MBD may reflect a disruption of the dopamine economy, although this theory does not explain why such a disruption should produce MBD in children and parkinsonism in adults. As Paul Wender, a psychiatrist at the University of Utah, points out, there are many

---

*Although most professionals in the field of learning disabilities believe that there is a strong tendency for MBD to be associated with cognitive deficits like dyslexia, no one claims that they always go together. Paul Wender points out that amphetamine treatment of an MBD child who is also dyslexic will leave a child who is dyslexic without MBD. Marcel Kinsbourne, Professor of Pediatrics and Psychology at the University of Toronto, is notable among those who suggest that MBD and dyslexia may be completely independent conditions that are associated only because some adverse influences on the brain may bring about both of these conditions.

ways in which the dopamine economy could be disrupted, and not all of them can be detected by present techniques (Wender, 1977, pp. 21–22). The two kinds of disruptions that we know best how to detect are a deficit in the brain's production of dopamine and a deficit in the brain's sensitivity to dopamine.

Tests for the former can be made by measuring the concentrations of dopamine or its metabolic products in body fluids (cerebrospinal fluid [CSF], blood, urine). Wender reports that tests of urine have shown no difference between MBD children and normal controls, perhaps because much of the uninary content of dopamine metabolites comes from outside the brain. Tests of cerebrospinal fluid by Wender and his colleagues and by Bennet Shaywitz, a pediatric neurologist at Yale, have suggested that there may indeed be a deficit in dopamine production in MBD children. However, obtaining CSF samples is a discomforting and occasionally hazardous procedure, so it has not been possible on ethical grounds to study many MBD children. Wender hopes that it may be possible to continue these studies in adults. He has reported evidence that the MBD syndrome changes its manifestations but does not disappear when an MBD child reaches adulthood. He finds that these adults also respond favorably to the administration of amphetamine (Wood et al. 1976).

Tests of blood have also been suggestive. Dyslexic children are reported to differ from normal controls in the amount of activity of monoamine oxidase (MAO) in certain of their blood cells (the platelets). MAO is an enzyme that is involved in the metabolism of dopamine, norepinephrine, and certain other neurohormones (Hughes 1976). Tests of the sensitivity of the nervous system to dopamine and related neurohumors in MBD children have barely begun.

The fact that amphetamine administration improves the behavior of MBD children supports the dopamine depletion hypothesis, since amphetamine affects the metabolism of dopamine, norepinephrine, and other monoamines. Amphetamines comes in two forms (stereoisomers), the d- and the l-. They differ in their effects on the metabolism of the various monoamines. By comparing their effects on the behavior of MBD children, Wender has obtained some evidence that it is indeed dopamine, rather than norepinephrine, that is involved in MBD (1977, p. 22). More remains to be done along this line, to rule out, for instance, the monoamine serotonin. One of the great potential advantages of finding biochemical correlates of learning disabilities is that they may make possible very early diagnoses.

Amphetamines are among the most widely abused drugs, both by street users and by misprescription. They have the reputation for being central nervous system stimulants. So firmly entrenched is the idea that amphetamines are stimulants that their calming effect on MBD children was widely believed to be paradoxical—opposite to the effect of amphetamines on normal people. It is only recently that anyone got round to doing a controlled study—to compare the effects of amphetamine directly in both MBD and normal children. Christy Ludlow, a speech pathologist at NINCDS, and her colleagues found that amphetamines affected both normal and hyperactive children in the same way, with perhaps an even greater beneficial effect on the speech behavior of normal children (Ludlow et al. 1977). In another paper, Ludlow and her colleagues reported additional control experiments on normal children (including some of their own children) (Rapoport et al. 1978). Once again, they found that the effects of amphetamines on normal children were of the same kind as those reported in MBD children. "What this research does," Ludlow concludes, "is to blow to hell the myth of the paradoxical effect of 'stimulant' drugs in hyperactive children. We don't get specific effects according to sites of the brain, and we don't get specific effects according to population, and that's why I don't think that this area is quite ready for research: we have more questions than there are methods to examine the questions."

Indeed, the supposed "paradoxical" effect of amphetamines on MBD children was once adduced as evidence that they have atypical monoamine metabolisms. Just because the effects of amphetamines on MBD children are not "paradoxical" (they are not opposite in direction to the effects of these drugs on normal children) does not, however, allow one to conclude that MBD children have normal monoamine metabolisms. So, the results of Ludlow's control experiments are not inconsistent with Wender's theory. They do show, however, that a child should not be diagnosed as MBD because he is calmed by amphetamines—an error that has frequently been committed in the past.

Diagnosis and Prognosis

Subgroups

There is general agreement by now that learning disabilities are heterogeneous. There are presumably many different causes and many different syndromes, but there need not be an exact correspondence between syndromes and causes. Infectious diseases can again serve us as a metaphor to make this point. "Influenza," for example, is a term for a variety of infectious diseases caused by a dozen or more different viruses. To one degree or another, they all have similar symptoms. In other cases, such as typhoid, a single cause may produce quite different symptoms in different people. One person can be an asymptomatic carrier, while another person infected with the same microorganism can be frankly sick. As a rule, preventions and cures must be addressed to the causes of the disease, but relief from suffering is attained by attacking the symptoms.

A possible solution to the problem of making suitable teaching available to learning-disabled children en masse is to classify them into subgroups for each of which a suitable set of standardized teaching materials and teaching methods can be designed. A rational scheme for doing this, like a rational scheme for treating infectious diseases, would use remediational techniques of demonstrated safety and effectiveness. The remediational techniques prescribed for any category of children would be known to be safe and effective for those children. In each case, the prescribed remediational scheme would be the one best suited to the child among those available. At present, there is no such rational scheme of classification. As we shall discuss below, very few, if any, remediational techniques have been demonstrated by objective standards to be safe and effective. The diagnosis and classification of learning disabilities is an art, believed to be reliable in the hands of its most skilled practitioners, but generally agreed to be unreliable when it is based on mass screening tests. This is unfortunate, because P.L. 94–142 has mandated screening for learning disabilities on a scale far too large for the work to be carried out by the most skilled diagnosticians.

For a rational treatment of bacterial infection by penicillin, the infecting organism must be classified as penicillin-sensitive or penicillin-resistant. The patient must be classified as allergic to penicillin or not allergic. Only then can a physician know whether or not it will be safe and effective to prescribe penicillin. It is not enough merely to know the symptoms of the disease, because both penicillin-resistant and penicillin-sensitive strains of bacteria can produce the same symptoms, and because the symptoms do not indicate whether or not the patient is allergic to penicillin. In a sense, learning-disabled children are, by definition, those who are resistant to conventional methods of instruction. This idea could be pursued further toward a rational scheme of classification. We have a body of remediational techniques developed by skilled teachers. We could, for example, classify LD children as phonics-sensitive or phonics-resistant, Fernald-sensitive or Fernald-resistant, and so on. This is in fact what happens when an individual child is being treated by an eclectic remediator. Ideally, it would be possible to achieve such a diagnosis by some means short of trying out several remediational techniques on each child, but as far as we know, there are no such diagnostic tests available.

Instead, most present schemes of classification are based on symptoms (see, for example, the scheme of Elena Boder discussed in the first chapter). No honest classification of learning disabilities can be based on causes, because the causes are unknown. It is often asserted that certain remediational procedures are best suited to children with certain kinds of symptoms. This claim surely reflects much hard-earned wisdom on the part of skilled remediators. Although there is no statistical data of which we are aware that could objectively confirm these assertions, such data may be forthcoming. Some of it may come from Boder's studies and some from the study of Paula Tallal and Betty Stark. In addition, one component of a large study commissioned by the OJJDP (see chapter 4) is an attempt at remediation by the ACLD, aimed at a population characterized in advance by a variety of diagnostic tests. This study is particularly well favored to find relations between standard diagnostic measures and the results of remediational procedures. Indeed, much of the needed data might be unearthed from the files of experienced remediators, if only it could be located and analyzed.

Grace Yeni-Komshian's quest for reliable measures of reading skill, mentioned at the beginning of this chapter, was addressed to another need for reliable and accepted classifications of learning disabilities: without them, it is difficult to compare one scientific study of learning disabilities with another.

It is not clear that learning disabilities should be divided into discrete subgroups. Perhaps, like intelligence, learning disabilities vary over a continuum of types and degrees, with no clear boundaries between classes. Fortunately, it should not be necessary to rely on subjective judgments for the classification of learning disabilities. There is a large body of sophisticated techniques available for the classification of people according to test results. It has been developed over almost a century of psychological testing for intelligence and other traits. Given a large number of test scores from each of a large sample of subjects, a mathematical technique called *factor analysis* exists for reducing the mass of data to a relatively small number of scores. Mathematical techniques are also available for the objective classification of the data. They can often find divisions of the test subjects into discrete classes, when such divisions exist.

Typically, the use of such techniques can extract from a large mass of test scores two to four composite scores that summarize most of the information available in the data. For example, one might be a general measure of intelligence, such as IQ; another might be related to processing auditory information; and another to visual information processing. Donald Doehring at McGill University has published one such study. Using factor analysis, he reduced the combined results of 31 separate tests to a small number of combined descriptive scores. When he used these scores to classify 34 children with reading problems, he found that they fell into four distinct subgroups (Doehring 1977, pp. 350–352). There is no guarantee, however, that a similar study of another group of children would yield a similar classification. For one thing, Doehring's sample of 34 children is relatively small—intelligence tests like the WISC have been standardized on populations of thousands of children. A group of only 34 children might separate into four distinct groups just by accident. For another, the results of such a study are likely to depend very much on the population from which the sample of children was selected. Doehring chose his sample from children attending a summer reading program. It is quite likely that another group of children attending a different program would have shown a different pattern of subgroups—perhaps because they were self-selected in a different way by their very choice of a program to enter. Until classifications of learning disabilities have been based on sample sizes and selection procedures comparable to those that have been used to standardize intelligence tests, it is doubtful that the classifications will be widely accepted.

Soft Signs

When attempting to distinguish a learning disability due to actual brain damage or to a congenital brain disorder from learning difficulties that may be due to social, psychological, or emotional disorders, diagnosticians often look for neurological "soft signs." These are neurological symptoms that are often associated with known diseases of the brain or brain injuries but are not by themselves sufficient to indicate that a specific brain disease or injury is present. Among the soft signs often associated with learning disabilities are left-handedness, clumsiness of gait, extending the great toe when the sole of the foot is stroked (Babinski's sign), poor handwriting, a tendency to walk on the toes, mixed laterality (ambidexterity), hyperactivity, short attention span, and left-right confusion. However, it has been pointed out that these soft signs can be found almost as frequently in children who are unusually gifted (Duane 1977). The Tallal and Stark study gives particular attention to soft signs in an attempt, says Tallal, "to see whether there really is anything to soft signs or not."

Electroencephalography

The cells in the brain do their work by controlling miniscule electric currents (on the order of one-billionth of an ampere). Since the brain contains billions of cells, it actually uses an appreciable amount of electrical power—about as much as a few dozen electronic pocket calculators or one small light bulb. When large numbers of brain cells are engaged in coordinated activity, they cause measurable electrical currents to flow through the brain, the membranes surrounding it, the skull, and the scalp. These currents can be detected using electrodes placed on the scalp and suitable amplifiers. A record of these currents is called an *electroencephalogram* (EEG).

Observation of the EEG can give a diagnostician some information about the inner workings of the brain but not very much. As an analogy, consider what can be learned about an electronic pocket calculator by examining it with the aid of a transistor radio. Some of these calculators produce radio static when they are at work. By holding a small radio near the calculator, one can hear noise that signals the calculator's activity. In this way, one can use the radio to tell when the calculator is turned on or turned off, and perhaps even to recognize by some characteristics of the noise whether it is merely displaying a number or is actively engaged in calculation. What one cannot do with the radio is find out how the calculator works.

The EEG gives a similarly crude picture of brain function. It is useless as a tool to discover, for example, how cells in the auditory cortex might be wired up to detect phonemes; but it might be capable of telling an investigator whether the auditory cortex as a whole is active or resting. The EEG is very useful for some diagnostic purposes—in particular, for diagnosing epilepsy. It would be nice if it also could be used as a diagnostic tool in studying learning disabilities, because it does measure objectively some of the activity of the brain.

A number of studies have purported to show differences between EEGs recorded from normal and learning-disabled children. It is possible that appropriate EEG measurements will turn out to be useful in diagnosing learning disabilities; but it is very doubtful that the EEG will have much to contribute to our understanding of the causes of learning disabilities, because so little is understood about the relation between the EEG and the underlying function of the brain. Considering that the clinical EEG is a record of the massed activity of tens of millions of cells recorded through the skull and the scalp, and that each of these cells has its own special function, it is hardly surprising that the relation between the EEG and the detailed workings of the brain is poorly understood.

For the present, one must take a cautious attitude in interpreting EEG findings as evidence of learning disabilities. The features of the EEG are quite sensitive to fatigue and attention. It is quite possible that EEGs obtained from LD children would differ from those obtained from normal children just because the LD children would be more anxious or less attentive in the testing situation. The kinds of miswirings that can be induced by eye closure can affect the EEG, so that abnormalities in the EEG are not necessarily indicative of congenital abnormalities in the brain.

One ambitious attempt to standardize the EEG for diagnostic purposes is the neurometric battery being developed by E. Roy John of the New York University Medical Center and his colleagues (John et al. 1977, pp. 1393–1410). In the course of an hour, the neurometric battery measures the EEG from a score of electrodes under a variety of test conditions. The large mass of data generated by this procedure is analyzed with the aid of a computer. These tests have by now been carried out on several hundred normal and LD children. It is claimed that the neurometric battery can reliably discriminate LD children from normals, and it can distinguish subgroups within the LD population. If these claims withstand further scrutiny, neurometrics may prove to be a valuable diagnostic tool.

Longitudinal Studies

In the end, the aim of diagnosis is prediction. Will a disability get better or worse? Will it respond to treatment? Will this treatment or that one produce a better result? The only way to answer such questions about learning-disabled children is to follow their progress over a period of several years—perhaps even over a lifetime. The longitudinal studies required for this purpose are expensive. The work is labor-intensive, and large numbers of children must be followed if the results are to be of broad applicability. And of course the study will be fruitful only to the extent that it was well designed—to the extent that the researchers asked the right questions. Since the field of learning disabilities is new, there have not been many longitudinal studies.

Two studies cited by Christy Ludlow (1978) suggest that the prognosis for many LD children, given current techniques of remediation, is not very good. Both groups of children (38 in the first, 30 in the second) were diagnosed as language impaired before they were 5 years of age. Despite extensive language therapy during the intervening five years, the majority of both groups of children continued to show severe difficulties in language or reading at age 9.

The Collaborative Perinatal Project (CPP) sponsored by NINCDS was a major study that bears on this question. At 12 centers in the United States, the project collected data on 35,000 children from the time their mothers-to-be first registered for prenatal care until the children were 7 years of age. The study ran from 1959 to 1965. Scores of data were collected from each child.

In a paper presented to the 14th International Conference of the ACLD, Sarah Broman of the NINCDS described some of her results from an analysis of the CPP data: "Psychomotor and cognitive development of children followed in the Collaborative Project was evaluated at ages 8 months, 4 years and 7 years. A speech, language and hearing evaluation was made at age 3. Physical status of the mother was monitored during pregnancy and labor and delivery. Major medical evaluations of the children were made at birth, and at one and 7 years. Demographic and family history data was collected from the mothers during pregnancy and when the children were 7." The study identified "low achievers" who were "young children with a significant discrepancy between intellectual ability and academic achievement" (Broman 1977A). Not surprisingly, children who were identified as low achievers at age 7 had already shown "fairly wide-spread cognitive deficits and behavioral deviations at age 4." At age 7, the low achievers manifested "deficits in visual-motor performance, verbal ability, and short-term memory and ... certain neurological soft signs." There were stronger correlations between low achievement and low SES, large family size, and poor family stability than there were with physical or medical factors. In all, 3 percent of this large unselected population were characterized as low achievers (Broman 1977B).

Paul Satz, one of the leading advocates of the developmental lag theory, has been conducting a longitudinal study of a population of more than 600 white male students in Alachua County, Florida, since 1970. The design of the study calls for the students to be tested every three years from kindergarten through high school. When he took reading measures at the end of second grade, Satz found 12 percent of the students to show severe reading disorders. By the time these students had reached the fifth grade, the percentage with severe reading difficulties had risen to over 30 percent. Despite this increase in the percentage of reading disorders over time, the test given during kindergarten still managed to predict, for the majority of children, in which reading group they would fall in fifth grade. Satz is attempting to develop measures that can predict the course development so that intervention may be used at appropriate ages. He is attempting validation of his measures by applying them to other populations. Satz is testing their predictive value using data from a large study he is conducting in Australia, as well as two other studies in the United States (Satz 1978; 1976; 1975). There is potentially a vast amount of longitudinal data in the files of special schools and in follow-up studies of their students. However, such *retrospective* studies will almost inevitably suffer some disadvantages in comparison with *prospective* studies like those of Satz and the Collaborative Perinatal Project which are designed as research tools. A prospective study is designed, and its subjects are chosen, before its data is taken. The populations of special schools will be selected for a variety of reasons, usually not including the requirements of a good research design. In a retrospective longitudinal study, it may be difficult to compare the life courses of the students with control populations of normal students or of LD students who were not given special treatment. The lack of these controls is likely to make the results of a retrospective study difficult to interpret. Nonetheless, the data are potentially of great value in comparison to the cost of obtaining them, and retrospective studies are to be encouraged.

We mentioned earlier a follow-up study by Susan Trout of clients of an LD clinic at the University of the Pacific in San Francisco. Two other retrospective studies have recently come to our attention. One, by the Marianne Frostig Center of Educational Therapy in Los Angeles (1977), is a follow-up study of the postschool adjustments of some of the school's former students. Another is a follow-up study of former students at the Cove School in Evanston, Illinois, written by Laura Lehtinen Rogan, the school's clinical director, and Lenore Dumas Hartman (1978). Our ability to interpret their findings is limited, as is to be expected of retrospective studies, by the lack of control populations. Moreover, the graduates of these schools are, on the average, in their twenties, so it is likely to be too early to evaluate the influence of LD on the whole course of their lives. Many of them are still in school or college. None has reached the age of 40.

Some general conclusions can be drawn with caution from this data. The underlying disabilities do not appear to have gone away. Many of these graduates are still in trouble. However, significant numbers of them have entered college, many have graduated, and some have gone on to graduate and professional schools. The majority are either still in school or gainfully employed. Most have sought some kind of psychological counseling. In the absence of suitable control data, it does not seem possible to determine whether their records of employment are better or worse than one should have expected.

Likewise, the absence of control data makes it almost impossible to evaluate the effects of the special education these students received. The graduates of the Frostig school were generally satisfied with their schooling and felt that it had been helpful. They were, on the average, more satisfied than their parents. This discrepancy may well reflect a difference between the students' own expectations and those of their generally middle-class parents. The other studies did not formally report this data.

Epidemiology

There are two major obstacles to studies of the incidence of learning disabilities. The first is the lack of an objective and accepted definition of these conditions. The second is that the best present methods of diagnosis and classification are highly labor-intensive and, therefore, very expensive to carry out on a large scale.

Incidence

We have already encountered a number of estimates of the prevalence of learning disabilities in the school-age population: the Collaborative Perinatal Project produced, in Sarah Broman's analysis, a figure of 3 percent "low achievers" (Broman 1977A). Paul Satz found 12 percent of his second-graders to have severe reading difficulties (Satz 1978). Preliminary results from a study commissioned by the OJJDP show 16 percent of students 12 to 15 years old with learning disabilities.

In England in the 1960s, a study of the Isle of Wight found a 3.5 percent incidence of specific reading retardation among children (Yule 1974, pp. 1–12). A similar survey conducted in London came up with a figure of 6 percent (Rutter and Yule 1975, pp. 181–197). Leon Eisenberg found a greater incidence of reading retardation in an urban center among sixth grade children (28 percent) than in a suburb (about 3 percent) (Eisenberg 1966, pp. 352–365). Kiyoshi Makita reported a 1 percent incidence of dyslexia in Japan (Makita 1968, pp. 599–614).

There are tantalizing suggestions in these figures that the incidence of learning disabilities differs between cities and suburbs and depends on native language, and very likely on socioeconomic status. They can be no more than suggestions at present. It is clear that the criteria for recognizing learning disabilities varied from one study to another, as did the criteria for selecting the populations to be studied. Until uniform definitions and diagnostic techniques are adopted, it will be difficult to compare incidence figures from one study with those from another.

Family Studies

It is clear, however, that learning disabilities, and, in particular, reading disabilities, tend to run in families. The evidence, including a study of their own, is reviewed by Barton Childs and his colleagues (Childs et al. 1976). They favor the hypothesis that reading disabilities can be inherited genetically, but, if this is true, the pattern of inheritance is likely to be complex.

Safety and Efficacy of Remediation Techniques

If remediation were without risks or costs, we might be happy to undertake it on the theory that there is nothing to lose. Unfortunately, remediation takes time, money, and the scarce resources of well-trained people; and it risks harm by wasting time, by frustration, by raising unfulfilled expectations, and by stigmatization. The use of ineffective techniques of remediation does harm by taking up time that could better be spent on effective ones. Unfortunately, there are hardly any satisfactory studies of the safety and efficacy of remediational techniques. For example, Hallahan and Cruickshank reviewed several dozen studies of perceptual-motor training techniques and found almost all of them to be methodologically unsound. Many of them failed to use obvious controls, or even any controls at all (Hallahan and Cruickshank, 1973, Chap. 6). For example, any study of the efficacy of remediational techniques must be controlled for the Hawthorne effect, that is, the tendency for any innovation to lead to an improvement in performance, no matter what the innovation may be. (The effect is named for a study of the relation of industrial lighting to labor productivity conducted in Hawthorne, California.)

One of the major difficulties in designing a useful test of the efficacy of a remediational technique is that of defining the population that participated in the test. Tests are always open to the objection that the remediational techniques studied succeeded or failed only for the particular kinds of learning-disabled children participating in the study, and that the use of some other group of children would have given a different result. If a test is conducted on a mixed group of children, the techniques used may work for some of them and not for others, and this variability of results may obscure the real success achieved in some cases.

We should like to suggest a way out of this difficulty. Tests of the efficacy of remediational techniques should be conceived, not as tests of the techniques alone, but rather as tests of the *combination* of the remediational technique and the methods used to select the children to whom it is applied. If a test fails to show that a remediational technique attained significantly beneficial results with a particular population of children, one can then conclude that the combination of the technique and the selection procedure has not been shown to be effective. Consider a hypothetical example. Suppose the Metropolis School System undertakes a test of the expensive Acme Reading Kit, which is claimed to reduce reading failure. Second grade classes are assigned at random to a control group that will receive conventional instruction and a test group that will use the Acme Reading Kit. At the end of the year, tests of reading reveal no significant difference between the performances of the two groups of second grade classes. This does not show that the Acme Kit was not more helpful than conventional instruction for *any* of the second grade students, but it does show that the use of the Acme Kit in randomly chosen second grade classes does not produce a significantly favorable result. The school board can fairly conclude that it would not be justified in purchasing the expensive Acme Reading Kit for use in all second grade classes. If the Acme Company still claims that their kit is effective for some children, the onus should be on them to find a means of selecting those children who will benefit from the use of their kit.

One remediational technique that has been subjected to carefully controlled studies is the Feingold diet. At the 1978 meeting of the ACLD in Kansas City, C. Keith Conners, Professor of Psychiatry and Psychology at the University of Pittsburgh School of Medicine, reported the results of his "double-blind crosser" tests of the Feingold diet. ("Double-blind" means that neither the children participating in the test nor the parents and teachers evaluating their behavior knew whether the children were on the Feingold diet or not. This precaution guards against the participants' expectations biasing the results. "Crossover" means that each child experienced both the Feingold diet and a test diet which resembled the Feingold diet except that certain food colorings were added to the meal. Thus each child served as his own control.) Conners found, in a small number of children (5 percent to 10 percent) that the addition of food colorings to their meal did cause a worsening of their hyperactivity for a period of a few hours; that is, he found that the Feingold diet was actually effective for a small number of hyperactive children. Conner's study did not support Feingold's claim that as many as 50 percent of hyperactive children could benefit from his diet.

Personnel and Funding

Many of the people in the learning disabilities field are unaccustomed to the rigors of the scientific method. Most of the teachers and remediators on the front lines have had little, if any, training in research. Yet they are the ones with the best opportunities to observe experiments of nature. They know what the phenomena are, but they usually don't know how to capitalize on them for research. When they do scientific work, it is too often of the "hit-and-run" variety—a single study done as a master's or doctoral thesis that is not followed up. The literature is swamped with such studies. Scientists must take them into account, yet they are difficult to evaluate.

On the other hand, too many of the scientists who claim to be working on learning disabilities have very limited experience with learning-disabled people. One special educator tells a story that illustrates this point. He had been sending some of his dyslexic students to a researcher who was surprised to find that they very rarely made letter-reversal errors. The researcher came to the conclusion that dyslexics don't really make such errors. He was not aware that the students had had hours of remedial instruction addressed to reversals. If the researcher had seen the students before they received the instruction, he would have seen many more reversal errors.

The professional scientist is subjected to pressure to "publish or perish." This pressure leads to a profusion of reports of incomplete and ill-considered studies. As Paul Satz points out, it weighs especially heavily on the scientist who wants to do longitudinal studies, which, by their nature, are not productive of a yearly flow of finished papers. The rhythm of grant support, which requires annual progress reports and triennial grant applications, also makes it difficult to plan and organize long-range studies. In recent years, the entire scientific community has been burdened by an inconsistency and unpredictability of financial support that have made long-term projects difficult to carry out.

One of the criticisms frequently leveled at reading disabilities research is that it tries to define an abnormality without knowing what is normal. "Ironically enough," notes Christy Ludlow, "the normal population has not been well-studied." Monte Penney, a Senior Program Officer at the National Institute of Education, disagrees. He suggests that researchers in the LD field have simply failed to avail themselves of the literature on the normal reading process. He contends that "knowledge about the normal course of language development in learning to read is qualitatively better—the evidence is better—than the evidence about learning problems." In response, Ludlow argues that there are still many problems unsolved. "Certainly we don't know how children learn language, which is one component of reading. And we still don't know how they learn to read."

Funding research grants on childhood and adult language disorders by the NINCDS has actually fallen from $856,096 to $454,505 in the period from 1974 to 1977. This is not due to the government's lack of interest in these problems, writes Ludlow, but rather it "reflects the number and quality of proposals received. They are few and frequently poor in technical merit" (Ludlow 1978).

In sum, although the scientific approach to learning disabilities is ultimately our best hope for solutions, it has a long way to go. It must begin by building its infrastructure, both of questions and hypotheses and of people knowledgeable of the phenomena and the means to explore them.

The material gathered for this report offers no basis for the hope that solutions to the problems of learning disabilities will be quickly in hand. Yet no one questions that there are children and adults with serious, but diagnostically elusive, problems with learning and with life. We don't know the answers, and it may be that we are trying to go "too far too fast." Still, we are earnestly seeking them, and as we pause for a moment before the progress and upheaval promised by P.L. 94-142, we can glimpse some of the paths we must follow.

Chapter 6
Conclusions

"More than a matter of words . . ."

Terminology

When we began to work on this project in June, 1977, our original intention was to describe the outlines of the field of dyslexia. Before very much time had elapsed, it became apparent that "dyslexia" was, to use a hackneyed phrase that rings throughout the field, just "a piece of the elephant." The elephant in question—assuming there is just one—was learning disabilities.

At first, the term "learning disabilities" seemed unattractive because it seemed to place too heavy an emphasis on academic problems and not enough on the difficulties that occur outside school and after the educational process has run its course. We were tempted to use the term "living disabilities," but it lacks precision, and the last thing this field needs is a new catch-all phrase. We tried for a while to use the term "dyslexia" to represent the whole field, because it has a scientific and technical sound to it and because its Greek etymology was appropriate: difficulty with language. But, in the end, we decided that it would be best to reserve this term for people who have trouble reading. Another strong contender was "minimal brain dysfunction" because its definition includes both an educational and a medical dimension and because it is defined as a syndrome. Finally, we were persuaded that the term "learning disabilities" was as good as

168

we have, because learning is a lifelong activity that is not confined to school.

The solution to this semantic problem will probably emerge slowly as more accurate methods of diagnosis, and hence characterization, are developed. But, the main challenge—the necessity—that the field faces is more than a matter of words. Finding the right classification is important, to be sure, but not as important as finding ways to help people deal with and—to whatever extent possible— overcome their handicaps.

Public Law 94-142

The most ambitious plan in place at the moment is P.L. 94-142. There seems to be some justification for the criticism that this act unreasonably raises expectations: in spite of its elaborate mechanisms, the EHC Act may in fact be, as a member of a Westchester school board puts it, "grotesquely under-funded." While the trend in legislation for handicapped children has been a strong and positive one, the mandate that all handicapped children receive a free appropriate education has created massive financial difficulties for local school districts. Now, while the federal government offers to share the burden of costs associated with educating the handicapped, states and schools must still pay the basic costs —and there will be more of these costs, because there will be many previously unserved handicapped children entering the school system. In addition, states and school districts must foot the bill for locating and evaluating these children. And they must do all this at a time when voters are showing strong signs of resentment at the rising taxes that are necessary to keep school systems going. These factors, plus the severe shortage of specialists trained to work with learning-disabled children, plus the political factors that come into play at the local level, make it all too likely that many LD children will still not receive the services they need to develop to their fullest potential.

While the due process requirements in P.L. 94-142 are a necessary—and laudable—feature of the legislation, they also constitute, in a very deliberate way, an invitation for parents to complain, unfortunately including parents whose children are not learning disabled but have merely failed to live up to parental expectations. And it is easy to conjure up a scenario (which, in fact, is already coming to pass) in which the grievance channels become quickly clogged while children sit in classrooms waiting for help—or getting the wrong kind.

A final point to be made about P.L. 94-142 concerns its implicit and perhaps naive assumption that regular classroom teachers now working in the school system will be willing to undergo further training in order that the "least restrictive environment"—mainstreaming—mandate be met.

As we have noted, most of the teachers in the system will be there until the end of the century, and many of them are openly hostile towards the idea of working with handicapped children in their classrooms. The more recently trained a regular classroom teacher is, the more likely it is that he or she will have some exposure to special education techniques, but "some exposure" is not enough. And although P.L. 94-142 assumes that many educators will be capable of handling handicapped children in a regular classroom setting, it cannot, obviously, guarantee that this will be the case. The act does, in fact, allow states and local school districts to use P.L. 94-142 grants to develop specialists and other necessary personnel, but there is no reason to assume that these monies will be sufficient to cover the costs of both developing specialists *and* providing continuing education or in-service training for the regular classroom teacher. Some form of added incentive—from the federal government, or from local education agencies, or both—may be necessary to stimulate the regular classroom teacher to continue his or her education. If mainstreaming is to work, those who resist the idea of further training must be given other tasks so that room can be made for educators who are most willing and competent to carry out the aims of the law. We should also admit the possibility that some of the hostility to mainstreaming may be well founded. This major piece of social engineering is being imposed on the schools according to a civil rights model for dealing with the handicapped, in the absence of any objective evidence that it will do more good than harm to their education and to society as a whole.

Remediation

The occasional success story notwithstanding, the track record for most remedial techniques is poor. This is particularly true over the long term; the few longitudinal studies that have been done suggest that, ten years later, the problems are still there. When a person with a specific learning disability graduates from high school or college, he or she often hits a wall in the sense that the strategies and compensatory mechanisms that worked well enough in school do not work in life after school—the job world, living on one's own. As we have emphasized repeatedly in this book, a learning disability is more than an academic problem. It is an emotional, a social, and frequently a physical problem as well.

On the plus side, it has been noted that many learning-disabled people have deep reserves of motivation and ego strength; if these can be tapped, then success in a variety of tasks is possible. On the negative side, not every person with a learning disability comes from an environment that is supportive, loving, and tolerant and which therefore allows these assets to flourish (of course, even under the best circumstances, some people remain seriously handicapped). Also, on the negative side is the fact that, as presently defined, remediation is usually seen as a means of making a person "more typical" or "more normal" rather than as a means of finding the unique strategy that will work for that person. That strategy may entail the mastery of academic skills—or of the skills that allow a person to survive in an academic environment—or it may involve the mastery of other skills: manual, technical, artistic. This is not to say that the methods for finding the strategies that will work for normal people are completely understood: self-fulfillment is a challenge for everyone. The difference is that a normal person is better equipped—or, to be more accurate, better endowed—to be flexible than a learning-disabled person is.

But our society, at least as far as it reflects its attitudes in legislation, still defines a learning disability primarily in academic terms. Therefore, the solution to a learning disability is seen to be an academic one. The point is, however, that remediation must be seen as a multifaceted undertaking that need not—that should not—focus on success in school as its sole mission.

The Adolescent and Adult

This is especially true for the older learning-disabled person: the adolescent and the adult. Based on the Office of Juvenile Justice and Delinquency Prevention preliminary estimate that 16 percent of youths between the ages of 12 and 15 (in three scattered cities) are learning disabled (see chapter 4), and a Bureau of the Census survey figure that in 1977 there were roughly 16 million youngsters enrolled in high schools in the United States, it could be suggested that at least 600,000 LD students are graduating from, or dropping out of, high school every year.

Other studies, as we have noted, however, come up with much lower incidence figures of LD among the general population. For instance, the Collaborative Perinatal Project of the National Institute of Neurological and Communicative Disorders and Stroke has found a 3 percent incidence rate (see chapter 5). It is not yet clear why figures vary so much. Differences probably depend both on the population sampled, the measurement techniques used, and the criteria for recognizing disability.

Nevertheless, even at the much lower incidence figure, we still have some 120,000 learning-disabled people who come spilling out onto society *every* year. There is within this population a range of learning-disabled adults going all the way from those who will become highly successful craft, business, and professional people to others who are severely disabled in life, and, whether high school graduates or not, are going to be at a great disadvantage in certain work environments. This holds true for some LD college attendees and graduates as well. It is the problems of this latter group who need continued help which concern us here.

In a "Vocational Kit" on Employment Information produced by the California Association for Neurologically Handicapped Children (CANHC) in 1976, Lauriel E. Anderson points out that if an LD person develops proficiency in a job skill, he or she still faces various barriers to employment. Among them are:

1. RIGID ACADEMIC REQUIREMENTS [often demanding high school diplomas when, in fact, an LD person might be able to get a General Education Diploma if testing] were adapted so that a reader could ask him questions which he could answer in writing if his disability was [reading], or which he could read but answer orally if his writing were impaired. A reader is as basic to a dyslexic as to a blind person.

2. INFLEXIBLE APPRENTICESHIP TESTS. Often the requirements for getting into an apprenticeship program exceed the requirements for the job. Why require a high proficiency in English for a plumber? . . . Why is skill in writing a requirement for carpenters? . . . Let us test for relevant knowledge.

3. INAPPROPRIATE APPLICATION PROCEDURES lose many good workers. Let an employee take the application form home, or take it orally. And why throw up barriers such as "What magazines do you read?" which throws panic into the non-reader. . . .

4. RESTRICTIVE UNION REQUIREMENTS which seem to be getting tighter, exclude him for similar reasons; so progress in the area of a skilled vocation is almost impossible.

5. INFLEXIBLE WORKING CONDITIONS often prove a barrier to his employment. Where he could work a partial day, he cannot always be productive 8 consecutive hours; or the pressures for on-the-spot job completion decrease effectiveness. But the move in some jobs to write up individual contracts for completion of specific jobs gives hope for more adaptive conditions in some areas.

Indeed, the life problems of the LD person in the work world, as well as in general adult living, have been largely neglected. In part this is due to the fact that the special interest groups in the field, particularly the ACLD and the Orton Society, have concentrated their efforts so far on getting help for people when they are young—the time when help is likely to make the biggest difference. However, more might be accomplished for the learning-disabled adult if these organizations were less reluctant to join the cause of other handicapped people.

In part, the neglect of the adult is also due to the fact that the adults themselves tend to disappear—or, more accurately, to hide for fear that, once their disability has been discovered, they will lose their jobs and be unable to find new ones. To find the right environment for the LD adult will, in many instances, require guidance and counseling. To deal with situations that present unusual challenges, such as financial planning, or problems in relationships, or health matters, or getting and holding a job, may require some form of continuing professional contact and support. For most learning-disabled adults, such help is not available; although there are a number of government programs that extend aid and services to people with handicaps, the eligibility requirements for the learning disabled are, as we have shown, inconsistent in some cases and totally lacking —or yet to be determined—in others. To a learning-disabled person seeking to help himself or herself, Washington's maze of laws, rules, regulations, and requirements is just plain bewildering. In addition, protection for the adult against loss or refusal of employment is forthcoming only when the employer is receiving assistance from or under contract to a government agency.

Yet, supporting the learning-disabled adult is not the sole responsibility of the government, nor should it be. A great deal can be done in the private sector and, particularly, in the business community. Most employers are at this time unaware of learning disabilities or prejudiced against the learning disabled. A number of benefits would accrue from turning this situation around. For one thing, if there were greater awareness and acceptance in the business community concerning the disabilities and, just as importantly, the abilities of LD people, suitable productive employment might be found for the many LD adults who are now drifting jobless because they cannot meet the expectations of the labor market. In addition, many other LD adults who are working are actually underemployed because they are being used inefficiently. A more realistic understanding of their strengths and weaknesses would enable them to be more productive and happier in the work place—thus reducing job turnover. Enlightened change in both employment practices and career opportunities for the learning disabled would do more than any number of social welfare programs to benefit LD individuals, their families, and also society at large. This is a need that must be met, not only for today's adults, but also for future adults. Otherwise, the label that ensures services for school-age children under P.L. 94–142 may work against them when they go looking for jobs.

Sadly, many LD adults (and children too) report they often feel like "con artists" because of the double burden of not only having to do their work but, also, of maintaining the facade that they are working in the same way that most people do. Partly because the learning-disabled adult fears losing what he has gained in life if discovered and partly because some LD adults are unaware that their life problems stem from learning disabilities, LD adults are now only vaguely and incompletely understood.

It has been suggested that an abnormally large proportion of the LD population may turn to antisocial behavior—crime. This hypothesis is unproved but is under active investigation. Frustration that is such a central feature of the syndrome (particularly perhaps of the unrecognized and untreated syndrome), might explain part of this hypothesized deviant expression. Concomitant problems in misperceiving social nuance, inability to accept praise or discipline, and low self-image might also contribute to a need to act out.

In summing up the plight of the LD adult whose disabilities are severe, Lauriel Anderson writes: "For them, welfare checks instead of pay checks . . . and society and family dependency instead of families of their own. The waste of human potential and the lifetime cost to society for this neglect is enormous" (Anderson 1976).

Science

Ultimately, the means of prevention, diagnosis, and treatment of learning disabilities are most likely to come from scientific research. But the science of learning disabilities is not yet a mature discipline. It lacks an adequate cadre of well-trained investigators. Although it is replete with interesting phenomena and questions about them, it lacks an adequate body of hypotheses and theories.

Much of the best recent scientific work on learning disabilities has served to cast doubt on the most popular theories, but some things are becoming clear. Learning disabilities are not all of one kind. There are multiple syndromes and multiple causes. Some learning disabilities appear to be hereditary. There is increasing evidence that some learning disabilities can be caused or at least exacerbated by environmental insults such as poisoning by food additives.

Learning disabilities are not merely a school problem. They can affect a wide range of cognitive functions, in addition to academic performance. There has been a tendency to try to make a sharp distinction between cognitive difficulties due to psychological, emotional, or cultural factors and those which are "neurologically based," but recent developments in neurophysiology have confirmed what psychologists have long believed—that such a distinction is in principle unsound. This is only one of the ways in which the science of learning disabilities benefits from the science of normal cognitive function. In fact, these two fields are inextricably linked, and each contributes to the other. That is both the problem and the promise of research in learning disabilities: an answer to the question of what goes wrong in the brain is also an answer to the question of what goes right.

Specific Recommendations

So far, the greatest commitment of resources to the learning disabled has been within the fields of education and remediation. Although there is evidently much room for improvement in the education and remediation of the learning disabled, these efforts have already achieved a considerable momentum. We perceive the greatest needs for innovation in the field of learning disabilities to be: (a) there is a tremendous need for more high-quality scientific investigation of learning disabilities; (b) attention needs to be given to the needs of the learning-disabled adult who has passed out of the educational system.

Our detailed recommendations are as follows:

(1) The field of learning disabilities lacks an adequate corps of scientific investigators with solid grounding in the research techniques that have been successful in mature scientific disciplines. This corps needs to be enlarged. Two techniques for doing so which have proven efficacy in other fields are these:

(a) Grants should be made to appropriate universities to support requisite preparatory training of graduate and postgraduate students for careers in scientific investigation of learning disabilities.

(b) Grants like the "Special Fellowships" offered by some of the National

Institutes of Health should be made to established investigators in mature scientific disciplines to enable them to acquire expertise in learning disabilities. They should be paid salaries appropriate to their rank for two or three years of study in the field of learning disabilities.

(2) Agencies which support research on learning disabilities should not presume that they are dealing with a mature scientific discipline. Instead, they should give careful consideration to the model proposed by Charles A. Murray et al (1976A, pp. 72-74). Murray concluded that good research of the kind that needs to be done on the link between LD and juvenile delinquency would not soon be forthcoming if the OJJDP merely put out an ordinary Request for Proposal or waited for the research to be done by investigators in the field. They recommended that the OJJDP itself take an active role in designing the study, to insure that it would be carried out on a scale and with a careful methodology that are rarely encountered in this field.

We further recommend that all National Institute of Health Study Sections and other panels that evaluate research proposals on learning disabilities contain representatives of mature scientific disciplines such as experimental psychology, statistics, and neurophysiology.

(3) There are certain areas of research on learning disabilities where we believe the leverage to be especially favorable. These deserve emphasis:

(a) *Epidemiology*. Studies of the heritability and incidence of learning disabilities should be supported. Particular attention should be given to studies of the incidence of LD within families, to the identical twins of the learning disabled—especially those reared apart—to the relations between learning disabilities and socioeconomic status, diet, and perinatal health status. These studies offer the potential for prevention of LD through genetic counseling and perinatal health care.

(b) *Longitudinal studies.* Well designed and executed prospective longitudinal studies are essential for the validation of diagnostic techniques, for prognosis, for testing the efficacy of remediation, and for answering such questions as: is there a link between LD and JD?

(c) *Biochemical studies.* Not only can such studies offer clues to the causes of LD, but they also may provide the means for the earliest diagnoses.

(d) *Studies of the relation of LD to diet and to environmental toxins.*

(e) *Studies of the neurological and neuropsychological bases of learning behavior and dysfunctions.*

(f) *Careful studies of the efficacy of remediational techniques.* At present we are investing major resources in remediational techniques that have not been shown to be safe and effective. Studies of the efficacy of remediational techniques should not be funded unless they satisfy basic methodological criteria, such as those discussed in the critical review by Hallahan and Cruickshank (1973, pp. 176-216).

There are many additional areas of research on learning disabilities that deserve support, but most of them can only progress hand in hand with our understanding of normal function. For example, cytoarchitectural studies of dyslexic brains deserve support, but, like past cytoarchitectural studies of the brains of geniuses, idiots, and aphasics, they will be difficult to interpret until we improve our general knowledge of the relation between brain structure and function.

(4) Section 503 of the Rehabilitation Act of 1973, P.L. 93–112, and the regulations pertaining thereto (1976) require contractors with federal contracts in excess of $2,500 to establish affirmative action plans for employment of the handicapped, including the learning disabled. Employers have not yet felt the full force of these regulations, but they should expect to soon. We propose that there should be an organized effort by industry, in advance of the full implementation of the Section 503 Regulations, to consider how their mandate can be met by finding suitable employment for the learning disabled. The industries affected should be well aware that many learning-disabled individuals have extraordinary abilities in addition to their handicaps.

(5) Advocates of the learning disabled such as the ACLD should explore ways in which the Rehabilitation Act of 1973 can be used for the benefit of their constituents, including employment in private industry, teaching and school positions, and government jobs.

(6) We have a mass of anecdotal information, some of it reported here, indicating that many learning-disabled individuals continue to suffer handicaps after they leave the schools. At present, however, there are virtually no diagnostic, guidance, or counseling services available to learning-disabled adults. Attention should be focused in this area. We urgently need some careful studies (preferably prospective) of the fate of learning-disabled adults after school.

(7) More adult education programs should be established for the learning disabled. The program at Ventura College might serve as a model.

(8) Government programs under which learning-disabled people might qualify for assistance of one sort or another are hopelessly tangled and not coordinated with one another. Learning-disabled individuals deserve to have a task force established within BEH—perhaps including representatives from other government agencies, such as the Developmental Disabilities Office, the Rehabilitation Services Administration, and the Office of Management and Budget—that would address this problem and try to make sense out of it. At least one learning-disabled person should be appointed to serve on this task force, and, for that matter, on other advisory committees whose work has a bearing on the LD population. (See p. 37 for an example of an existing interagency government task force.)

(9) The Army Corps of Engineers is not permitted to build a dam without a cost-benefit analysis and an environmental impact statement. Neither should the government be allowed to undertake a major piece of social engineering like P.L. 94–142 without a cost-benefit analysis and an analysis of its probable impact on the people and institutions it will affect. P.L. 94–142 imposes on the schools costly but untried measures such as parent advocacy, mainstreaming, evaluation of disabilities, and individualized education programs. Before such radical

measures, which may turn out to be counterproductive, are imposed on one of our major social institutions, they should pass through a probationary status (like that of an experimental drug) to gain some objective assurance that they are both safe and effective. Otherwise, they may prove to be disastrous—either because they are bad ideas in the first place, or because they are so grotesquely underfunded that they are never given a chance to succeed. If measures on this scale fail, the backlash they will provoke may set progress back for years.

We have a long history of well-intended governmental initiatives that have done more harm than good. For example, the government imposed on manufacturers of children's clothing a requirement that the clothing be treated with flame-retardant chemicals that subsequently turned out to be carcinogenic. It is possible that some of the hostility to P.L. 94–142 may be well founded. Perhaps it is time for a reconsideration of whether the measures imposed by P.L. 94–142 are in fact the right dose of the right medicine. Perhaps these measures should be subjected to clinical trials before they are universally imposed.

References

Abt Associates, Inc. and the National Task Force on the Definition of Developmental Disabilities. *Final Report of the Special Study on the Definition of Developmental Disabilities.* Cambridge, Mass.: Abt Associates, Inc., 1977.

Adelman, H. and Taylor, L. *Learning Problems and the Fernald Laboratory: Beyond the Fernald Techniques.* Paper presented at the World Conference of the Council for Exceptional Children, Stirling, Scotland, 1978.

American Academy of Pediatrics. Joint Organizational Statement: The Eye and Learning Disabilities. *Pediatrics,* 1972, *49*, 454–455.

American Academy of Pediatrics Committee on Nutrition. Megavitamin Therapy for Childhood Psychoses and Learning Disabilities. *Pediatrics,* 1976, *58*, 910–912.

American Academy of Physical Medicine and Rehabilitation. Statement on Doman-Delacato Treatment of Neurological Handicapped Children, 1967. In Hallahan, D. and Cruickshank, W. *Psychoeducational Foundations of Learning Disabilities.* Englewood Cliffs, N.J.: Prentice-Hall, 1973, 94–96.

American Association of Psychiatric Services for Children, Inc. *Developmental Review in the EPSDT Program.* U.S. Department of HEW, Health Care Financing Administration, The Medicaid Bureau, 1977.

American Psychiatric Association Task Force on Vitamin Therapy in Psychiatry. *Megavitamin and Orthomolecular Therapy in Psychiatry.* Washington, D.C.: American Psychiatric Association, 1973.

American Speech and Hearing Association. Position Statement of the American Speech and Hearing Association on Learning Disabilities Adopted by the ASHA Legislative Council, November 1975. *ASHA,* 1976, *18,* 282–290.

Ames, L. B. Learning Disabilities: Time to Check Our Roadmaps? *Journal of Learning Disabilities,* 1977, *10,* 328–330.

Anderson, L. E. Employment Barriers for the Learning Disabled Adult. In Anderson, L. E. (ed.), *Vocational Kit: Steps in Vocational Readiness for Adolescents and Adults with the Hidden Handicap.* Los Angeles, California: California Association for Neurologically Handicapped Children, 1976.

Boder, E. Developmental Dyslexia: A Diagnostic Approach Based on Three Atypical Reading-Spelling Patterns. *Developmental Medicine and Child Neurology,* 1973, *15,* 663–687.

Boder, E. School Failure—Evaluation and Treatment. *Pediatrics,* 1976, *58,* 394–403.

Broman, S. H. *Early Development and Family Characteristics of Low Achievers.* Paper presented at the 14th International Conference of the ACLD, March 1977. (a)

Broman, S. H. *Early Development and Family Characteristics of Low Achievers II: A Multivariate Analysis.* Paper presented to the Annual Meeting of the American Academy of Child Psychiatry, Abramsen Research Symposium on Epidemiological Studies and Child Psychiatry, Houston, 1977. (b)

Chapter 766 of Acts of 1972: The Comprehensive Special Education Law (Chapter 766 Regulation), Commonwealth of Massachusetts Department of Education.

Childs, B., Finucci, J. M., Preston, M. S., and Pulver, A. E. Human Behavior Genetics. In H. Harris and K. Hirschorn (eds.), *Advances in Human Genetics* (Vol. 7). New York: Plenum, 1976.

Chomsky, N. *Reflections on Language.* New York: Pantheon Books, 1976.

Comptroller General of the United States. *Learning Disabilities: The Link to Delinquency Should Be Determined, But Schools Should Do More Now.* Report to Congress, March 1977. GAO Report GGD-76-97.

Connors, C. K. *New Research on Food Additives and Behavior.* Paper presented at the 15th International Conference of the ACLD, Kansas City, Missouri, March 1978.

Council for Exceptional Children—Division for Children with Learning Disabilities. By-Laws, Article II, *Purpose and Goals.* Adopted at the Chicago Convention, 1976.

Cowley, J. F. and Fitzmaurice, A. M. *Mathematics in Review.* Paper Prepared for the Task Panel on Learning Failure and Unused Learning Potential for the President's Commission on Mental Health, 1977.

De Quiros, J. B. Diagnosis of Vestibular Disorders in the Learning Disabled. *Journal of Learning Disabilities,* 1976, *9,* 50–58.

Doehring, D. Comprehension of Printed Sentences by Children with Reading Disability. *Bulletin of the Psychonomic Society,* 1977, *10,* 350–352.

Duane, D. D. A Neurologic Overview of Specific Language Disability for the Non-neurologist. *Bulletin of the Orton Society,* 1974, *24,* 5–36.

Duane, D. D. *Developmental Dyslexia—By Any Other Name a Challenge.* Paper presented at the European Congress of Child Neurology, Marseilles, France, December 1977.

Eisenberg, L. Reading Retardation: Psychiatric and Sociological Aspects. *Pediatrics,* 1966, *37,* 352–365.

Eisenberg, L. Psychiatric Aspects of Language Disabilities. In D. D. Duane and M. B. Rawson (eds.), *Reading, Perception and Language.* Baltimore, Maryland: The Orton Society/York Press, 1975.

Ellingson, C. *The Shadow Children: A Book About Children's Learning Disorders.* Chicago: Topaz Books, 1967.

Feingold, B. F. *Why Your Child is Hyperactive.* New York: Random House, 1975.

Freedman, D. History and Background of the Developmentally Disabled Assistance and Bill of Rights Act (P.L. 94–103). In the *Final Report of the Special Study on the Definition of Developmental Disabilities* submitted to the Committee on Human Resources of the U.S. Senate and the Committee on Interstate and Foreign Commerce of the U.S. House of Representatives. Cambridge, Mass.: Abt Associates, Inc., November, 1977.

Geschwind, N. *Anatomical Foundations of Language and Dominance.* Paper presented at the Symposium on the Neurological Bases of Language Disorders in Children: Methods and Directions for Research. National Institute of Neurological and Communicative Disorders and Stroke, Bethesda, Maryland, January 1978.

Geschwind, N. and Levitsky, W. Human Brain: Left-right Asymmetries in Temporal Speech Region. *Science,* 1968, *161,* 186–187.

Getman, G., Kane, E. R., Halgren, M. R., and McKee, G. W. *The Physiology of Readiness: An Action Program for the Development of Perception for Children.* Minneapolis, Minnesota: Programs to Accelerate School Success, 1964.

Glaser, E. M. *Strategies for Facilitating Communication About Dyslexia Research and Treatment.* Research Proposal to National Science Foundation, 1976. [Available from Human Interaction Research Institute, Los Angeles, California]

Goldman, A. L. Anker Calls Program for Handicapped in 'Recess.' *The New York Times,* November 20, 1977, pp. 63.

Hallahan, D. and Cruickshank, W. *Psychoeducational Foundations of Learning Disabilities.* Englewood Cliffs, N.J.: Prentice-Hall, 1973.

Hicks, R. E. and Kinsbourne, M. Human Handedness: A Partial Cross-Fostering Study. *Science,* 1976, *192,* 908–910.

Hughes, J. Biochemical and Electroencephalographic Correlates of Learning Disabilities. In R. Knights and D. Bakker (eds.), *The Neuropsychology of Learning Disabilities: Theoretical Approaches.* Baltimore, Maryland: University Park Press, 1976.

International Reading Association. Resolution Adopted by the Delegates Assembly of the International Reading Association in May 1976.

John E. R., Karmel, B. Z., Corning, W. C., Easton, P., Brown, D., Ahn, H., John, M., Harmony, T., Prichep, L., Toro, A., Gerson, I., Bartlett, F., Thatcher, R.,

Kaye, H., Valdes, P., Schwartz, E. Neurometrics. *Science*, 1977, *196*, 1393–1410.

Joint Committee on Learning Disabilities. Letter transmitted to Edwin Martin, Deputy Commissioner of Education, BEH. April, 1976.

Joint Committee on Learning Disabilities. Unofficial Report to BEH submitted during the early drafting of the regulations for P.L. 94–142.

Kappelman, M. and Ackerman, P. *Between Parent and School.* New York: The Dial Press/James Wade, 1977.

Kavanagh, J. and Yeni-Komshian, G. *Developmental Dyslexia and Related Reading Disorders.* U.S. Department of HEW. Publication no. (NIH) 78–92 (forthcoming).

Keogh, B. K. A Compensatory Model for Psychoeducational Evaluation of Children With Learning Disorders. *Journal of Learning Disabilities* 1971, *4*, 544–548.

Kolata, G. B. Behavioral Teratology: Birth Defects of the Mind. *Science,* 1978, *202*, 732–734.

Liberman, I. Y., and Shankweiler, D. *Speech, the Alphabet, and Teaching to Read.* Paper presented at the Conference on the Theory and Practice of Early Reading Instruction. Learning Research, and Development Center, University of Pittsburgh, May 1976.

Liberman, I. Y., Shankweiler, D., Camp, L., Heifetz, B., and Werfelman, M. *Steps Toward Literacy.* Report to the Task Panel on Learning Failure and Unused Learning Potential of The President's Commission on Mental Health, November 1977. (a)

Liberman, I. Y., Shankweiler, D., Liberman, A. M., Fowler, C., and Fischer, F. W. Phonetic Segmentation and Recoding in the Beginning Reader. In A. S. Reber and D. L. Scarborough (eds.), *Toward a Psychology of Reading: The Proceedings of the CUNY Conferences.* New York: John Wiley & Sons, 1977. (b)

Ludlow, C. L. *The Need for Encouraging Increased Research and Research Training Concerning the Neurological Bases of Language Disorders in Children.* Paper presented at the Symposium on the Neurological Bases of Language Disorders in Children: Methods and Directions for Research. National Institute of Neurological and Communicative Disorders and Stroke, Bethesda, Maryland, January 1978.

Ludlow, C. L. Rapaport, J. L., Brown, G. L. V., and Mikkelson, E. J. *The Effects of Dextroamphetamine on Hyperactive and Normal Children's Language Behavior.* Paper presented to the Annual Convention of the American Speech and Hearing Association, Chicago, November 1977.

Maeroff, G. I. Law on Education of Handicapped Poses Fiscal Burden for Districts. *The New York Times,* January 30, 1978, p. A1.

Makita, K. The Rarity of Reading Disability in Japanese Children. *American Journal of Orthopsychiatry,* 1968, *38*, 599–614.

Marianne Frostig Center of Educational Therapy. *Follow-Up Study of the Post-School Adjustment of Former Students with Learning Handicaps.* Final Report, 1977.

Milner, B. Disorders of Learning and Memory after Temporal-lobe Lesions in Man. *Clinical Neurosurgery*, 1972, *19*, 421–446.

Murray, C. A., Schubert, J. G., Gunn, A. E., Casserly, M. D., Bass, S. A., Harper, P. P., Bektemirian, M., and Hines, S. L. *The Link Between Learning Disabilities and Juvenile Delinquency: Current Theories and Knowledge.* Report to the National Institutes for Juvenile Justice and Delinquency Prevention, Office of Juvenile Justice and Delinquency Prevention, Law Enforcement Assistance Administration. Washington, D. C., 1976. (a)

Murray, C. A., Schubert, J. G., Gunn, A. E., Casserly, M. D., Bass, S. A., Harper, P. P., Bektemirian, M., and Hines, S. L. *The Link Between Learning Disabilities and Juvenile Delinquency: Current Theories and Knowledge. Executive Summary.* Report to the National Institutes for Juvenile Justice and Delinquency Prevention, Office of Juvenile Justice and Delinquency Prevention, Law Enforcement Assistance Administration. Washington, D.C., 1976. (b)

Orton, S. T. *Reading, Writing and Speech Problems in Children.* New York: W. W. Norton & Company, Inc., 1937.

Palfrey, J. S., Mervis, R. C., and Butler, J. A. New Directions in the Evaluation and Education of Handicapped Children. *New England Journal of Medicine,* 1978, *298*, 819–824.

Pettigrew, J. D. and Kasamatsu, T. Local Perfusion of Noradrenaline Maintains Visual Cortex Plasticity. *Nature,* 1978, *271*, 761–763.

Public Law 91–230. Elementary and Secondary Education Assistance Programs, Extension. April 13, 1970.

Public Law 93–112. Rehabilitation Act of 1973. September 26, 1973.

Public Law 93–380. Education Amendments of 1974. August 21, 1974.

Public Law 94–103. Developmentally Disabled Assistance and Bill of Rights Act. October 4, 1975.

Public Law 94–142. Education for All Handicapped Children Act of 1975. November 29, 1975.

Public Law 94–142 Regulations. Assistance to States for Education of Handicapped Children, Procedures for Evaluating Specific Learning Disabilities. Department of HEW, Office of Education, *Federal Register,* December 1977, *42*, 65082-65085.

Rapoport, J. L., Buchsbaum, M. S., Zahn, T. P., Weingartner, J., Ludlow, C., Mikkelsen, E. J. Dextroamphetamine: Cognitive and Behavioral Effects in Normal Prepubertal Boys. *Science,* 1978, *199*, 560–563.

Rawson, M. B. Developmental Dyslexia: Educational Treatment and Results. In D. D. Duane and M. B. Rawson (eds.), *Reading, Perception and Language.* Baltimore, Maryland: The Orton Society/York Press, Inc., 1975.

Rogan, L. R. and Hartman, L. D. *A Follow-up Study of Learning Disabled Children as Adults, Abstract.* Evanston, Illinois: Cove School Research Office, 1978.

Rutter, M. and Yule, W. The Concept of Specific Reading Retardation. *Journal of Child Psychology and Psychiatry,* 1975, *16*, 181–197.

Satz, P. Friel, J. and Fletcher, J. Some Predictive Antecedents of Specific Reading Disability: A Two-, Three-, and Four-year Follow-up. In J. T. Guthrie (ed.), *Aspects of Reading Acquisition.* Baltimore, Maryland: Johns Hopkins Press, 1976, 111–141.

Satz, P., Friel, J. and Goebel, R. Some Predictive Antecedents of Specific Reading Disability: A Three-year Follow Up. *Bulletin of the Orton Society*, 1975, *25*, 91–110.

Satz, P., Taylor, G., Friel, J. and Fletcher, J. Some Predictive and Developmental Precursors of Reading Disability: A Six Year Follow-up. In D. Pearl and A. Benton (eds.), *Dyslexia: An Appraisal of Current Knowledge*, New York: Oxford University Press, 1978, 313–347.

Saunders, R. E. Questions and Answers About Dyslexia. *Psychiatric Annals*, 1977, *7*, 461–463.

Schmitt, F. O. and Worden, F. G. (eds.), *The Neurosciences: Third Study Program*. Cambridge, Mass.: M.I.T. Press, 1974.

Schubert, E. D. The Role of Auditory Perception in Language Processing. In D. D. Duane and M. B. Rawson (eds.), *Reading, Perception and Language*. Baltimore, Maryland: The Orton Society/York Press, Inc., 1975.

Section 502 Regulations (Implementing Section 502 of Public Law 93–112). Architectural and Transportation Barriers Compliance Board. Practice and Procedures for Compliance Hearings. *Federal Register*, December 1976, *41*, 55441–55451.

Section 503 Regulations (Implementing Section 503 of Public Law 93–112). Office of Federal Contract Compliance, Equal Employment Opportunity, Department of Labor. Affirmative Action Obligations of Contractors and Subcontractors for Handicapped Workers. *Federal Register*, April 1976, *41*, 16147–16155.

Section 504 Regulations (Implementing Section 504 of Public Law 93–112). Nondiscrimination of Basis of Handicap, Programs and Activities Receiving or Benefiting from Federal Financial Assistance. *Federal Register*, May 1977, *42*, 22676–22702.

Shankweiler, D. and Liberman, I. Y. Misreading: A Search for Causes. In J. F. Kavanagh and I. G. Mattingly (eds.), *Language by Ear and by Eye: The Relationships Between Speech and Reading*. Cambridge, Massachusetts: M.I.T. Press, 1972.

Sheridan, H. Questions and Answers About Dyslexia. *Psychiatric Annals*, 1977, *7*, 463–465.

Siegel, E. *The Exceptional Child Grows Up: Guidelines for Understanding and Helping the Brain Injured Adolescent and Young Adult*. New York: E. P. Dutton Co., 1974.

Silver, L. B. The Minimal Brain Dysfunction Syndrome. In J. Noshpitz (ed.), *The Basic Handbook of Child Psychiatry* (Vol. 2). New York: Basic Books Inc., 1978.

Smith, S. L. *Learning Disorders in Relation to Living*. Memo to Kingsbury Lab School Staff, no date.

Steg, D. R. and Schenk, R. Intervention Through Technology: The "Talking Typewriter" Revisited. *Educational Technology*, 1977, *17*, 45–47.

Sutton, S. B. A New Chance for Children Who 'Can't Learn.' *Harvard Magazine*, February 1976, *78*, 26–33, 54–56.

Task Panel on Learning Failure and Unused Learning Potential. Report submitted to the President's Commission on Mental Health. February 15, 1978. PCMH/P-78/13.

Tec, L. *The Fear of Success*. New York: The Reader's Digest Press, 1976.

Temerlin, M. *Lucy: Growing Up Human: A Chimpanzee Daughter in a Psychotherapist's Family*. New York: Bantam, 1977.

The Orton Society, Inc. Pamphlet published by The Orton Society. Towson, Maryland, no author, no date.

The White House Conference on Handicapped Individuals, Volume Two, *Final Report*, Part C. Washington, D.C.: U.S. Government Printing Office, 1977.

The White House Conference on Handicapped Individuals, Volume Three, *Implementation Plan*. Washington, D.C.: U.S. Government Printing Office, 1978.

U.S. Civil Service Commission. Equal Opportunity, Prohibition Against Discrimination Because of a Physical or Mental Handicap. *Federal Register*, March 1978, *43*, 12293-12296.

U.S. Senate Committee on Labor and Public Welfare. *Report on the Education for All Handicapped Children Act*. (U.S. Senate Reports No. 94-168). Washington, D.C.: U.S. Government Printing Office, 1975.

Wender, P. H. Speculations Concerning a Possible Biochemical Basis of Minimal Brain Dysfunction. In J. G. Millicap (ed.), *Learning Disabilities and Related Disorders: Facts and Current Issues*. Chicago: Year Book Publishers, 1977.

Witelson, S. F. Developmental Dyslexia: Two Right Hemispheres and none Left. *Science*, 1977, *195*, 309-311.

Witelson, S. F. Sex and the Single Hemisphere: Specialization of the Right Hemisphere for Spatial Processing. *Science*, 1976, *193*, 425-427.

Wood, D. R., Reimherr, F. W., Wender, P. H. and Johnson, G. E. Diagnosis and Treatment of Minimal Brain Dysfunction in Adults. *Archives of General Psychiatry*, 1976, *33*, 1453-1460.

Yule, W., Rutter, M., Berger, M., and Thompson, J. Over- and Under-Achievement in Reading: Distribution in the General Population. *British Journal of Educational Psychology*, 1974, *44*, 1-12.

Name Index

Subject Index

Achievement and expectation, 10, 59, 90-91, 129-30, 140, 162, 169

ACLD (Association for Children with Learning Disabilities), 9, 12, 16, 25, 43, 50-52, 55, 123-24, 158, 172, 176

Adolescents, learning disabled, 70, 73, 75, 78-84, 127, 171-73

Adults, learning disabled, 38, 40, 48-49, 78, 84-86, 126-28, 163, 170-73, 176

Albinism, 142

Allergies, 118, 143

Amblyopia, 136-37, 141

American Sign Language for the Deaf, 149-50

American Speech and Hearing Association, 13, 24, 50, 53-55

Amphetamines, 108-109, 155n., 156-57

Anatomy of the brain, 136-39, 141-42, 145-46, 150-55

Aphasia, 14

ASHA (American Speech and Hearing Association), 13, 24, 50, 53-55

ASL (American Sign Language for the Deaf), 149-50

Association for Children with Learning Disabilities, 9, 12, 16, 25, 43, 50-52, 55, 123-24, 158, 172, 176

Auditory cortex, 138-39, 151-52, 160

Barriers to the handicapped, 35-36, 82

BEH (Bureau of Education for the Handicapped, Office of Education, U. S. Department of Health, Education and Welfare), 8, 25, 28-30, 34, 40-44, 55-56, 61, 70, 90, 95-96, 112, 176

Dean's Grants program, 42-43

Model Programs project, 40-41

regulations, 32